Military Strategy

in a

Changing Europe

Towards the Twenty-first Century

Also from Brassey's

CAHEN
The Western European Union & NATO

COKER
Shifting into Neutral?

DROWN
A Single European Arms Industry?

GROVE
Maritime Strategy and European Security

GROVE
NATO's Defence of the North

SLOAN
NATO in the 1990s

WINDASS & GROVE
The Crucible of Peace

Military Strategy

in a

Changing Europe

Towards the Twenty-first Century

Edited by

BRIAN HOLDEN REID

and

MICHAEL DEWAR

BRASSEY'S (UK)

(a member of the Maxwell Macmillan Pergamon Publishing Corporation plc)

LONDON · OXFORD · WASHINGTON · NEW YORK · BEIJING
FRANKFURT · SÃO PAULO · SYDNEY · TOKYO · TORONTO

UK (Editorial)	Brassey's (UK) Ltd., 50 Fetter Lane, London EC4A 1AA, England
(Orders, all except North America)	Brassey's (UK) Ltd., Headington Hill Hall, Oxford OX3 0BW, England
USA (Editorial)	Brassey's (US) Inc., 8000 Westpark Drive, Fourth Floor, McLean, Virginia 22102, USA
(Orders, North America)	Brassey's (US) Inc., Front and Brown Streets, Riverside, New Jersey 08075, USA Tel. (toll free): 800 257 5755
PEOPLE'S REPUBLIC OF CHINA	Pergamon Press, Room 4037, Qianmen Hotel, Beijing, People's Republic of China
FEDERAL REPUBLIC OF GERMANY	Pergamon Press GmbH, Hammerweg 6, D-6242 Kronberg, Federal Republic of Germany
BRAZIL	Pergamon Editora Ltda, Rua Eça de Queiros, 346, CEP 04011, Paraiso, São Paulo, Brazil
AUSTRALIA	Brassey's Australia Pty Ltd., PO Box 544, Potts Point, NSW 2011, Australia
JAPAN	Pergamon Press, 5th Floor, Matsuoka Central Building, 1-7-1 Nishishinjuku, Shinjuku-ku, Tokyo 160, Japan
CANADA	Pergamon Press Canada Ltd., Suite No. 271, 253 College Street, Toronto, Ontario, Canada M5T 1R5

First edition 1991

Library of Congress Cataloging in Publication Data
Applied for

British Library Cataloguing in Publication Data
Military Strategy in a Changing Europe
1. Central Europe. Warsaw Pact military forces compared with North Atlantic Treaty Organization military forces.
I. Reid, Brian Holden   II. Dewar, Michael
355.0091713

ISBN 0-08-037706-8

Printed in Great Britain by B.P.C.C. Wheatons Ltd., Exeter

For two newcomers,

HARRY AND JACK FLEET

Contents

vii

Contents

Contents

Preface

A unique gathering in the history of the British Army took place
recently. Two hundred and fifty delegates from the Ministry of Defence,
the Foreign Office, most NATO nations, the universities, industry and
the media met at the Senate House, University of London, to attend a
Conference organised jointly by the British Army and the Department
of War Studies, King's College, London on future British strategy. It
was not so much the number of delegates that was so notable as the level
of representation, which included the Rt. Hon. Archie Hamilton MP,
Minister of State for the Armed Forces, and General Sir John Chapple,
GCB, CBE, ADC Gen., the Chief of the General Staff. In all cases, the
delegates were unusually distinguished and knowledgeable.

This volume is a collection of the papers presented at the Conference.
The mixture of military and academic viewpoints provides perceptive
and balanced comment on Britain's future contribution to NATO in
general, and the Central Region in particular. At a time of bewildering
and sudden change, requiring an alteration in our priorities and new
approaches to the defence of Europe, this collection is intended to make a
contribution to a debate which has not ended with the gradual
disintegration of Soviet power in Eastern Europe – it has just started.

The Editors are grateful to a number of friends and colleagues for their
assistance in producing this volume. We are most grateful to Professor
Sir Michael Howard for his unstinting support in this and many other
projects. To Professor Lawrence Freedman we owe a special debt for
nurturing the original idea. We are obliged to Dr M. L. Dockrill and Dr
David Robertson for their advice and encouragement. Finally, we are
also most grateful to four officers for their efforts on our behalf, Colonel
D. de G. Bromhead, LVO, OBE, Lieutenant-Colonel A. P. Ridgway,
RTR, Lieutenant-Colonel D. Spackman, RRF, and Major N. M.
Fairclough, RE.

BRIAN HOLDEN REID
King's College, London

MICHAEL DEWAR
IISS, London

Notes on the Contributors

Field-Marshal Sir Nigel Bagnall retired as Chief of General Staff in 1988. Before that appointment he was Commander-in-Chief, British Army of the Rhine. He is currently embarking on a new career as an author.

Major-General Ian Baxter, CBE currently holds the appointment of Assistant Chief of the Defence Staff (Logistics) on the central staff of the Ministry of Defence.

Field-Marshal Lord Carver retired as Chief of the Defence Staff after a long and distinguished career in the British Army, which included commanding an armoured brigade in the Western Desert during the Second World War. Among his many distinguished works are *El Alamein, Tobruk, Warfare Since 1945* and his autobiography *Out of Step*.

Colonel Michael Dewar retired from the British Army recently. He was appointed Deputy Director of the International Institute for Strategic Studies in April 1990. Among his many works on military topics are *The British Army in Northern Ireland, Brush Fire Wars, The Art of Deception in Warfare* and *Defence of the Nation*.

Christopher Donnelly was Head of the Soviet Studies Research Centre at the Royal Military Academy, Sandhurst before taking up his current post as Sovietologist in Residence in the Office of the Secretary-General of NATO. He is the author of *Red Banner*.

General Sir Martin Farndale retired as Commander-in-Chief, British Army of the Rhine in 1987. He retained the appointment of Master Gunner, which he still holds. He is the author of a number of works including *The History of the Royal Regiment of Artillery*.

Lawrence Freedman has been Professor and Head of the Department of War Studies, King's College, London, since 1982. His many publications include *The Evolution of Nuclear Strategy, The Price of Peace, Arms Control: Management or Reform?* and *Britain and the Falklands War*.

David Greenwood is Head of the Centre for Defence Studies at

Aberdeen University, and has written extensively on defence policy and procurement issues.

Brian Holden Reid is Lecturer in War Studies at King's College, London, and since 1987 has been Resident Historian at the British Army Staff College, Camberley – the first civilian to work on the Directing Staff for over 100 years. A Fellow of the Royal Historical Society and of the Royal Geographical Society, from 1984–87 he was Editor of the *RUSI Journal*. He is the author of *J. F. C. Fuller: Military Thinker* (1987) and a co-editor of *The British Army and the Operational Level of War* (1989), *New Technology and the Arms Race* (1989), and *Continental Commitment vs Out-of-Area: Future Commitments* (1990).

Colonel Hans D. Lemke is a senior staff member of the Stiftung Wissenschaft und Politik, Ebenhausen, and a well-known authority on alternative defence models.

Simon Lunn is Deputy Director, the North Atlantic Assembly. He is the author of *Burden-Sharing in NATO*. He was previously head of the Plans and Policy section of the NATO Peace Planning Directorate and has been a lecturer at the Royal Institute for International Affairs.

Major-General J. J. G. Mackenzie, OBE was educated at the Royal Military Academy, Sandhurst. He has instructed at the Staff College and commanded an armoured brigade in Germany before being posted as Director of the Higher Command and Staff Course, and Deputy Commandant of the Staff College. In February 1989 he was appointed Commandant. He is currently commanding an armoured division in Germany.

Major-General Anthony Pollard, CBE held the appointment of Director-General Training and Doctrine (Army) in the Ministry of Defence until January 1990. He is now General Officer Commanding, South West District.

Peter Sharfman is Director of Policy Anlysis, Washington C³I Division, the MITRE Corporation, and was formerly Program Manager, International Security and Commerce in the Office of Technology Assessment, United States Congress.

Air Chief Marshal Sir Anthony Skingsley, after a long and distinguished career in the Royal Air Force, currently holds the post of Deputy Commander-in-Chief, Central Europe, a senior NATO Appointment in Headquarters Allied Forces Central Europe.

Major-General Julian Thompson was Commander of 3 Commando Brigade in the Falklands War and the initial landing force commander. In 1983 he was appointed Major-General, Royal Marines before retiring. He is currently undertaking research at King's College, London, and is the author of *No Picnic* and *Ready for Anything*.

Martin van Creveld is Professor of History at the Hebrew University in Jerusalem. Among his many distinguished works on military history are *Supplying War*, *Command in War* and *Technology and War*.

Phil Williams was a lecturer in the Department of Politics at Southampton University until his recent appointment as Professor in Security Studies at Pittsburgh University in the United States. He was associated with the Royal Institute of International Affairs until 1989. His works include *The Senate and US Troops in Europe*.

List of Tables

List of Figures

List of Abbreviations

AAFCE	Allied Air Force Central Europe
ACE	Allied Commander Europe
ADP	Automatic Data Processing
ADR	Air Defence Region
AFCENT	Allied Forces Central Europe
AG	Adjutant General
AH	Attack Helicopter
AI	Air Interdiction
APC	Armoured Personnel Carrier
ASM	Air-to-Surface Missile
ASOC	Air Support Operation Centre
ATACMS	Army Tactical Missile System
ATAF	Allied Tactical Air Force
ATAGMS	Anti-Tank Air Guided Missile System
ATOC	Air Transport Operations Centre
ATTU	Atlantic to the Urals
AWACS	Airborne Warning and Command System
BAI	Battlefield Air Interdiction
BAOR	British Army of the Rhine
BEF	British Expeditionary Force
BITE	Built in Test Equipment
CAS	Close Air Support
CASEVAC	Casualty Evacuation
CDS	Chief of the Defence Staff
CENTAG	Central Army Group
CFE	Conventional Forces in Europe
CGS	Chief of the General Staff
CIGS	Chief of the Imperial General Staff
CINCENT	Commander-in-Chief Central Europe
CIS	Commander Intelligence System
COMNORTHAG	Commander Northern Army Group
DA	Defence Attaché

DOB	Date of Birth
DPC	Defence Planning Committee
ECM	Electronic Counter Measures
EW	Electronic Warfare
FEBA	Forward Edge of the Battle Area
FLOT	Forward Line Own Troops
FOD	Flying Object Damage
FOFA	Follow on Forces Attack
FOTL	Follow on to Lance
GDP	General Defence Plan
GNP	Gross National Product
GSFG	Group of Soviet Forces in Germany
IEPG	Independent European Planning Committee
ILS	Instrument Landing System
IT	Information Technology
LPD	Landing Platform Dock
LSL	Landing Ship Logistic
MARILYN	Manning and Recruiting in the Lean Years of the Nineties
MBFR	Mutual Balanced Force Reduction
MBR	Main Battle Tank
MDA	Main Defence Area
MICV	Mechanised Infantry Combat Vehicle
MLRS	Multi-Launcher Rocket System
MOB	Mobilisation
MOD	Ministry of Defence
MR	Medium Range
NORTHAG	Northern Army Group
NSWP	Non Soviet Warsaw Pact
OMG	Operational Manoeuvre Group
PASUV	Soviet Command and Control System
PGM	Precision Guided Munitions
POL	Petrol Oil and Lubricant
PVR	Premature Voluntary Release
Q&M	Quartermaster
RNR	Royal Navy Reserve
RPV	Remotely Piloted Vehicle
RSTA	Reconnaissance, Surveillance Target Acquisition
RUSI	Royal United Services Institute
SACEUR	Supreme Allied Commander Europe
SAM	Surface-to-Air Missile
SAMS	School of Advanced Military Studies
SAS	Special Air Service
SHAEF	Supreme HQ Allied Expeditionary Force

SHAPE	Supreme HQ Allied Powers in Europe
SHORAD	Short Range Air Defence
SNF	Short Range Nuclear Forces
SPD	German Social Democratic Party
STA	Surveillance and Target Acquisition
STARS	Surveillance Target Acquisition and Reconnaissance System
STO	Survive to Operate
STOL	Short Take Off and Landing
TA	Territorial Army
TNF	Theatre Nuclear Forces
TVD	Soviet Theatre of Military Operations
UAV	Unmanned Aerial Vehicle
VSTOL	Vertical and Short Take Off and Landing

Introduction

BRIAN HOLDEN REID

GREAT BRITAIN has long enjoyed a strategically ambivalent relationship with the European mainland. Since the days of the later Tudors, although Kings of England proudly disported the title of 'King of France', they had in practice abandoned any continental ambitions – confirmed by the humiliating loss of Calais in 1558. Thereafter British foreign policy was governed by one overriding principle: the balance of power. British statesmen strove to sustain an equilibrium among all the European great powers so that one could not secure a continental hegemony over all the others. The balance operated to ensure that no continental power occupied the Low Countries; from here an invasion of England – like that attempted by the Armada in 1588 – could be launched. As Great Britain gained in economic power and international influence, so this equilibrium could be more easily secured by financial measures (such as loans to powers already at war), rather than by the deployment of British troops on European shores. At the height of British power, for instance, the Duke of Wellington rarely commanded more than 30,000 British troops, although he directed armies of three times that number. Because of this exercise of imperial power by financial means and naval power (itself a reflection of commercial strength), an influential idea gathered strength that Britain's true *métier* in a war with over-mighty European states, whether these were Philip II's Spain, or the France of Louis XIV and Louis XV or Napoleon, lay in judiciously executed amphibious operations against the enemy's peripheral colonial possessions, whilst Britain's European allies carried the heavy burden of military operations against his main body. In the oft-quoted words of Francis Bacon, 'He that commands the sea is at great liberty and may take as much or as little of the war as he will'; though such sweeping observations concealed the reality that, however vital command of the sea had been to Britain's security in, say 1804–05, that *by itself* sea power did not bring down Napoleon's continental empire.[1]

The thorny question of whether to invervene militarily on the

1

continent of Europe or exercise maritime power overseas has been the central dilemma of British defence policy. No matter how dogmatically publicists argued for a distinctly 'British' amphibious strategy, Britain could not escape one crucial fact: the threat of invasion, which would occur again in 1940–41, underlined that geographically Britain was part of Europe and that the defence of the British Isles depended on affairs in Europe. This was an inescapable reality. If Britain were occupied by a continental power, the British Empire would collapse. If outlying provinces of the Empire were occupied (as occurred in South-East Asia in 1941–45), Britain would be weakened but her power would not be destroyed. Thus any threat to the security of the British Isles was paramount. Hence Admiral Fisher responded to the naval threat posed by Germany in home waters by withdrawing Britain's naval 'legions' to home waters in the years before 1914.[2]

But to what extent could the exercise of naval power, even of this magnitude, influence the conduct of a great continental power determined to exert her dominion on both land and at sea? In the event of a war with Germany, the Royal Navy advocated the use of blockade, the destruction of German seaborne trade and the employment of amphibious raids. The Commander-in-Chief of the Channel Fleet, Admiral Sir Arthur Wilson, was of the opinion that 'we should be bound to devote the military forces of the country to endeavour to create a diversion on the coast of Germany in France's favour; also, in view of the rapidity with which events moved in the War of 1870, any diversion to be effective must be made at once'. The General Staff considered these proposals in some detail. When the Army complained that they were impracticable, the Royal Navy took itself off in a huff, and planned its own naval war in complete secrecy behind the scholarly and elegant portals of the Royal Naval College, Greenwich. After this rebuff, the Army, too, went its own way from 1906 onwards, and concentrated on planning for a land war with Germany. This inevitably required a continental commitment and some kind of alliance with France. The commitment was small: initially four infantry divisions and one cavalry division, rising to six infantry divisions and one cavalry division by 1914. The Foreign Secretary, Sir Edward Grey, remained ignorant of the detail of staff conversations held with the French Army by the General Staff to co-ordinate the movement of British troops to France. Thus the British Empire entered the First World War in August 1914 committed to both a maritime strategy (and the occupation of Germany's colonies was effected within months after the declaration of war) *and* a continental commitment (although on a small scale).[3]

The result of this strategic dispersal was that Great Britain was in no position to bring about the short war and decisive victory that her statesmen desired. It was an inevitable result of coalition warfare that the degree of influence which could be exerted within any given alliance depended on the number of divisions of troops that a power could command on the ground. Because of the small size of Britain's Army, her forces were subordinated strategically to those of France. This would remain true until at least 1918. Nonetheless, despite the great toll of the immense battles of attrition on the Somme and at Third Ypres, the like of which she had never experienced before (nor since), Great Britain emerged by November 1918 as the greatest continental power, with Europe's largest army. This apparent strength disguised one feature of the war that would be repeated in the Second World War: that the resources of Germany were greater than those of Britain and France combined, and that Germany had been defeated only by bringing in the United States to redress the balance, as George Canning had foretold. Nonetheless, the British Army had played the central role in the defeat of the main body of the enemy in a great continental war for the first and only time in British history. Yet this force was demobilised in a very short period of time. Its force structures disappeared, its expertise (so sorely learnt) was dissipated, and no attempt was made to learn the operational lessons of the Great War until the deliberations of the Kirke Committee in 1932. Traditional arguments were reasserted. The popular verdict on the greatest triumph in British military history was that it had all been a ghastly mistake. The ghosts of the 'lost generation' had come back to haunt those who had survived, and the conclusion was reached that 'never again' should Britain commit her forces to the continent of Europe. If she did, so the conventional wisdom ran, then Britain would run the risk of repeating the slaughters on the Somme and at Passchendaele.

The drift of this kind of thinking was summed up in the title of a book by Captain B. H. Liddell Hart, *The British Way in Warfare* (1932). Elsewhere in a stream of lectures, essays and articles in *The Times*, Liddell Hart put the case for not resurrecting a continental commitment and for relying on the strength of naval and aerial forces for the security of the British Empire. If a continental commitment had to be made, Liddell Hart averred, then it should be kept small – say, two high-quality, armoured divisions rather than the mass army of 1914–18. This he termed 'limited liability'; it would avoid the great casualty lists of 1916–17; but it would also have limited Britain's influence in strategic discussions with our allies. Liddell Hart argued that in historical terms the First World War had been an aberration. The British Empire had been built up on the clever employment of 'economic pressure exercised through sea power'. Stimulating and wide-ranging though such arguments were, they were not new and confirmed existing prejudices and policies rather than opened up new areas of thought. When Liddell Hart exercised direct influence over decision-makers, such as Neville Chamberlain, it was because they found in his work a justification and supporting historical evidence which confirmed existing policies.[4]

The policy of the British Government in the late 1930s was indeed impaled on the horns of a perplexing dilemma. The kind of strategy formulated by Liddell Hart seemed to offer one solution. By 1937–38 the British Empire was confronted by a triple threat to its heart and arteries: Nazi Germany in Europe; fascist Italy in the Mediterranean; and a militaristic Japan in the Far East. The Chiefs of Staff reported in December 1937 that:

> We cannot foresee the time when our defence forces will be strong enough to safeguard our trade, territory and vital interests against Germany, Italy and Japan at the same time . . . [we cannot] exaggerate the importance from the point of view of Imperial Defence of any political or international action which could be taken to reduce the number of our potential enemies and to gain the support of potential allies.[5]

Such was the justification for the Chamberlain Government's policy of Appeasement. War in Europe, which would directly threaten the security of the British Isles, would be avoided by conceding to Germany her territorial grievances in Europe arising from the provisions of the Treaty of Versailles. Britain could then concentrate on the defence of her Empire. Of course, such a policy assumed that Nazi Germany shared the British Government's abhorrence of the evils of war; and secondly, that territorial concessions in central Europe would not result in the creation of a continental super-state which would dominate all the others. Chamberlain was wrong on both counts.

When the Chamberlain Government woke up to the fact that the Nazis did not share the same ethical values as themselves, it was forced to rely on deterrence. But ultimately deterrence relies upon force, not merely the threat to use it. Thus it must enshrine substance as well as gesture. A number of British troops had been stationed in Germany to enforce the provisions of the Versailles Treaty; these had been withdrawn by December 1929. In 1937 the continental commitment had been abandoned, not to be resurrected until the German occupation of Prague in March 1939. Both before and after the Munich crisis in the autumn of 1938, the British Government could not fall back on existing force structures by which military power is exerted and through which its chosen policy could be enforced. This was perhaps the gravest legacy of the period of disarmament which had followed the First World War. The lack of a continental commitment resulted in little sustained thinking about fighting a war in Europe, although a group of serious-minded officers, mainly on the General Staff, realised that such a war was imminent. The forces to fight it did not exist; the doctrine for their employment was fragmentary; and commanders and staffs were not trained to fight it. As Donald Cameron Watt has observed:

The trouble is that deterrence may well require the reality of military preparations for real war to be credible to those to be deterred and to those whom deterrence is intended to protect. Otherwise there will always be the element of a Hollywood stage set, of two dimensional facades about it.

Or, to vary the metaphor: The series of hurriedly improvised alliances and guarantees that the British Government sought to create after Munich lacked the fundamental coherence and commonality of interest that deterrence required. As Watt writes elsewhere. 'The British system of guarantees in Eastern Europe was coming to resemble less a damn against aggression than the architecture of Stonehenge.' It was a key factor in the events leading up to the outbreak of war that the German Foreign Minister, von Ribbentrop, had convinced Hitler that the British were bluffing; he was wrong. The British sought to deter Germany with nothing more robust than their determination to deter.[6]

Appeasement did not reduce the insoluble dilemmas confronting the British Government. By 1939 Britain found herself at war with Germany; with Italy by 1940; and with Japan by 1941. The Chamberlain Government had rested its more bellicose policy in 1939 on the fighting power of the French Army. Should the Germans turn westwards then the Low Countries would be protected by French military power, and Britain's security, as Stanley Baldwin had predicted, would truly rest on the Rhine. The French Army would also provide time, as in the First World War, which permitted the British to mobilise their resources undisturbed. The British were confident that they could win a long war of exhaustion. This, too, proved a delusion when they were forced to fight a short one and the French army was utterly defeated. The full consequences of Britain's ambivalent attitude to the European continent now visited themselves on the Army. Although the paper strength of Home Forces in 1940 was 26 divisions, after Dunkirk only sufficient equipment remained for two. Britain alone defied a power which dominated Europe, subject not only to a submarine blockade but aerial bombardment. The collapse of the balance of power in Europe was extended world-wide. After the signing of the Nazi–Soviet pact and the collaboration of Soviet forces in the occupation of Poland, the Soviet occupation of the Baltic states and attack on Finland, Britain was confronted by the combined forces of an alliance stretching from the English Channel to Tokyo and Vladivostok.

Britain survived the greatest crisis in her history, mainly owing to the great good fortune that the resources of this immense power bloc were never brought to bear upon her directly at one time; and with the German attack on the Soviet Union it disintegrated. Certainly Hitler played his cards, which were so stacked against the British, appallingly badly. Thus Hitler himself provided the British with the allies they required after the loss of their continental foothold; he compounded this folly with the

decision to declare war on the United States in December 1941 after the
Japanese attack on Pearl Harbor. Thus the conditions which had led to
Allied victory in 1914–18 were re-created. Once more the New World
was brought in to redress to balance of the Old. Likewise, the successful
termination of the campaign in North-West Europe in 1944–45
concluded the Second World War with the occupation of central
Germany by British troops (although this time on a greater scale).

Nevertheless, buoyed up by the prevailing optimistic mood after
1945, the new Labour Government only belatedly addressed the
fundamental strategic problems which had provoked British interven-
tion in two World Wars. In both 1914 and 1939 it had been to redress the
effect of overwhelming German power in Central Europe, which
France, on her own, was too weak to counteract. But in both World
Wars, the two Western democracies had proved unable to withstand the
German onslaught (in 1940 castastrophically so), and extra-European
powers were brought in to restore the balance. In 1945 with German
power utterly destroyed, the Soviet Union threatened to replace
Germany as a threat to the balance of power in Europe. Great Britain had
emerged from the Second World War as the greatest power in Western
Europe, but neither Britain nor the United States had envisaged the
stationing of large numbers of troops in Germany for long periods of
time after 1945. Thus a security system had to be improvised during the
late 1940s. 'Appeasement' was utterly discredited. Ernest Bevin, the
Foreign Secretary, was determined not to 'appease' the Soviet Union. As
M. L. Dockrill has noted of some of the broad similarities that mark the
twentieth century: 'The confrontation between the Soviet bloc and the
West, now led by the United States, assumed many of the features of the
"armed camp" which characterised the relations between the European
powers before 1914, although now with the crucial difference that the
development of the atomic bomb made it increasingly impossible for the
two blocs to contemplate all-out war, which would not lead to victory in
any real sense, but to their mutual destruction.'[7]

Throughout the crises of the period 1950–85, 'the threat' was always
clearly defined and the forces of the North Atlantic Treaty Organisation,
placed under the command of its military structure, the Supreme
Headquarters Allied Powers in Europe (SHAPE), modelled closely on
the wartime Supreme Headquarters Allied Expeditionary Force
(SHAEF), developed their doctrine and training with this obvious
adversary in mind. Before the mid-1970s, nuclear weapons dominated
NATO's doctrine for the very good reason that a defensive alliance of
democracies could not match the levels of military preparedness in
peacetime attained by a dictatorship, less concerned with the standard of
living of its civil population. In any case, it was only in the exercise of
military power that the Soviet Union was acknowledged as a super-

power; by all other standards of comparison, the Soviet Union was a Third World state, with an under-developed economy. Since the mid-1970s, partly under the influence of technology, partly because of the reappraisal of the American experience in Vietnam, increasing attention has been devoted in the West, including Britain, to what is now called the 'operational level' of war – the conduct of military operations on a large-scale in a 'conventional' war. The study of this subject had fallen into neglect after 1945.

Thus, by way of conclusion, some comment is required on the extraordinary events which have brought the 1980s to an end and inaugurated the last decade of the twentieth century. We are now witnessing the dissolution of Soviet power in Eastern Europe (although the actual Soviet military structure remains intact, and at the time of writing none of the new Eastern European governments has yet left the Warsaw Pact). But three general conclusions on the impact of these developments on the balance of power and the character of Britain's armed forces seem warranted:

● Britain does not necessarily require forces whose structures are solely threat-led. The validity of the operational level of war is not dependent only on the existence of this threat and a continental commitment to resist it. Indeed for much of its history – while the threat was most actute – NATO ignored the operational level. It may be applied equally to smaller forces and other types of war than large-scale continental operations. Thus a diminution of the Soviet military threat in central Europe does not justify any lessening in our study of this area of military activity.
● The greatest crisis in Britain's history in 1940–41 was the result of a failure of deterrence. The policy of the Chamberlain Government failed because its policy of deterrence did not convince and because it lacked the existing force structures by which militay power could be exerted. Deterrence to be credible must rest on substance. In their turn, to be effective, such forces demand the appropriate doctrine and training. If conventional forces are reduced by negotiation, it is not the diminution of the numbers of forces that is alarming, but the withering of expandable force structures should the international climate demand them.
● Finally, that the relationship between the conceptual basis for the development of doctrine and 'the threat' must be dynamic.

Leon Trotsky once wrote, 'He who wishes for a quiet life should not have been born in the twentieth century.' The astounding developments of 1989–90 indicate that problems do not go away – they only call for further study.

Part I
THE STRATEGIC CONTEXT

CHAPTER 1

The Central Region in NATO Strategy

LAWRENCE FREEDMAN

MY OBJECTIVE in this chapter is to provide an analysis of the political context within which questions such as the development of the military balance in Europe and the various issues of doctrine and force planning must be addressed. Sensitivity to the political context is always important: this is even more so at a time of dramatic change.

The Soviet system is reaching the end of its natural life. The decline began long before Gorbachev and there have not yet been any indications that it is reversible. Hegemony in Eastern Europe has been undermined by a failure to provide the basic necessities of life, thereby rendering the sense of foreign domination even more intolerable. The economic failure of the Soviet bloc is the fundamental strategic fact. Gorbachev, *perestroika, glasnost* and so forth are merely symptoms. Suppress them and the disease will persist and manifest itself in other forms.

It may take time before this decline is fully reflected in Soviet forces. The Soviet military will still be arguing that too precipitate unilateral disarmament would be reckless. Unrest within its own borders, especially in the Baltic states, may discourage any dismantling of military forces. There are also practical problems of morale and the necessity to cater for the needs of redundant officers, which will slow down progress. The general will have their own priorities for cuts, which may seek to sustain front-line strength. Nonetheless, with or without disarmament negotiations, it is almost impossible to see the Soviet Union maintaining armed forces of the current quantity and quality at the turn of the twenty-first century.

The conventional wisdom told us that the Soviet Union posed a threat as a result of both its ideological character and its military strength. Reduce both and it would be less of a threat, but there are certain tests which must be passed. From this perspective, at issue is the nature of the tests and the reversibility of any progress in passing them.

11

However, even if the Soviet Union passes these tests, that does not mean to say that Europe can then settle down into a harmonious stability. The evident loss of self-confidence in the Kremlin, when it comes to telling others how to conduct their political affairs, has a mixed impact. Developments that would have been quite unthinkable a few years ago are now everyday occurrences and we are witnessing the emergence of a genuinely pluralist Eastern Europe. What has been most striking is the fragility of the Soviet Union itself – with evidence of increasing popular discontent with rule from Moscow. Here the 'new thinking' finds it limits. Troops have been used regularly over recent months – apparently with varying degrees of central control – within a number of the Soviet Republics. However, the intolerance of independence movements within the Soviety Union throws into relief the tolerance of those just without.

There are many reasons to applaud this process, but we should do so with open eyes for it contains obvious dangers. We do not know the limits of Soviet tolerance, and one of these movements may overstep the mark, or result in a shift in the power balance within the Kremlin. More awkward still, an effective collapse of Soviet hegemonic power in Eastern Europe, including the Baltic states, may unleash disturbing political forces. The cocktail of liberated nationalism, economic failure, and environmental neglect is extremely potent. It offers a recipe for great tension. For the moment, all that it is necessary to note is that it introduces a fluidity that has been absent from European politics since the formation of the cold-war alliances. It is to the processes of alliance formation that I now want to turn, through a consideration of the attitudes of some of the key members of NATO to the development of alliance strategy, particularly with regard to the Central Region, in order to suggest their likely responses to the new political circumstances.

At the time of the 'creation' of the North Atlantic Alliance in the late 1940s, Western strategy was of necessity closely related to a dynamic political situation. The policy debates of the time – over the importance of the American atomic arsenal, the comparative value of economic measures and security guarantees, or the future of Berlin – had to be worked out in a Europe still suffering from post-war convulsions. Questions about the long-term Soviet objectives in Europe, the prospects for the communist parties in France, Italy and Greece, and the durability of the division of the Germany, had an immediacy and an urgency that recent debates on the 'threat' lack. There was every reason to believe that the validity or otherwise of the conclusions reached might soon be revealed in actual Soviet behaviour.

Because one great war had just been completed and few had the stomach for yet another, and also because the logic of the situation encouraged a stalemate, the confrontation settled down into the cold war. This meant that a number of measures taken for short-term effect took on a long-term appearance. As the original problem had not gone away, there seemed to be little reason to remove the various elements that had served before as a solution. Having created the Atlantic Alliance there was no justification for dismantling it; having despatched American troops to Europe there seemed no reason to bring them home or to abandon the air bases; having set in motion German rehabilitation and rearmamemt there was no case for reversing the process; having felt obliged to draw attention to the American nuclear arsenal as a source of deterrence there was no inclination to put it into mothballs.

These were the props of the new European security system. Because they had seemed so necessary when first put in position it was naturally assumed that if one or more of them were removed then the whole system would come tumbling down. Nothing much happened to suggest that the Soviet Union had become reconciled to the status quo. So the early concern remained and became institutionalised along with the props themselves.

The concepts of containment and deterrence encouraged the view that the political situation of the late 1940s was in a state of suspended animation: let the West lower its guard and the Eastern push would carry on as before. And who would dare try to check that this concern was really warranted? So the Alliance continued to do things in the name of deterrence without being quite sure just how much the Soviet Union needed deterring or exactly what it was that did the trick. Were we on the edge of disaster or coasting along with a comfortable margin of safety?

If these props were to be kept in position then what many suspected to be a somewhat unnatural American commitment to an involvement in European politics had to be sustained. The basic assumption behind the formation of the Atlantic Alliance was that a would-be aggressor in Europe would be deterred by the thought of having to take on the United States in pursuit of his objectives – sooner rather than later (as it had been in the previous two World Wars). A constant worry has resulted that the United States might retreat into isolationism.

Moreover, the very nuclear capability that, in the first instance, seemed to confirm an almost effortless American military supremacy, and upon which NATO came to rely overmuch, soon became checked. We tend to talk about the age of strategic parity as starting at the end of the 1960s, when the Soviet Union achieved a sort of visible equality in missile numbers with the United States, but the problems of a nuclear stalemate began as soon as it was recognised that the Soviet Union was in sight of being able to inflict substantial devastation on the North American continent. This fundamentally altered American perceptions of its own vulnerability and, in principle, the sorts of risk that it ought to be prepared to accept on behalf of others. The nuclear stalemate could not help but make the American commitment to Europe appear even more unnatural.

As soon as the first Soviet nuclear explosion was detected in August 1949, the Truman Administration recognized that the days of nuclear supremacy were numbered and that conventional forces would now need to be stressed. The Korean War provided the opportunity to get this rearmament process underway, but the experience of conventional war in Korea, the unfortunate economic consequences of rearmament, and the collapse of the planned European Defence Community brought home too quickly and severely the problems of a conventional bias. The adoption of 'massive retaliation' in 1954 by the United States (which the British had anticipated by two years) was, therefore, something of a relief because it took the pressure off the Europeans and let everyone rest under the cover of American nuclear strength.

This nuclear strength was known at the time to be a diminishing asset, and perhaps all that the Secretary of State John Foster Dulles had in mind when he propounded the doctrine of massive retaliation, was to extract the maximum economic and political advantage from American superiority while it lasted. But as so often happens, a short-term expedient took on a long-term character. The flaw of massive retaliation was pointed out from the start, but it took the first Sputnik of October 1957, underlining America's new vulnerability, for this flaw to be generally acknowledged.

Unfortunately, the implications of this acknowledgement were awkward. At the very least they were expensive because of the costs of matching Soviet conventional strength. More to the point, the Europeans were now nervous about subtracting from the security equation the very factor that had just been made so prominent. Without nuclear weapons what would the Russians have to lose from a conventional war in Europe? Their territory would not be at risk. What would they have to lose, indeed, from making nuclear threats against Europe when the American interest would be clearly to sit tight?

The nuclear factor could not be subtracted, but to sustain it meant flying in the face of all the accumulated wisdom of international politics: that powerful countries rarely knowingly promise to commit suicide on behalf of smaller powers.

The West Europeans encouraged the United States to give substance to its commitment to Europe by basing forces on the continent in such a way that they would soon get caught up in a local war, even though prudent judgement in Washington would be to stand clear. By including nuclear weapons with its forces it even exposed itself to nuclear risk in order to reassure its allies that it was keeping the Soviet Union so exposed.

At the same time, Europeans have required of Washington reassurance that it will not rush headlong into a confrontation with the Soviet Union nor ignore local sensitivities in its military planning. Using weapons as political symbols encourages a tendency to over-interpret every shift in military policy as revealing something fundamental about long-term intentions. The Americans have been remarkably tolerant of this tendency, but this tolerance cannot be open-ended. So long as the United States saw itself as engaged in a global confrontation with the Soviet Union, then it was difficult to argue that it should abandon the very part of the world where the confrontation began and where there was most at stake. But once the United States decides that this confrontation is over and won then its attitude towards the defence burden incurred by its European responsibilities will shift quickly, especially as there is already a powerful body of opinion convinced that the Europeans do not carry their fair share of the burden.

Here, as elsewhere, the critical ally is West Germany. For just as Bonn has habitually paid close attention to the signals emanating from Washington, now the process has reversed and Washington is watching Bonn for indications of a declining interest in collective defence.

West Germany made a covenant with its allies in the 1950s. Part of this was to be its rehabilitation in return for promises that it would not return to its bad old ways. Political conditions at the time prevented this promise from being reinforced by a toleration of permanent division: NATO took on the cause of German reunification but did nothing to pursue it. In practice rearmament was only acceptable because Germany was divided. The military aspect of the covenant was an offer of bases and forces in return for a promise that West Germany's territorial interests would be respected – that is to say, it was not being set up as a superpower battleground but, through forward defence, it would be able to stand up to Soviet power whether directly or indirectly applied.

Because of the tremendous conventional power that the Warsaw Pact could bring to bear, and because it rearmed during the days of massive retaliation, Germany's basic guarantee was nuclear deterrence, so that any attempt to dilute deterrence appeared as a readiness to sacrifice German interests. This saved Bonn at the time from having fully to face the implications of rearmament, but it also meant that any shift from the nuclear bias would push these implications to the fore. Other facts conditioned West Germany's response and thus NATO's attitude. As reunification was still high on the agenda the permanence of the inner-German border could not be recognised in NATO's foreign or defence policies. In addition, everyone was sensitive to the role played by military might in German history, so rearmament had to be handled in such a way as to be as unprovocative as possible to *all* of its neighbours.

This meant renouncing nuclear and chemical weapons and not becoming too associated with offensive strategies. Lurking not far below the surface was the suggestion that, if the Germans were mishandled and came to feel unloved and betrayed, they might see little choice but to mend fences with the East, perhaps exchanging unity for neutrality.

This mixture of concerns has influenced all NATO planning for the Central Front, especially once the dilemmas of nuclear strategy were recognised. This complex symbolism made itself evident during the multilateral force debacle; then in the arguments over nuclear use within the Nuclear Planning Group, with the Germans preferring approaches based on signalling to those based on 'war-fighting'. In the debate over cruise and Pershing missiles the Germans (perhaps inadvertently) pushed the issue of the imbalance of intermediate range forces to the fore out of a concern with 'coupling', then set conditions for its resolution (that is, no 'singularity') which required that the new missiles be based in a number of countries. Finally, as the political temperature rose, they became most anxious to resolve the problem through arms control. More recently the issue of short-range nuclear forces has highlighted the tension between the requirements of deterrence and the Federal Republic's sense of special vulnerability.

This debate resulted in Britain and the United States asserting a NATO orthodoxy *against the very country it was designed to protect*, but a country which, because of its geography and history, is overly sensitive to the shifts of central European politics. As the fear of Soviet hegemony subsides it is replaced by a consciousness of the concessions to sovereignty paid when the fear was much greater. Whether it appreciates this or not, West Germany is in the process of renegotiating its post-war covenant with its allies. As the objective of nuclear deployments has been largely to reassure West German elites, if they no longer wish to be reassured then the case for deployments is otiose.

Similar problems have emerged with the increasing stress on conventional forces. Leaving aside the 'coupling' issue this has traditionally raised ('Are the Americans seeking to reduce the nuclear risks to themselves even if this means undermining deterrence and so increasing the conventional risks to Europe?'), most ideas for reform meet some deep-rooted German objection. Given the rapid drive towards German reunification and its profound impact on existing concepts of security, it is clearly apparent that there is a *declining* readiness to accept the inconveniences of front-line status, such as low-flying aircraft and exercises, and that the arguments of first resort tend to be based on political sensitivities.

The French responded in a somewhat different way to the dilemmas of the nuclear stalemate. It was De Gaulle, after all, who drew attention most bluntly to its implications for the American nuclear guarantee.

Unlike other Europeans who were prepared to continue to believe in the guarantee as an act of faith, provided that the Americans worked to sustain this faith, the French chose to disbelieve. According to the Gaullist analysis, alliances were untenable in the nuclear age: nations had to look to their own devices – preferably nuclear – for their security. The bloc structure in Europe was therefore loosening up and France would be both the agent and the beneficiary of this transformation. It could achieve this most effectively by keeping the Anglo-Saxons at the periphery of European politics.

So it withdrew from the Integrated Military Command, began to practise what would later be described as 'equi-distance' in that it did not differentiate between the superpowers as much as Washington might expect, and confirmed this new independence by the energetic pursuit of the *Force de Frappe* – if possible *tous azimuths*!

But the bloc structure failed to crumble and France's nuclear capability turned out to be essentially regional (and thus anti-Soviet) in nature. France's nuclear force and its absence from the Integrated Command became the symbols of its independence, but in a context in which this independence counted for far less than had been expected, with NATO still active and, in practice, still at the centre of French security policy. The continued stress on the primacy of nuclear deterrence and of national independence began to rest uneasily with the realities of interdependence and the growing uncertainty, even within France itself, about the wisdom of such dependence on nuclear threats. Thus, for France, the old Gaullist symbols have been maintained, even though in practice they are contradicted daily in the working out of defence policy. The allies have learned to respect the symbols while drawing France surreptitiously – and in many aspects successfully – back into the Alliance fold.

Now as the bloc structure does show signs of subsidence France is in no position to exploit it. In the 1960s it could establish a relationship with the Federal Republic in which, for reasons of history and nuclear capability, it still had the upper hand, and a relationship with the Soviet Union based on its maverick role within the Western alliance. Now dominant in central Europe is German economic strength and the consequent creation of a D-Mark zone. France has its own special relationship with the Soviet Union, but then so does everyone else and Soviet power counts for less these days. So long as German power is contained within the established structures of the European Community and NATO then France has little cause for concern, but it is somewhat ironic that the country which at one point appeared to have the greatest interest in a looser Alliance structure now appears to have the greatest interest in keeping it tight.

Along with France, Britain in the 1950s also saw a nuclear deterrent as an answer both to the problems of national decline and the question marks developing against the American nuclear guarantee. Yet neither of these themes was ever fully developed in domestic political debate along the lines that might have been expected. So long as the original Alliance framework remained intact, British policy-makers were not prepared to follow the French and publicly question American good faith. National nuclear deterrence was very much second-best and thus maintained more as a means of having a say in Alliance decision-making and – publicly – as an insurance policy. Insurance policies do not lend themselves to serving as a heady source of patriotic symbolism. Furthermore, the nationalistic rationale was undermined by the palpable dependence on the United States which enabled Britain to stay in the nuclear business. The difficulty of explaining why NATO needed Britain to sustain nuclear forces in addition to those of the United States, without explicitly challenging the viability of the American guarantee, led to muted rationales for the continued development of the national nuclear force.

The political rationales remained powerful but also somewhat difficult to promote in a country which was clearly losing out in all sorts of ways to non-nuclear countries. Nuclear status was by no means a self-evident source of comparative national advantage. However, as the Polaris force posed no great economic strain and was safely out of sight there seemed no need to worry about the quality of the strategic or political rationales. It was only when the cost of staying in the nuclear business suddenly appeared substantial, with the decision to opt for Trident as a replacement for Polaris, that the past inattention to the rationales became a problem. The price-tag – just under £10 billion – still seemed excessive when the benefits of remaining in the nuclear club appeared so modest. However, as the price was paid and the savings from the cancellation of Trident began to appear small, the national nuclear force once again began to slip away as a source of partisan controversy.

In NATO, if not in the Community, Britain's main concern has been less with its own freedom of manoeuvre than with the need to keep the United States committed to European security. London has not asked of Washington more than it was prepared to offer itself, so Britain has in its own defence policies taken on – on a much smaller scale – all those tasks which it deemed essential for the United States. In its own break with the past it has accepted an overt and open-ended peacetime alliance and a continental commitment for the Army. It has even shadowed the American nuclear guarantee to Europe with one of its own, basing key elements of its nuclear capability in West Germany and – notionally at least – assigning its strategic forces to SACEUR. This turned Britain into a paragon of NATO orthodoxy. Its proudest boast was that it contributed to all NATO regions with all types of armament. One rarely detected any divergence of view between British Government pronouncements and the prevailing view at NATO headquarters. This was hardly surprising, as the conceptual framework within which NATO operates was largely an Anglo-American creation.

Britain supported flexible response, helping to uphold nuclear deterrence while contributing to forward defence. Its forces in Germany were placed there not only to help keep the Russians at bay but also to reassure West Germany of a commitment to its defence, and, intially, West Germany's neighbours that any retrograde tendencies could be monitored and if necessary suppressed. By also contributing a strong naval presence in the Eastern Atlantic it also helped to sustain the idea that sufficient reserves of American men and *matériel* might be ferried across the Ocean to turn the course of a prolonged European war.

This has had its costs. Britain's per capita defence spending is significantly higher than that of its European allies and the burden on GDP greater. As crunch points have come with the regular defence reviews, it has striven to avoid offending its allies. BAOR has survived despite its high absolute and foreign-exchange cost. It is, however, an interesting question as to whether BAOR (or for that matter American forces in Europe) would have survived so easily were it not for the fact that in the short term it normally costs money to impose cuts (as the returning soldiers have either to be housed or paid off).

Nonetheless, the priority attached to the Alliance has come at the expense of those aspects of the British defence effort that might have been expected to have the most nationalistic appeal. In the 1960s and the 1970s the global presence was sacrificed for the regional commitment. In 1981, despite the attachment of an 'island people' to its navy, the continental commitment triumphed. Much of the opposition to Trident was based on a concern that its cost would render Britain unable to meet its Alliance obligations.

But British policy-makers must now come to terms with the reality that hegemony over Europe is now completely beyond Soviet capacity. Do we then have a reason for an extraordinary peacetime alliance and a continental commitment? Why should we spend a greater proportion of our GDP on defence in order to maintain stability on the Central Front, especially if the country most involved says that stability is no longer a problem, and that the best way to finally remove a threat from the East is to ensure that we no longer pose a threat *to* the East?

It is important to be aware of these issues, because they could come to the fore of public debate. This could result not only from a steady improvement in East–West relations and further evidence of fragmentation in the East. Two other factors could encourage it. The first would be if the United States began a deliberate process of withdrawal. While we might hesitate to set an example for the United States, we might well be tempted to follow one. Second, the delicate balancing act between commitments and resources that set the parameters for British defence policy could tilt in the direction of a defence review if the political costs of cuts were seen to decline. In these circumstances it is by no means clear that the preference for the continental commitment as expressed in *The Way Forward* (1981) will be so strong. We can look at the latest White Paper and note that almost £4.5 billion is spent each year on the Central Front as against just over £2 billion on the Eastern Atlantic, or that the Central Front has an adverse impact on our balance of payments to the tune of some £1.4 billion each year.

It might have been better if, in the late 1940s and early 1950s, military counters to the assertion of Soviet power could have been kept firmly in the background, with priority given to the economic and the political. But Berlin and then Korea made this impossible. Once the military factor has been pushed to the fore then deterrence was no long based on the unwisdom of an aggressor's taking on the United States, but on the quality of the Alliance's military preparedness. It might then have been better if the conventional rather than the nuclear aspects of preparedness could have been emphasised, but as discussed above, this opportunity passed with the adoption of massive retaliation.

The prominence of the military factor created a tension between those who saw – and still see – NATO as essentially a political arrangement to deal with the political imbalance in Europe resulting from Soviet strength, and those who see it as a military arrangement designed to deal with a military threat.

The more NATO was forced to emphasise the military factor the more those responsible for and concerned with this factor came to the fore in NATO debates. Those who see political cohesion rather than military strength as the key to NATO's success require of the armed forces that they organize themselves with as much regard to the requirements of allies as to the threat from the East. But it is very difficult for those responsible to treat their forces as if they are purely symbolic and have no functional purpose.

The belief that the credibility of deterrence depends on the quality of available military options should deterrence fail has focused strategic analysis on to narrow considerations of technology and comparative force structures. In one sense this leads to a dangerous form of unreality in strategic debate. Any serious East–West confrontation would, by definition, mean that both alliances would be under immense strain so that, at least in the crisis stage, the movement and disposition of military forces would need to be closely related to a developing political situation. So even when the analysis starts with the military relationship it soon gets caught up with questions of political cohesion.

The fast-moving situation in which we actually find ourselves results from the erosion of Soviet power in Eastern Europe. While it is not one that need raise fears of total war, it is one that is fraught with lesser dangers. Inevitably this process raises questions about the need for NATO and the maintenance of forces in the Central Region. In political terms, I would argue that the need for the Alliance is as great as ever. This is not because I believe that we risk being the victims of a great confidence trick perpetrated by Moscow, but rather because there is quite enough experimentation in the former Warsaw Pact countries, and a degree of stability in the West is essential to a smooth process of transition. I would expect that the generally positive processes of recent years must soon include one dramatic reverse, and if that happens there would be a risk of panic if it appeared that we had lowered our defences as a result of a naive optimism.

The current optimism reflects the remarkable progress that has already been made in getting agreement essentially along lines suggested by the West. Success in Vienna would clearly have a major effect on assessments of the threat, whatever sceptics said about force-to-space ratios and warning time. My own scepticism with regard to the arms-control process largely reflects its tendency to move towards a radical transformation of the military relationship assuming that the political relationship remains constant. But arms control has only become possible because of political change and it is my guess that, despite its recent progress, political developments will continue to outpace the negotiations.

In military terms too the Central Region remains important in that, if tension in the East does escalate into conflict, this is where it could still spill over into the West. However, assuming that the fragmentation in the East continues, it is simply unrealistic to expect that Western public opinion – or at least Western finance ministers – will tolerate the same level of defence burden as before, or that West German soil will be as available as before for all the preparations deemed desirable by a prudent military commander. There is real risk of the Alliance beginning to unravel and part of the challenge of ensuring that it does not will be to develop rationales sensitive to the requirements of a Europe in the midst of historic change and not simply rely on presumptions of an unchanging threat.

CHAPTER 2

The Central Front in British Strategy

FIELD MARSHAL LORD CARVER

BRITAIN'S contribution to NATO's Central Region is fairly directly derived from the part we played in the landings in Normandy in June 1944 and the campaign which followed them. There were obvious geographic, political and logistic reasons why the British Army was placed on the left of Eisenhower's line and therefore finished the war in the North German plain.

However, it was not inevitable and not foreseen that an army of ours, backed by a tactical air force, should remain committed to the defence of that area for nearly half a century thereafter. Far from it; the task of the British Army of the Rhine, as it was called, was initially seen as that of an occupation force: to ensure that the edicts of the British Control Commission, based in theory on the Yalta agreement, but in fact on Anglo-American consultation, were, if necessary, enforced. That had been the task of the first British Army of the Rhine from 1918 to 1930. It was the aggressive and unco-operative attitude of the Soviet Union, frustrating attempts to find an agreed solution to the future of Germany, which converted Rhine Army from an occupation force in 1947 of the equivalent strength of two divisions, into a force reasy to oppose a possible Soviet invasion of Western Germany. The process of conversion was hesitant, and some years passed before it was accepted as permanent.

Britain's traditional maritime outlook and suspicion of a continental commitment were displayed at the outset. When the tripartite talks about the future of Germany broke down in December 1947, Ernest Bevin, the Foreign Secretary, asked Field-Marshal Montgomery, the CIGS, to initiate military staff talks between the British, American and French Commanders-in-Chief in Germany 'with a view to ensuring concerted action in the event of any attempt by the Russians to move into Western Europe',[1] and himself to go and talk to his French opposite

23

number, General Revers, about it. The latter persuaded Montgomery that a British commitment to fight alongside the French on the Rhine was an essential ingredient in persuading the French themselves to do so. As Bevin formulated his concept of an association of the democratic countries of Western Europe with the United States, and also possibly the Dominions of the British Commonwealth, the Chiefs of Staff instructed the Joint Planners to consider what they should recommend as Britain's strategy in this context. They came up with a paper[2] which stated that 'The supreme object of our defence policy is the defence of the United Kingdom and the development of an offensive capability.' Their conclusion was that 'From the point of view of the countries of Western Europe, there is no doubt that they would be encouraged and fortified if we adopted a continental strategy, but this, in our view, is quite impracticable, at least until 1957.'

They went on to say 'The retention of a foothold in Europe might be a practicable strategy, but requires much more detailed examination and discussion with the Americans. At present our view is that the disadvantages outweigh the advantages. We therefore conclude that, from our point of view, the best strategy appears to be the air strategy, since that gives us the best chance of preventing war and achieving ultimate victory and provides for at least some support to the countries of Western Europe. In any case we recommend that, in the forthcoming talks (in Washington) we should enter into no commitment to send land and air forces to the continent.'

This was not to the liking of Montgomery, who, contrary to the hallowed ritual of the procedure of the Chiefs of Staff, submitted a rival, and remarkably prescient paper of his own.[3] Its salient points were the need to develop the three Western zones of occupation into one West German state, which could be accepted into a Western Union, and contribute to its military strength. In order to persuade the French to accept the resurrection of their former enemy, Britain must commit herself to fighting alongside France on land on the line of the Rhine. The aim should be to build up a Union strong enough to hold a Russian attack until American help could be deployed.

When the two papers were considered by the Chiefs of Staff, Montgomery's colleagues, Marshal of the Royal Air Force Lord Tedder, who was Chairman of the Committee, and the First Sea Lord, Admiral Sir John Cunningham (not to be confused with the famous Admiral Andrew Cunningham), supported the view of the Joint Planners. The issue was then referred to a meeting of the Chiefs of Staff with the Prime Minister, Clement Attlee, Bevin and the Minister of Defence, A. V. Alexander. The minutes[4] record that Tedder and Cunningham 'considered that it would prove both financially and economically impossible to place an army on the Continent on the outbreak of war, especially as in any future war we should have to be prepared for full-scale operations from the beginning . . . it was open to doubt whether it was militarily sound to attmept to hold an enemy with such predominant superiority in manpower on the Continent'. They suggested that our support for Western Union should be limited to naval and air support. Tedder said: 'He could not believe that Western Union would collapse if we withheld a specific promise to fight on land on the Continent.' Cunningham agreed, and said that 'Our traditional policy was to encourage and assist our Continental allies to provide land forces but to refrain from engaging in any land operations ourselves at the outset, in order to leave ourselves free to wield our maritime power. Nowadays, of course, we could use air power as well, and he feared that any commitment to engage in land operations was bound to detract from our air and sea power. The only times we had broken away from our traditional policy had led to the tragedies of Mons and Dunkirk.'

Montgomery even seemed to have been affected by the limited liability bug, although he stuck to his plea that we must line up with the French from the start. He said that Western Union would need 23 divisions by $D + 14$ and 48 by $D + 30$, and optimistically declared that France could produce 30, while we need provide only two. Attlee sided with Tedder and Cunningham and suggested that we should plan an offensive from the Middle East, while Bevin failed to give full support to Montgomery, saying that 'he would like the Chiefs of Staff to consider how the forces of the United Kingdom, France, the Benelux countries and possibly Italy should be organised and rationalised so as to form an effective whole', and registered his dislike of Montgomery's idea of the resurrection of Germany.

They were, of course, influenced by knowledge of the decision, taken a year previously, that we should develop our own atom bomb.

Reliance on an 'air strategy' must be seen in that light; but it would be some time before we would be in a position to deliver any number, and our Western European allies did not even know, any more than the British public did, that the decision had been made. One wonders how Cunningham thought that we were going to 'encourage and assist our Continental allies to provide land forces' if we did not, and how he would propose to 'wield our maritime power' against the Soviet Union advancing to the Rhine. One's mind boggles also at the prospect of Attlee's suggestion of an offensive against the Soviet Union launched from the Middle East, unless he envisaged solely an aerial one, once atom bombs were available.

Nevertheless, these discussions led to the signature of the Brussels Treaty, the main purpose of which, in Bevin's eyes, was to persuade the United States that Western Europe was sufficiently prepared to make an effort in its own defence to warrant American support: to act as a stepping stone toward the wider Atlantic Alliance, which, as NATO, came into existence in 1949, although no effective military organisation was established until almost two years later. The British Government, in that period, showed no enthusiasm for giving Western Union any military teeth. At that time, and for several years later, both the American and the British Government expected that the Alliance, combined with American military aid, would make it possible to build up the armies of the continental nations of Western Europe, so that the Americans in Britain could withdraw their armies from Germany and limit their contributions to naval and air support. From the start the Americans saw clearly that this could not be done, unless Germany made a substantial contribution. Argument about how to achieve this, without resurrecting the threat of Germany to its neighbours, dominated the affairs of the Alliance, which were complicated by France's heavy commitment in Indo-China.

Britain was also facing imperial problems, but, having divested herself of military commitments in the Indian sub-continent and Palestine, embarked on an ambitious rearmament programme in response to both the formation of NATO and the Korean War. The threat of world-wide communism, stemming from the Soviet Union and China, seemed very stark at the time.

The Defence White Paper of 1951 stated that it was the Government's intention to have the equivalent of 10 divisions in the standing army, Rhine Army's strength being increased from three to four. The Reserve Army would be designed to produce another 12, making use of ex-national servicemen to fill the ranks. Two years later the standing army's strength had been increased from 373,500 to 437,500, the equivalent of $11\frac{1}{3}$ divisions, of which four were stationed in Germany.

1954 was a crucial year. After the rejection by the French National Assembly of the Pleven Plan for a European Army, Anthony Eden, the Foreign Secretary, under strong pressure from the United States for German rearmament in some form, persuaded the French and the other Brussels Treaty powers to admit both Germany and Italy to the Western Union as a means of their acceptance as full members of NATO. The price he had to pay was a British guarantee that we would maintain the forces we then stationed in Germany – four divisions and a tactical air force, or whatever the SACEUR regarded as the equivalent capabili-ty – and not to withdraw them against the wishes of the majority of the Brussels Treaty powers 'who should take their decision in the knowledge of SACEUR's views'. Rhine Army alone numbered 70,000 at that time.

The 1954 Defence White Paper stated that 'the Government will continue to regard it as a defence measure of the first importance to maintain the strength and efficiency of the British forces on the continent assigned to SACEUR. The primary deterrent, however, remains the atomic bomb and the ability of the highly organised and trained US strategic air power to use it. We intend as soon as possible to build up in the RAF a force of modern bombers capable of using atomic weapons to the fullest effect. A strong and efficient force of medium bombers is of the great importance to us both for our own security and for the defence of Western Europe'.

At that time the army was beginning to consider the possible employment of nuclear weapons on the battlefield, but did not envisage operations fundamentally different from those in the closing stages of the Second World War. Considerable emphasis was given to close co-operation between tanks and infantry. At one stage the brigade group was regarded as the basic formation, consisting of three infantry battalions (for which there were no armoured personnel carriers), one armoured regiment and one towed field-artillery regiment. Plans were based on Rhine Army being reinforced by both regular and Territorial Army Divisions from the UK, for which there was, in reality, no equipment nor logistic support, and most of whose personnel could not have been regarded as trained for battle.

The manufacture of the first British thermonuclear weapon in November 1954 coincided with the Conservative administration's acceptance that the rearmament programme embarked upon by its Labour predecessor had been over-ambitious and was imposing an excessive strain on the nation's economy, as well as on the army's manpower, which was stretched by the concurrent emergencies in Malaya, Cyprus and Kenya. The result was to increase the emphasis on nuclear weapons. This was reflected in the 1955 Defence White Paper, which stated that 'The knowledge that aggression will be met by overwhelming nuclear retaliation is the surest guarantee that [a major war] will not take place . . . This counter-offensive strength is also our own most effective defence against aggression . . . the first few [nuclear] exchanges would be of critical importance. Great advantages would flow from surprise and the first assault . . . the enemy might well initiate the use of nuclear weapons at the outset. A prompt and overwhelming counter-offensive with the most powerful weapons available offers at present the surest means of limiting the scale of such attacks'.

In emphasising the Soviet preponderance in conventional weapons, the White Paper went on to say: 'Even allowing for the essential German contribution, the free world cannot put into the front line anything comparable. The use of nuclear weapons is the only means by which this massive preponderance can be countered. But with their aid and with the German contribution, we can adopt a forward strategy on the ground in Europe and so defend the Continent, instead of contemplating again the grim process of liberation . . . The NATO Council in Paris in December

1954 therefore approved a report by the Military Committee which assumed the use, in a major war, of nuclear weapons . . . We still need troops on the ground to hold the enemy well to the east in Europe in the vital initial stages of a war. This would give time for the effects of our strategic air offensive to be felt. It would also hold back from the United Kingdom the threat of shorter range aircraft and ground-to-ground missiles. The presence of a firm shield of troops and tactical aircraft similarly reduces the danger that the Communists might be tempted to try and overrun Europe with conventional forces in the hope that the West would refrain from using nuclear weapons in its defence or that it could be used as a pawn in a shameful negotiation.' The White Paper said that four divisions would be maintained in Germany, and that the army's total strength was 437,900, almost equally divided between regulars and national servicemen.

1956 was the year of Suez and a year later saw the advent to power of Harold Macmillan. He was, at that time, wedded to the concept of the nuclear weapon as an overall deterrent to war, and was determined to reduce the army's strength for a number of reasons. Suez appeared to have shown that the attempt to maintain the capability to engage in Second World War-type operations was a waste of manpower and money. He also wished to steal the Labour Party's clothes by being able to announce the abolition of conscription before the next general election; and he was annoyed that, while we were experiencing continuing economic difficulties, aggravated by the scale of our defence expenditure, much of it stemming from our contribution to the Central Front in Germany; the newly fledged Federal Republic, spending much less, was becoming one of our chief economic rivals.

A major restructuring of the forces was therefore undertaken, aiming at the abolition of national service by December 1962 and the reduction in regular strength of the armed forces by that time to 375,000, of which the army would be allowed to recruit up to 165,000. That involved the disbandment or amalgamation of 51 teeth-arm units, 21 in the Royal Artillery, 17 in the infantry, 8 in the Royal Armoured Corps and 5 in the Royal Engineers. It was originally intended to reduce Rhine Army from its then current strength of 77,000 to 45,000; but, in the teeth of protests from NATO, when there was a renewed crisis over Berlin in 1958, the target was agreed at 55,000, at which it has remained ever since.

Another dramatic event was to influence the function of the forces on the Central Front: the launching of *Sputnik* in 1957 and the realisation that it would not be long before the Soviet Union would be able to deliver megaton weapons by ballistic missiles on to targets in the United States.

It cast doubt on the assumption that the ability of the US Air Force's Strategic Air Command to deliver devastating destruction to the Soviet

Union could be relied on to allow Britain, and other European members of NATO, to make what appeared to be little more than token contributions to oppose the military might of the Soviet Union. The Americans began to show concern that the weakness of Western European defences could trigger off a nuclear exchange, which would result in Soviet megaton weapons landing on American cities. The task of NATO's conventional shield was no longer to act as just a trip-wire for massive retaliation, a forward screen to protect air bases and an insurance against war by miscalculation. In his 1957 NATO letter, SACEUR, the American airman General Lauris Norstad, described the task of his conventional forces as 'to force a pause' by fighting a conventional action 'to meet less-than-ultimate threats with a decisive, but less-than-ultimate response', adding that this 'would thereby provide us with essential political and military manœuvrability'.

This was highly awkward for the British Government, which was in the process of increasing its dependence on megaton nuclear weapons, reducing its conventional forces and threatening to reduce its conventional contribution to the Central Front even further, if it did not receive satisfaction in its demand that the Federal Republic should compensate it for the 'offset costs' involved. The longer the pause that had to be forced, in order to avert the danger of Soviet nuclear weapons landing on American cities, the stronger needed to be not only NATO's combat forces, but, almost as significant, their logistic backing to enable them to fight for longer and to replace their losses.

The nettle of this strategic conundrum was grasped when John F. Kennedy became President of the United States in 1961 and appointed the intensely logical management expert from Ford Motors, Robert McNamara, as his Defense Secretary.

The significant shift of emphasis about the role of the conventional forces on the Central Front initiated a long debate, which continues to this day, about the credibility of what is called 'extended deterrence', when the Soviet Union has the capability to deliver shattering blows against the cities of both European and American members of NATO, and of the relative part to be played, and emphasis given, to nuclear and conventional forces within the Alliance. The Americans continue to wish to ensure that the Europeans insure against either a nuclear or a non-nuclear war limited to Europe, which would leave their countries in ribbons, while America and at least part of the Soviet Union would be intact. They insist therefore that there must be no 'decoupling': that a Soviet conventional incursion across the Iron Curtain must carry the risk of American megaton weapons landing on Soviet cities.

This tension between the conflicting interests of the United States and of the European members of NATO, the Canadians being on the sidelines, was eventually dampened down by a compromise called 'flexible response', which was not what the author of the phrase, the American General Maxwell Taylor, meant by it. It should have been called 'graduated response', the brainchild of Rear-Admiral Sir Anthony Buzzard. Denis Healey, who became Defence Secretary when Harold Wilson's Labour Administration came to power in 1964, made a significant contribution to its acceptance. As a doctrine, it had the advantage of resembling the dogma of the Church of England. It could mean all things to all men.

The result of this long, and 'agonising reappraisal' of NATO's strategy, and our adaptation to it, was summed up in the 1966 Defence White Paper, which said: 'Once nuclear weapons were employed in Europe, on however limited a scale, it is almost certain that, unless the aggressor quickly decided to stop fighting, the conflict would escalate rapidly to a general nuclear exchange, in which the whole of America's nuclear forces would be engaged. Organised land warfare would then soon become impossible. We have, therefore, urged on the Alliance that it should abandon those military preparations which rest on the assumption that a general war in Europe might last for several months. At the same time, NATO must maintain its ground forces in Germany at about their existing level until satisfactory arms control arrangements have been agreed in Europe, provided, however, that some means is found for meeting the foreign exchange cost of these forces. We shall be negotiating for this purpose, and shall strengthen air support at the cost of some reduction in nuclear strike forces stationed there.' A supplementary statement at the end of the same year, announcing major changes in the organisation of the army's reserves, added this: 'It is no longer realistic to maintain ground forces designed to fight another major conventional war on large armies in Europe. The risk of major war in Europe is now small, but if it did come, it would involve the use of nuclear weapons. This is the basis of the Western Alliance's strategy.' The paper went on to lay emphasis on logistic support for the regular army as the chief function of the reserves, and the concept of reinforcing Rhine Army with divisions based on the mobilisation of the Territorial Army was abandoned.

In 1967 the Labour Government was faced by an acute economic crisis and decided on major reductions in the armed forces in order to keep defence spending down to £2 billion a year. While the main reductions were to be obtained by a major withdrawal from east of Suez, economies were sought also within NATO. The rationale produced for these was that the overall deterrent to war provided by the existence of a considerable nuclear armoury was such that the Soviet Union did not contemplate military action; and that there would be ample political warning of any change in the Soviet attitude. The Government therefore proposed to economise on anything connected with either a surprise attack or a prolonged period of operations, whether on land or at sea. The result was the proposal to withdraw one infantry brigade group and an RAF squadron to Britain, although they remained assigned to the Central Front. It was expected to save £5½ million in foreign exchange. In addition, agreement was reached with the United States and West Germany by which the foreign exchange costs of Rhine Army and RAF Germany were covered for a year. After this move the strength of Rhine Army was 54,300, which, with 32,900 civilians, cost £207 million.

This somewhat complacent attitude was reflected in the 1968 Defence White Paper, which stated: 'NATO strategy should be based on the forces that member countries are prepared to provide', and 'Within the total resources available to NATO, adjustments should be made, particularly in the air forces, with the object of extending the conventional phase of hostilities, should war break out; this would give more time in which any decision to use nuclear weapons could be taken.' This change in emphasis, away from over-reliance on nuclear weapons, was the fruit of years of discussion in NATO, culminating in acceptance of 'flexible response'.

The Soviet invasion of Czechoslovakia in that year administered a shock to any complacency. The 1970 Defence White Paper drew attention to the 'threatening increase in the size and quality of Warsaw Pact forces', and reaffirmed that 'The security of Western Europe must rest fundamentally on the US strategic nuclear guarantee.' With both sides having increasing numbers of tactical nuclear weapons, and also developing first-strike strategic systems, a strategy which envisaged an almost automatic recourse to nuclear weapons was no longer acceptable. NATO, the White Paper said, must provide a wider and more flexible range of response, appropriate to the nature of the threat. The Alliance must be ready to use nuclear weapons, but they must not be the only response available The validity of its strategy 'depended critically on maintaining conventional forces at a level which would give NATO an alternative to a nuclear response against anything but a major deliberate attack, and which, if an attack on that scale should occur, would allow time for negotiations to end the conflict and for consultations among the Allies about the initial use of nuclear weapons, if negotiations hould fail'.

The Government fortunately managed to convince itself, if not those actually serving on the Central Front, that, in the words of the White Paper, 'At present the level of these conventional forces is just sufficient for this purpose, though there is a need for improvements in quality and equipment.' If satisfactory arrangements about offset costs could be agreed with the Federal Republic, the brigade which had been removed would be returned. Soon after this paper had been published, the Labour administration gave way to a Conservative one, headed by Edward Heath. During this time neither the composition nor the operational plans and training of 1st British Corps had changed significantly, as the emphasis shifted to and fro between reliance on nuclear weapons and enforcing the pause. Its commanders at different levels had no great confidence either that their forces would be able to hold up those of the Warsaw Pact for more than a few days, if that, or that operations could be conducted in any meaningful way while both sides were using nuclear weapons on the battlefield, whatever they might be doing with them further behind it.

6th Brigade returned to Germany in 1971, its sojourn at Catterick having posed more problems than it solved. Since then there have been changes in the organisation of Rhine Army, which have theoretically altered the number of divisions or brigades, but have not in reality changed its operational capability. There was a curious interlude in the mid-1970s when, faced by manpower and financial problems, the Army Board, aghast at the prospect of yet more amalgamations or disbandment of teeth-arm units, tried to abolish brigades in order to avoid them. Fortunately, that aberration was soon abandoned. It coincided with the Defence Review carried out by the Labour administration which succeeded Heath's in 1974. Denis Healey, now Chancellor of the Exchequer, was determined to reduce defence expenditure at least to $4\frac{1}{2}$ per cent, and eventually to 4 per cent of GNP, from the $5\frac{1}{2}$ per cent at which it had been running. Britain's contribution came under scrutiny once more. There was little left to cut from anything tied to commitments outside NATO, and, within it, economies were centred on the operationally dubious ones of the air-transported and amphibious reinforcement plans to the Southern and the Northern Region. The Chiefs of Staff – I was then CDS – maintained that the cohesion of the Alliance would be undermined if our contribution fell below a critical level, which included maintaining our land and air force contribution to the Central Front at its current level, unless the MBFR talks negotiated a lower level for both the Warsaw Pact and NATO. We were prepared to accept a reduction of 5,000 in the strength of Rhine Army in that event, although that was not admitted publicly.

Since then there has been a growing emphasis on reducing reliance on the early use of nuclear weapons, with a complementary increase in interest in fighting for longer with conventional forces. This has more or less eliminated the idea that operational plans should be centred round the defensive tactical use of nuclear weapons, and aroused interest in plans which envisaged counter-offensive action, based primarily on tanks, but augmented by both armed- and troop-carrying helicopters. Confidence in the realism of these concepts must be limited by the paucity of the resources available: the almost total lack of any reserve, once the minimum force has been deployed to cover the main approaches.

The reality over the last 40 years has been that none of the politicians of any of the NATO countries have believed that there was ever a serious danger of war. The nearest we came to it was in the two Berlin crises, in 1948 and 1958, although the Cuba affair of 1962 had its repercussions in Europe. Czechoslovakia in 1968 caused a minor tremor. They have not therefore been prepared to take the unpopular measures to meet that as an urgent threat. The strength of their contributions, including ours to the Central Front, has been determined essentially by political factors: by the need to maintain the cohesion of the Alliance, the essential key to which is persuading the United States to maintain both its nuclear umbrella and the stationing of its conventional forces in Europe – the real backbone of deterrence; by the need for the particular nation to maintain its own standing and influence within the Alliance; in our case, an important element has been to see that our influence is not eclipsed by that of the Federal Republic; and, finally, by domestic political pressures. The aggressive and repressive attitude of the Soviet Union has been an important factor in maintaining the cohesion of the Alliance and persuading its members, including ourselves, to make an adequate contribution. The current thaw in East–West relations puts that at risk, and the result, as we see it today in the two Germanies, must cause us some anxiety.

CHAPTER 3

The Central Front in Soviet Strategy

CHRISTOPHER DONNELLY

MICHAIL GORBACHEV claims to be a Leninist, to be inspired by and be guided (albeit not blindly) by Leninist principles and examples. If this claim is true, and I believe that in essence it is, then the requirements of his domestic policies will be paramount, and will be the overriding influence on all his foreign and military policies, including those concerned with arms control and force reduction.

The economic problems the USSR faces he identifies as mere symptoms; the cause of the country's manifest ills is political, and political reforms must go hand-in-hand with economic if Gorbachev is to succeed in bringing the USSR out of crisis and ensuring its position as a superpower in the twenty-first century.

The military establishment is the target of Gorbachev's reforms on two counts. First, the professional military constitute one of the most conservative groups in Soviet society. They are by definition dedicated to preserving the Soviet socialist system and its values. They have the strongest perception of NATO as 'the threat'. There is a considerable natural conservatism found in most established military systems, and in the Soviet military this is bolstered by a high degree of vested interest in the maintenance of its position in the hierarchy of privilege that is such a feature of today's USSR.

Secondly, to fuel his economic reforms, Gorbachev needs to achieve a rapid reduction in the resource allocation to defence, and also a means of securing the switching of those resources into an improvement in Soviet basic science and production. It is not his intent to produce a Western-style consumer economy, nor will all savings on defence be turned into consumer goods. The key to this policy is a reform of the defence industries, switching key personnel and applying some of the practices to the civilian sector which have made the defence industries effective. However, the process of integrating these two hitherto completely

separate sectors of Soviet industry is very slow, and there has been so far
no significant slowdown of defence production and no large scale shift to
civilian production. Nor has there yet been any really significant shift of
research and development facilities.

The military bloc, however, is still a group very important to
Gorbachev. Its support would be an essential for any opponent trying to
topple Gorbachev from power. Its support, as the recent events in China
have demonstrated, might be instrumental in keeping the Communist
Party in power if the reform process gets out of hand. Furthermore,
military power is still an essential ingredient of the Soviet claim to
superpower status. But it is the General Staff's monopoly of authority on
defence matters which has been, at least in part, responsible for the
disastrous course of Soviet economic development since the Second
World War. Gorbachev's relationship with his military must, therefore,
be handled gently and skilfully, and the serious pruning of the political
and economic clout which the Soviet armed forces have traditionally had
in the Soviet system must be conducted with extreme care.

For its part, the military face several serious problems which, it is
clear, cannot be solved simply by an influx of resources. On the one
hand, concepts for future war demand a serious revision of operational
and tactical thinking; poor junior officer leadership and the apathy of
many soldiers, induced by inter-ethnic friction, poor living conditions
and the general national lack of enthusiasm for hard work, threaten both
operational efficiency and unit social cohesion. New and projected
equipment will worsen the training problem and increase the need for
operational rethinking.

But the technological advances under way bring their own problems.
The Soviet armed forces face a serious problem of modernisation and
resource allocation over the next decade, for which policy decisions are
needed now. A significant reduction in current defence expenditure is
needed to generate resources to fuel this military modernisation too.
Technological developments in the short term (five years) favour the
current weapons platforms (for example, tanks, ships, and planes),
whose performance can outmatch counter-platform systems (like anti-
tank missiles). But emerging technologies promise to reverse this trend,
rendering many of the platforms which will dominate the battlefield of
the 1990s obsolete after the turn of the century. Given the cost, length of
time to develop, and in-service life of such platforms, this faces
procurement chiefs with difficult decisions. These decisions are made
more difficult because they will necessitate changes in doctrine, strategy,
operations and tactics, and training. This last is perhaps the most
difficult nut to crack. The significant and widespread changes in senior
military personnel, however, leave us in no doubt as to Gorbachev's
intent to force the pace of these changes on the Soviet General Staff.

This trend makes it imperative for the USSR to develop its own high technology base (and its military system to exploit this), whilst, if possible, reducing the rate of technological innovation in the West, and acquiring when possible access to Western inventions and the industrial expertise to produce this new technology. A review of Gorbachev's disarmament proposals shows how this has become a strengthening theme over the years. It is accompanied by the consistent theme of reducing the nuclear arsenals of the world and reducing the tension of East–West confrontation, both in Europe and around the globe. The series of unilateral proposals initiated on 7 December 1988 demonstrates how serious Gorbachev is to achieve a reduction in standing forces and also a reduction in the Western perceptions of the USSR as a threat.

In fact, there can be no doubt that Gorbachev's foreign policy initiatives have been dramatically successful in changing perceptions of the USSR as a threat, particularly in Europe and, within Europe, especially in West Germany. Arms control can be seen as the new and favoured tool of policy which Gorbachev, driven by his domestic needs, has chosen to achieve his political ends. These ends, he keeps reminding us, are to make the Soviet system work, not to change it into a Western-style democracy.

The disarmament proposals themselves are significant for several reasons. For those analysts who thought the USSR was likely to launch a bolt-from-the-blue attack and that it could and might do so at 48-hours' notice, then the reductions will seem very significant indeed. This is because as long as NATO remains at its current strength and readiness, they render the Soviet armed forces in Eastern Europe incapable of launching such an attack without giving unadvantageous warning. However, to those who never thought this a plausible scenario and who interpreted 'surprise' as limited surprise achieved by deception during a long and serious pre-war crisis, the reductions will be significant as an indicator that the Soviet leadership does not think that war is imminent, and not as signifying any real reduction in Soviet combat capability.

One thing is certain: the force reductions announced to date will undoubtedly lead to more. Gorbachev needs more drastic cuts rapidly for real impact on his economic problem. Let us recapitulate on a few of the military and political factors directing the current policy.

● Nuclear weapons are the *only* weapons currently available which can threaten the very existence of the Soviet state. Gorbachev needs to reduce the nuclear threat to the USSR. The fewer nuclear weapons NATO has, the fewer ready conventional forces the USSR needs.

- Significant reduction in conventional forces coupled with no need to invest heavily in new weapons is necessary to fuel Gorbachev's economic reforms.
- Domestic discontent means that Gorbachev cannot afford long-winded and detailed negotiations. Time is not on his side. He needs real improvement within three years.
- The USSR needs easy access to technology, finance, and industrial expertise from the West. This cannot be achieved unless the Soviet threat perception in the West is reduced.
- There are strict limits to the extent to which Gorbachev can risk alienating the Soviet General Staff by forcing on them military options which they dislike.
- Technology is changing the nature of battle very rapidly and past methods of calculation and planning are quickly becoming less reliable.
- Technical developments in the future will change the relative value of weapons and military systems and put a high premium on efficient C^3I, and the ability to switch rapidly from defence to attack and back again.
- The characteristics of new equipment and weapons make them versatile and equally useful in attack and defence.
- Current force structures and military organizations are not suited to the needs of tomorrow's battle and to exploiting the characteristics of new kit.
- To maintain high tempo on the future battlefield the Soviet army needs the lowest *force density consistent with cohesion*.
- The Soviet General Staff still believes that it is essential to maintain an offensive capability if defence is to be effective.

In addition to the above factors, we should note that Gorbachev:

- Has stressed the need for rapid and deep cuts.
- Has promised to reorganise every division in East Germany. Tank divisions are to be reduced to between 200 and 240 tanks, MR divisions to 160. There is to be a 50 per cent increase in anti-tank and anti-aircraft weapons in forward-defence sectors.
- Promises to withdraw the Soviet armed forces in eastern Europe.
- Has set in motion a reform of the General Staff.
- Has begun studies on the reforming of the conscription system and improving the means of rapid mobilisation.
- Is pushing the Soviet armed forces to improve its training system, rethink its operations and tactics, and complete its structural reorganisations.

The Historical Dimension of Defensive Operations

Soviet operational analysis places great store in the evaluation of Soviet Second World War operations are models for future planning. When Soviet operational concepts were firmly wedded to the offensive, the Manchurian, Yassi-Kishenev, Byelorussian and Vistula–Oder operations of 1944–45 were the ones most widely studied and evaluated for modern relevance.

If the Soviet armed forces are to adopt a more truly defensive character, then not only will we initially see changes in organization, deployment, tactics training, and equipment, but we must expect Soviet operational research to produce the analyses of Second World War operations essential within the Soviet military system as models. This is in fact being done, and the clear winners in the 'competition to find the most suitable World War II operation to evalute' are Kursk and Khalkin-Gol. The Kursk strategic battle of 1943 (which marked the real end of the German strategic offensive) and the repulse of the Japanese incursion from Manchuria into Mongolia in 1939 in Khalkin-Gol are held up as models of defensive thinking.

This is clearly true. In both cases an enemy attacked, was stopped, and was repulsed – at Khalkin-Gol only as far as the state borders so as not to provoke a war with Japan and thus risk a war on two fronts in 1939. At Kursk the Soviet counter blow was limited by Soviet resources and German strength.

But, the key to both attacks was:

- The use of forward fortified areas to attract the enemy's attack, and erode his strength in order to permit:
- A major counter-offensive to hold the weakened enemy and push him back, and:
- a strategic counter-offensive to push deep into the enemy's territory to transform local success into operational–strategic success. At Kursk, this counter-offensive enjoyed limited success, at Khalkin-Gol it was not attempted for political reasons.

Such a model is extremely attractive in Soviet military thinking. It allows for the aggressive use of defence to create a means by which the enemy can be lured to his own destruction. It also permits the maintenance of a significant counteroffensive capability, permitting decisive action to conclude a victory. In political terms, it permits a more rearward (and less provocative) deployment, clearly defensive forward positions, and fewer ready forces, *providing that* it is assumed that: in the first place, war is not imminent; in the second, a reasonable degree of mobilisation time is available; and finally, that forces have been trained and equipped appropriately, and adequately well.

Thus we would assess that Mr Gorbachev is keen to reduce both defence spending and East–West tension, and that therefore he will seriously try to make significant force reductions. We can also be fairly confident in assuming that the Soviet General Staff accepts that it must play its role in restructuring so as to reduce tension and avoid provoking war and an arms race. Of course, it needs to reduce in size so as to facilitate an improvement in military quality, to help improve the national economy, and also provide resources for long term 'high tech' research for technologies on which to base new weapons. The General Staff, however, still has the duty of planning and organising to win a war if it starts. Therefore it will attempt to complete the military modernisation programme that has been under way since the 1970s, and try to use any reductions as an opportunity to streamline and improve efficiency. Consequently, the General Staff will minimise the impact of reductions by ensuring that they are interpreted in the most advantageous way. And it follows from this that they will try and extract political concessions for reductions, and delay the execution of reductions if obstruction is deemed effective.

The result of this somewhat conflicting set of imperatives is likely to be a rather confused situation. It will probably remain difficult to identify the exact motives for any Soviet action, because the way a policy is implemented cannot only render its intention obscure and ambiguous, but actually cast doubt on the sincerity of the intention in the first place. The way in which some troop withdrawals are actually being carried out at the moment is a good example of this. The situation for NATO is further confused by the rapid changes in public attitude to the existence of the 'Soviet threat', and the interaction of this with domestic and foreign policies within, particularly, the Federal Republic of Germany. Once we doubt our own position, estimating the opponent's becomes doubly difficult.

That Gorbachev is deeply unpopular amongst many of the officer corps cannot now be doubted. That he has the support of many senior officers, newly in post, cannot be doubted either, not the least because they realise that ultimately Soviet military strength depends on social and economic health, and that reform is needed. On balance, we can expect that the Soviet General Staff will do its best to accommodate Gorbachev's needs to cut and redeploy the armed forces, whilst it attempts simultaneously to strive for delay; to permit more time to work out sensible military ways of reorganising to make the best of the situation; and devise appropriate operations and tactics to maintain the advantage. This will involve such measures as destroying any old equipment (save a few for the cameras) so as to leave a military with a higher level of modernisation. In addition, it will seek to cut understrength posts ('dead souls') weeding out poor quality officers and

NCOs, but not cutting the basic structure, and maintaining the regular/ conscript cadre structure until a more efficient mobilisation and training system can be devised and implemented.

Consequently, we should now expect to see really significant changes in Soviet structure and deployment in Europe, perhaps along the following lines. The Soviet Union will seek to maintain a strong border covering force and it will create 'fortified regions' – extensive, in-depth, all-round terrain fortifications and saturated with anti-aircraft, rapid-fire anti-personnel and anti-tank weapons. The reorgnisation of Soviet mobile divisions will follow, to yield smaller, more balanced formations withdrawn from border areas, deployed as counter-attack forces. Other groups of Soviet forces and Warsaw Pact armies may follow suit.

Moreover, we may observe the gradual disbanding of airborne divisions and their reallocation as airborne brigades deployed in-depth as an integral part of combined arms formations; the reduction of displaced forces to 'cadre status', with improved levels of reserve training; the reorganisation of Military Districts to cope with this new training/ mobilisation role and to establish defensive plans; and the development of the theatre command system, to include the command tasks previously done by the Military Districts. Taking all these changes in the round, the reorganisation of the arms of service will have to take account of an increased importance attached to space defence and its co-ordination with air defence. More stress has been placed upon the combined arms nature of future battle, amending force structures to take rapid account of weapons development, and the need for a unified rear-area and mobil-isation organisation, requiring the reorganisation of Military Districts.

Such reorganisation would confer several advantages. It would guarantee the effective defence of the USSR, but could do so at approximately half the current ready force levels, and with far fewer forces deployed forward. It would permit the reorganisation of combat forces along more versatile lines to keep pace with the demands of new tactics and technology. And it would enable forces of different qualities to be used – less competent forces in defence, higher quality troops with better leadership and command and control deployed as mobile counter-attack forces.

It has the added advantage of permitting the General Staff to retain its offensive capability (assisted by an overall reduction in force density), which would be much less provocative to the West, as it would appear obviously defensive. Land and air operations could be more easily integrated, as would the establishment of an effective air-space control system over the forward area. Finally, it would render Soviet forces less vulnerable to new weapons technology by virtue of their ability to create fortifications and deploy in-depth, and it would permit verification without loss of security.

We must always bear in mind that the concept of 'reasonable defence sufficiency', the term used to describe this reorganisation, is *not* an element of doctrine but the *product* of new doctrinal thinking. It is a tool of policy, a device to help achieve Gorbachev's political objectives, that is to say, reducing the threat from the West, especially the nuclear threat; reducing the need to compete by retarding Western force modernisation and the development of new weapons; assisting resource reallocation within and from the military; and facilitating military restructuring for great efficiency.

Implications for the West

If NATO made no response to a Soviet reorganisation, such as that suggested above, then the USSR would still be secure from attack, because the concepts are militarily sound (whereas in the view of the Soviet General Staff, purely 'defensive defence' concepts are not militarily sound). The Soviet force reductions would still be essential to fund the modernisation and development of new weapons for the Soviet armed forces to match what NATO might continue to develop.

But the 'number crunching' approach common in the West holds that, in the face of such a Warsaw Pact proposal (to cut ready forces to half current limits), NATO's refusal to make similar cuts is untenable. This may become *political* reality, but it ignores the *operational* reality that a significantly reduced density of NATO forces may not leave NATO with a credible military defence, and NATO reliance on nuclear deterrence will actually increase. Yet this nuclear deterrent is itself under increased pressure and its credibility (particularly in West Germany) is being eroded by Soviet political initiative. It will need a considerable amount of technical explanation to the several NATO publics to explain why a reduction in density may not be in NATO's interest, if public support for current defence policy is to be maintained. It will be very difficult to introduce into both arms negotiations and the public consciousness a reason why air-defence weapons must now be considered in the air balance, when previously this was ignored in Western proposals.

Based on the political analysis he has received, Gorbachev may be banking on NATO's inability to react quickly and coherently to his proposals. Soviet diplomacy may encourage some European member states to make unilateral decisions to cut conventional forces and oppose nuclear modernisation. This in turn would weaken American resolve and encourage the United States to make similar reductions in its commitment to Europe. The failure to pursue nuclear modernisation will lead over time to a *de facto* tactical denuclearisation of NATO. This denuclearisation is, after all, the *main* military objective of Soviet force cuts, nuclear and conventional. It is nuclear weapons which currently pose the only real military threat to the USSR.

Parity of ready forces at a significantly lower density than today does not make for stability if no account is taken of reserve mobilisation capacity. NATO can probably ensure the defence of Europe at 50 per cent of current ready force levels *if it adopts the Soviet model described above* – that is, if NATO adopts terrain fortification in-depth, manned by cadre forces with rapid mobilisation potential, with large reserve, and a mobile counter-attack force in-depth backed up by modern nuclear weapons. To this must be added the requirement for investment in technology applicable to new weapons and intense research into their effective application in battle.

But such a reform would be painful for NATO nations. It would require a modification of forward defence, the acceptance of fortification and deployment in depth, the reallocation of resources, and the adoption, for example by Britain and the United States, of a cadre/ mobilisation system for at least part of their forces. It highlights the possible need to switch military functions (such as close air support from air forces to army artillery). Without a General Staff such changes will be difficult in peacetime. It also implies a reduced American and British deployment of ready forces in Germany. Furthermore, it means that the 50 per cent reduction in deployed strength would not give a 50 per cent reduction in defence budgets. Gorbachev may conclude that NATO is incapable of making this institutional adjustment. But without such an adjustment, reduction in forces in Europe will cause destabilisation rather than increase stability, and will contribute to a Soviet military advantage.

It is in the Soviet interest to seek reciprocal unilateral reductions by each NATO member without a centralised and coherent plan and without co-ordination. Any NATO delay in formulating policy proposals to match those of Gorbachev increases the likelihood of this. It is for this reason that NATO proposals for 'security building', 'negotiation', and 'verification' are likely to be met by Soviet counter-proposals simply to reduce weapons and forces. In purely military terms, it is not necessarily in the Soviet military's interest for NATO to abandon forward defence in favour of a defence in-depth in order to meet what we think will be the new Soviet strategy. On the contrary, a NATO forward defensive posture at much lower force levels is by Soviet calculations a *less* effective defence. If to this can be added a reduction in NATO air power (which is NATO's only operational reserve until mobilisation is complete) and an increase in Soviet air-defence density (already many times that of NATO), the Soviet military advantage will be even further enhanced.

CHAPTER 4

Nuclear Weapons in Europe in the 1990s

PHIL WILLIAMS

THE NATO SUMMIT of May 1989 provided a compromise on the question of short-range nuclear forces (SNF) in Europe. Following the tradition of flexible response, which is capable of very flexible interpretation, a formula was found at the Summit which enabled both Mrs Thatcher and the coalition government of Chancellor Kohl to claim that their objectives had been achieved. Mrs Thatcher could argue that there was a commitment not to go to zero in short-range nuclear systems, while the West Germans could claim that, at the outset of the Summit, there was a commitment to modernise but not to negotiate, while at the end of the Summit there was a commitment to negotiate but not to modernise. If none of the parties emerged from the Summit entirely happy with what it had achieved, at least there was a feeling that a major and perhaps unbridgeable split between the allies had been averted – if only very narrowly. Furthermore, governments could go back and tell their electorates what they felt they wanted to hear. The sense of relief was translated into what appeared at times as a sense of euphoria, and it was suggested that the Alliance could now put the short-range nuclear forces issue behind it and move on to other and more important things. NATO had one again succeeded in managing an internal crisis and in establishing a broad consensus on strategy and force posture.

This assessment is not only very appealing, but is also a useful counter to tendencies towards over-dramatising differences amongst the NATO allies. Nevertheless, the nuclear issue is unlikely to go away. The crisis over nuclear weapons which developed in the first half of 1989 was the result of long-term secular trends, and the Summit compromise has done little to alter the underlying problems and the unanswered questions.

Some of these questions have been around for a long time and have proved resistant to any definite or entirely satisfactory answer. In the period since Reykjavik and the signing of INF Treaty, they have become particularly insistent and sensitive. Other questions result much more obviously from the developments since the mid-1980s. Part of the problem is that both the familiar and the more novel questions arise at several distinct levels. At the most general level, they are highly philosophical or conceptual and concern the meaning of security in a Europe where the Soviet Union is moving towards a less repressive form of government at home, where the Brezhnev doctrine is irrelevant in Eastern Europe, and where the concerns over the Soviet capacity for surprise attack are being eased by unilateral reductions in Soviet forces in Eastern Europe. In these circumstances, are the old notions of security through strength still relevant or is it necessary to consider alternatives? If the traditional unilateral approach to security is no longer adequate, what is to replace it? Is it possible to reconcile notions of unilateral security on the one side and ideas of mutual or common security on the other? Although such questions may appear very general, they do translate into more practical issues, such as the relationship between force planning and arms control.

There is a second level of analysis which concerns broad political issues, such as the nature of the evolving security order in Europe. What kind of order is envisaged in the medium if not the long term? Will political change lead not simply to the current loosening of the bloc system but to its erosion and ultimate demise? In the meantime, how can strategic and military stability be maintained against a backdrop of rapid political change? Is arms control an effective way of managing and facilitating change or is it liable to introduce added rigidities and have a stultifying effect? What kind of military postures are appropriate to the European security order of the 1990s? Perhaps most important of all, if stability is achieved at lower levels of conventional forces, do nuclear weapons still have a role to play in upholding the security order and in maintaining deterrence and stability?

The third level relates to more specific issues, such as the requirements of deterrence and force posture. If, as seems likely, there is a broad consensus within NATO on the need for a continuing nuclear component in deterrence, can this be translated into similar agreement on the precise operational requirements? What should the balance be between nuclear-armed aircraft, short-range missiles and nuclear artillery? Are all three elements necessary or can NATO dispense with one or more components of its nuclear order of battle?

The answers to such questions are neither easy nor obvious. One of the difficulties is that there are important but complex interrelationships between the conceptual, the policy, and the operational levels. Moreover, it makes a difference whether one starts with a top-down or a bottom-up approach. In some respects, it would be most sensible to start with the philosophical or conceptual issues, then consider the policy level before finally moving to the more technical level of operational requirements. In practice, however, it is difficult to proceed in such an orderly manner. The NATO agenda for the last 12 months has been dominated by the issue of a follow-on to the Lance missile partly because the existing systems will be obsolescent in 1995, and partly because the United States Congress has to make crucial decisions on funding well before then. Such considerations gave the operational issues an urgency and importance that demanded a response even though – the comprehensive concept notwithstanding – the conceptual and the political framework had not been fully sorted out, at least at the Alliance level.

This is not entirely surprising in view of both the pace of change and the uncertainty over whether or not the processes of reform that have been initiated in the Soviet Union are in any way reversible. Furthermore, part of the difficulty for NATO is that the member governments come at the issue at different levels, with some placing the emphasis on short-term military requirements, others focusing on the medium-term political changes, and yet others considering the more fundamental and long-term conceptual issues. Insofar as the member governments have addressed the conceptual problems, it is clear too that this itself has become a source of contention in the Alliance, with some governments focusing on new opportunities and others emphasising old and new dangers. The problem therefore cannot simply be dismissed as one of nuclear neuralgia on the part of the Federal Republic of Germany. In the final analysis it centres around the nature of security on the European Continent in the 1990s and beyond.

In view of this it is important to consider more fully the source of the dispute in NATO over short-range nuclear forces. Having done this, the chapter then outlines various options for NATO's force posture in the 1990s.

The Nuclear Impasse

The dispute over nuclear weapons which has, in one form or another, bedevilled the Western Alliance throughout much of the 1980s can be understood as a result of several distinct but related developments. The convergence of these trends and developments has altered the domestic and the international context within which the Alliance has to make decisions on nuclear matters.

The first and most obvious trend concerns the politicisation of strategic and defence issues. This process began with the neutron bomb episode and was intensified by the controversy over cruise and Pershing missile deployment. Although the mass protests have disappeared, they have left a sensitivity to nuclear issues amongst at least some European governments that cannot be ignored. Decisions concerning new deployments of nuclear weapons raise all sorts of difficulties, especially for the governments of nations who have to host these weapons – a difficulty that is all too easily exacerbated by the insensitivity of others to these domestic problems.

The second, and closely related difficulty, stems from the fact that the INF Treaty, and especially the second zero, disturbed the delicate equilibrium which has existed since 1967 when NATO adopted the strategy of flexible response. This strategy had two great virtues. The first was that it was capable of flexible interpretation – thereby alleviating the tensions over strategy that had dominated the previous five years. Secondly and closely related to this was that flexible response seemed to share the risks relatively evenly amongst the members of the alliance. There was some prospect that any war between NATO and the Warsaw Pact would be confined to Europe, and some prospect that it would escalate to the level of inter-continental strategic exchanges between the superpowers. This meant that both the Europeans and the United States were in the position of bearing some of the risks. In the 1970s the European allies became increasingly concerned at the possibility that, with the arrival of strategic parity, the might be decoupled from the United States. The deployment of cruise missiles and Pershing IIs was, in part, a response to these anxieties and was intended to reaffirm coupling. It was inevitable, therefore, that an INF Treaty based on the double zero option should generate a belief amongst at least some Europeans that the United States had reduced the risk to itself at the expense of its allies. West Germany, which acted as host for the short-range systems that were left, felt particularly vulnerable, claiming that it had been 'singularised' and was now bearing an inordinate share of the nuclear risk. In these circumstances, West German pressure for a third zero can be understood, not only as an almost inevitable protest against the redistribution of risk that had already taken place, but also as an attempt to re-establish risk-sharing arrangements that were less unfavourable.

There was a feeling in Bonn too that the risks were not only *unfair*, but that they were *unnecessary*. This can be understood partly in terms of changing assessments of the Soviet threat in the light of both the internal reforms initiated by Gorbachev and his unilateral arms cuts. It can also be understood as a result of the broadening of the NATO nuclear debate through the 1980s. Traditionally the debate in NATO was between three groups: those (mainly Americans) who emphasised the military utility of nuclear weapons; those (mainly European) who emphasised the political utility of nuclear weapons; and those (Americans in the 1960s and Europeans on the left in the 1980s) who contended that nuclear weapons had a very limited utility, that they deterred only the use of nuclear weapons, and that NATO should therefore focus on strengthening its conventional forces. Flexible response as adopted in 1967 resulted from a compromise between those who emphasised the political utility of nuclear weapons and those who emphasised their limited utility, while also having something in it for those who focused on the military utility of nuclear weapons.

The debate in the 1980s was complicated by the emergence of an approach to deterrence which is generally described as 'existentialism', and which effectively believes that deterrence in Europe is easy. It is important to emphasise that existentialism does not imply either an anti-nuclear or an anti-deterrence ethos. On the contrary, the most important assumption of existential deterrence is that nuclear weapons have had a profound and extremely positive impact on the behaviour of states, irrespective of the precise strategies adopted by the nuclear powers. In this view, deterrence is a condition not a policy, and has made all major states, including the Soviet Union, averse to high risks. The implication is that the threat from the Soviet Union, is indirect at most, and political rather than direct and military. Moscow is anxious to avoid any actions which might significantly increase the possibility of nuclear war. Any clash between the superpowers could do this as the escalation process is highly volatile and potentially uncontrollable: once hostilities begin, it is not clear where they will end. In other words, existential deterrence depends on what Thomas Schelling terms threats that 'leave something to change'. Accordingly, it has an extensive impact and encompasses extended deterrence in Europe. The stability–instability paradox that has led some analysts – especially those who emphasised the limited utility of nuclear weapons – to advocate the build-up of conventional forces, is explicitly rejected by existentialism. The presumption is that the stability that exists at the top level will be reproduced at lower levels. This approach denies the significance of thresholds and assumes that there is a continuum between low-level violence and the ultimate levels. It follows from this that the operational details of nuclear planning and distinctions between the types of nuclear weapon are of little relevance. Deterrence operates at a gross political level, is very easy, and does not depend on particular weapons systems.

Not surprisingly, those who adopt the approach that deterrence is easy believe that the European continent, because it is locked into the deterrence relationship between the two superpowers, is very stable. Moreover, so long as Western European security remains a vital interest of the United States and there is a visible American involvement in security arrangements on the Continent, the status quo is unlikely to be challenged. Maintaining stability, therefore, requires simply that the United States continues to highlight its interests in the independence and integrity of Western Europe. This in turn requires that it continues

to deploy a substantial – although not necessarily the existing – number
of troops in Europe as the visible manifestation of that interest. The
troop presence strengthens deterrence not because it is an automatic
trip-wire, but because it would mean that any Soviet aggression against
NATO would place the superpowers on an escalator which might be
difficult to control. The possibility that events might get out of control is
also increased by the large number of nuclear weapons that are deployed
in Europe – although these are not a prerequisite for escalation.

Although there is no inevitable linkage between assessments of a
declining Soviet threat and the notion of existential deterrence, one of
the implications of existentialism is that the Soviet threat is relatively
easy to deter. It is particularly persuasive, therefore, in a period of
reduced tension. Yet those who hold to existentialism see the radical
change in Soviet policy under Gorbachev not simply as an opportunity
but as a vindication. They believed that deterrence in Europe was robust
even before Gorbachev initiated his internal reforms and made
unilateral cuts in Soviet conventional forces. The Gorbachev initiatives
provide not a challenge but confirmation that deterrence is effective and
that the mellowing of the Soviet Union that George Kennan predicted in
his famous 'X' article, in which Kennan adumbrated a rationale for the
containment of Soviet power in Europe, has taken place. This is not to
deny that the changing threat perception resulting from Gorbachev's
initiatives has had a profound impact. The Soviet leader's policies
towards Western Europe have encouraged a new sense of movement and
a vision of the possibility for a lowering of the barrier between East and
West, especially in Germany.

This is related to another trend involving the Federal Republic. In the
past Bonn was so dependent on allied support and so concerned about
establishing and then maintaining its legitimacy as a member of the
Western Alliance that its own interests were subsumed in the wider
interests of the Alliance, and its own preferences, on some occasions at
least, were subordinated to the need for consensus and harmony. It was
especially anxious to retain the support of the United States. In the late
1970s and early 1980s, however, tension developed between Bonn's
approach to East–West relations and that of Washington. The attempt to
protect the gains of *détente* in Europe and to insulate the Ostpolitik from
the broader deterioration of East–West relations were early indications
that the Federal Republic was increasingly operating according to its
own agenda rather than allowing policy to be dictated by the United
States. While Bonn was only party successful in achieving these goals,
the differences with the first Reagan Administration over policy towards
the Soviet Union and Eastern Europe certainly encouraged the belief
that Bonn had to be more assertive in protecting and promoting interests
which were not necessarily shared by its allies.

The SNF dispute in 1988–89 can be understood as the culmination of all these trends. Yet the dispute was rendered even more complex because it had two distinct elements – one concerning the modernisation of short-range nuclear weapons through the introduction of new systems, and the other concerning arms-control negotiations which could not only pre-empt the introduction of new systems but might mean the withdrawal of many of the existing weapons. Bonn's approach to deterrence in the aftermath of the INF Treaty reflected the politicisation of the strategic debate in West Germany and the reluctance of Kohl's coalition government to take actions which would disaffect a large part of the electorate. If the position of the Kohl government was initially one of damage limitation, when the United States eased the pressure on modernisation, Bonn went beyond this to demand negotiations on short-range systems. In effect, this was an attempt by an unpopular government to mobilise domestic support. Yet to see the issue in terms simply of the primacy of domestic politics is to ignore other considerations that were vital to the dispute. The controversy involved fundamental questions about how security is best achieved during the 1990s and beyond. The West German Foreign Minister, Hans-Dietrich Genscher, has embraced an approach based upon notions of reciprocity and relaxation and enshrined in the notion of common security. Essential to this philosophy are the ideas that security is best achieved through agreement on lower levels of forces, that this will encourage a process of political change, and that at the end of this process all the states in Europe, but especially West Germany, will be better off. The modernisation of NATO's short-range nuclear forces would hinder this process, while the opening of negotiations on short-range systems, especially if it resulted in a third zero, would greatly facilitate it. Such an agreement would also bring to an end the singularisation of West Germany and redistribute the balance of risk in the Western Alliance in a more equitable manner. From Genscher's perspective, an SNF agreement at low levels and possibly at zero would be an ideal outcome both in East–West and West–West terms. It is also something that would be welcome in terms of West German domestic politics, as it would have appeal across the political spectrum and would help to neutralise the SPD. At the same time, Bonn's willingness to push so hard for the adoption of its preferences by the allies is symptomatic of the new reluctance to sacrifice West German interests for the sake of alliance harmony.

If Genscher has a vision of a new security order in Europe, however, it is not an order in which nuclear weapons would be superfluous or absent. They would provide an insurance policy against a reversal of the positive trends in Soviet domestic and foreign policy and provide a continuing guarantor of stability in a period of unprecedented political change.

Nuclear weapons would simply play a less prominent role in the force structures of both NATO and the then Warsaw Pact and would not necessarily have to be deployed on the European continent itself.

The point about all this is that the debate over short-range nuclear forces is not simply about these forces, nor even about deterrence; it is embedded in much broader issues which are both conceptual and practical, and which are related to the way in which Europe might evolve in the next decade. It is not clear, though, whether or not the Alliance will modify or maintain its traditional approach to security. Much will depend on the progress of the reform process in the Soviet Union and whether the trend towards greater freedom and flexibility in Eastern Europe is maintained. Perhaps the most important determinant, however, at least in the short term, will be the progress that is made in the CFE talks. At the Summit the opening of negotiations on short-range nuclear forces was linked explicitly to such progress. A Soviet willingness to make the kinds of concession that NATO has demanded in CFE will also stimulate further debate in NATO over the nature of security and the requirements of deterrence in an environment characterised by parity at lower levels of conventional forces. Much will depend on how far NATO is prepared to go in reappraising and modifying its traditional approach to security. The Comprehensive Concept is a useful beginning to this process but can hardly be the final word.

The extent of this reappraisal and the conclusions that are reached will do much to determine the role of nuclear weapons in NATO's force posture in the 1990s. The next section outlines a range of possibilities for NATO's nuclear order of battle, depending on whether deterrence is believed to be easy or hard. The more stringent the requirements of deterrence are believed to be in the 1990s, the more comprehensive NATO's nuclear posture has to be. Although the issues are highly complex, therfore, much will depend on which of the various concepts of deterrence prevails. Consequently, the next section considers a range of options for NATO's force posture. It looks at the underlying philosophies of deterrence and shows how these determine nuclear force-planning requirements.

Nuclear Weapons and Deterrence in the 1990s

In view of the doubts over nuclear deterrence in NATO it is possible to identify several distinct force postures.

The Military Utility Posture

If the traditional military view of deterrence as being difficult to convince the enemy of NATO's intentions is accepted, then the scope for change in NATO's force posture is limited. Deterrence is something that can be achieved only by confronting the Soviet Union with a comprehensive range of options that mean that, whatever level of force is used, Moscow could not obtain an advantage. While it is possible that reductions in conventional forces could eliminate many of the asymmetries that have been of concern to NATO in the past, in this approach nuclear weapons would retain a crucial role in NATO's deterrent posture. Furthermore, if flexible response is to be truly flexible then there has to be a comprehensive range of nuclear options. One implication of this is that French, British and American aircraft should be equipped with stand-off missiles in order to ensure the efficacy of the long-range components of NATO's nuclear armoury. A second implication is that the follow-on to Lance should be deployed and that NATO should continue to have available large numbers of short-range nuclear forces and nuclear artillery. These would prevent the Soviet Union from concentrating its forces and guard against a decisive breakthrough.

While there is some scope for arms control at the conventional level – so long as it is based on asymmetrical reductions – at the nuclear level the emphasis has to be on modernisation, albeit with some attempts at rationalisation. It might be possible, for example, to trade-off some of NATO's nuclear artillery in exchange for the follow-on to Lance. In terms of the conceptual underpinnings, there would not be a complete rejection of ideas of mutual security, but these would be less important than the continuing unilateral steps that NATO might take to reaffirm the credibility of its deterrent posture.

The difficulty with such an approach is that NATO would be unreceptive to Gorbachev's overtures and the sense of progress in moving towards more stable security arrangements in Europe could easily be dissipated.

The Political Utility Posture

There is a second strand of deterrence thinking which suggests that the ability to defeat the aggressor on the battlefield is less important that the capacity to pose a degree of risk that is totally unacceptable to him. From this perspective, what counts is the 'evident capability for effective use' of NATO's nuclear forces and especially the capacity 'to deny an aggressor swift success and to show him that he has underrated the defender's resolve and must, for his own survival, back down'. Political impact rather than military success is the key criterion here. This approach has predominated in Britain for some time. It was enunciated by Denis Healey during the debates with McNamara in the 1960s and was reaffirmed in the 1989 Statement on Defence Estimates.

In other words, what counts is not effectiveness on the battlefield but the psychological impact of any use of nuclear weapons on the enemy leadership. The implication is that it is necessary to have non-strategic weapons as well as strategic systems, that within the non-strategic armoury more emphasis should be placed on long-range rather than on short-range systems, and that therefore there has to be some kind of compensation for the INF Treaty. Although the 1989 Statement which reiterated these arguments also made clear that NATO should provide for a Lance follow-on 'to keep the armoury as a whole at the standard of effectiveness and versatility, and no larger than the minimum size needed to sustain its purpose' the FOTL is probably less important that the longer-range systems. Indeed, the crucial element in this approach is to retain a very evident capacity to ecalate the conflict and thereby confront Moscow with an intolerable level of risk and potential cost.

Although this approach to deterrence poses fairly stringent requirements, there is some flexibility in NATO's force posture. The nuclear artillery in particular could be drastically reduced, either unilaterally or through negotiations. At the same time, arms control is not regarded as an unmixed blessing and should certainly not be allowed to undermine basic force-planning requirements. Not surprisingly, therefore, Gorbachev's initiatives have to be treated with some caution, as they promise not a more stable Europe but one in which key elements of deterrence have been eroded. Negotiations on short-range nuclear forces are a potential problem rather than a solution, while the Bush initiative on the inclusion of aircraft in the CFE talks also provides an opportunity for the Soviet Union to go after NATO's dual capable aircraft. The emphasis once again is on force planning rather than arms control considerations, and it is believed that stability is best achieved through the apparatus of deterrence rather than through mutual agreement or restraint – although these may be useful supplements.

Modified Existential Deterrence

The third approach might be described as modified existentialism. The argument here is that deterrence in Europe is relatively easy and that some of the anguish over force planning that has been evident in the Alliance in the last two years is unnecessary. Deterrence is far more robust than is often assumed, and to suggest that it depends on the deployment of a follow-on to Lance is to imbue a single weapon system with far more significance than it deserves. To imply that deterrence in Europe will stand or fall depending on whether or not FOTL is deployed also suggests a delicacy to the balance that is unwarranted. It assumes too that the Soviet Union remains a predatory state held in check *only* by countervailing power.

Modified existentialism, however, deviates from pure existentialism in terms of the requirements for locking Western Europe into the deterrence relationship between the superpowers and ensuring that there is considerable potential for escalation. Modified existentialism is not indifferent to issues of strategy and force posture, but treats these in a distinctive way. It argues that, although there is little likelihood of the Soviet Union suddenly reversing its behaviour and becoming reckless rather than risk-averse, it is nevertheless useful to have capabilities that will both inhibit such a change and act as insurance against its occurring anyway. Furthermore, it accepts the argument that it is not sufficient to have American troops deployed in Western Europe as the only linkage to the strategic forces of the United States. There has to be some intermediate level of capability which will increase the probability of escalation and compel the Soviet leadership to consider the likelihood that aggression will have incalculable consequences. In other words, force-planning considerations are not irrelevant to a posture based on modified existentialism. Yet what is decisive is not so much the capacity for controlled escalation as the possibility of uncontrolled escalation.

In such an approach the strategic nuclear forces of Britain and France, providing as they do extra centres of decision making are crucial. Furthermore, it is necessary to ensure that there are nuclear forces on the European continent that might be used in ways which would significantly escalate hostilities, and cast doubt upon attempts by Moscow to ensure that the Soviet homeland remained a sanctuary. The systems that are most appropriate to this role are aircraft, which would be all the more effective if equipped with stand-off weapons, whether of French or American design. The nuclear artillery and the Lance follow-on are dispensable. Although they would intensify the level of hostilities on the battlefield they lack the capability to extend the battlefield into the Soviet Union in the same way as aircraft.

The virtue of this approach is that it gets away from the idea that Western Europe, especially Germany, would be used as the battleground. It also rejects notions of nuclear war-fighting, as the emphasis is less on rational control than on the possibility that events might get out of control. And because there is at a fundamental level a belief in the robustness of deterrence, there are possibilities for agreements on short-range nuclear forces that would eliminate a significant Soviet superiority in this category of weapons system. In other words, the more confidence there is about the capacity of NATO to deter the Soviet Union, the more opportunity there is to move towards security arrangements that are based on notions of reciprocity and mutual restraint.

The problem with this approach is that it concentrates on deterrence at the expense of war-fighting considerations and does not rest upon notions of the rational use of nuclear weapons, thereby making military planning particularly difficult.

Pure Existentialism

The fourth approach to NATO's force posture in the 1990s is to move towards pure existentialism. Although such a position is reminiscent of massive retaliation with American troops in Europe acting simply as a trip-wire, it differs from massive retaliation in certain crucial respects. Most important is that massive retaliation was a rational response in an era of American nuclear superiority, but an irrational and therefore incredible response in an era of strategic parity. Existentialism, in contrast, rests upon the assumption that a military conflict between the superpowers would unleash an uncontrollable process of escalation. The United States therefore would not have to plan to act in an irrational manner; it would simply have to ensure that any Soviet aggression against Western Europe would involve Moscow in a direct confrontation with Washington, with all the potential for uncontrollability that this would involve. Credibility rests not on an irrational response but on an uncontrollable process. In order to achieve this the United States would simply have to maintain a substantial contingent of American troops in Western Europe. Such a presence would ensure that any Soviet aggression would precipitate a direct superpower confrontation with all the uncertainties that this would involve.

The great virtue of pure existentialism is that it offers considerable opportunity for moving towards security arrangements that are reciprocal and mutual. Because it is relatively relaxed in terms of force posture it is positive and permissive in terms of arms control. From this perspective NATO could be flexible, not only about nuclear artillery and a third zero in short-range systems, but also about the inclusion of aircraft in the CFE negotiations. The difficulty with the approach, however, is that it places the burden of sacrifice on the United States and seems to remove all risk from the Federal Republic. Consequently, pure existentialism is unlikely to meet with a favourable response from the United States. There has already been evidence of this in the 'no nukes, no troops' sentiment that has been expressed in Congress.

This brief review has identified four possible bases for NATO's nuclear posture in the 1990s depending on how difficult deterrence of Soviet aggression is believed to be. It has also considered the arms control possibilities that are compatible with each of these approaches, as well as some of the broader problems they raise. The final section of this chapter offered some reflections on the controversy of the last two years and the future of NATO strategy in the light of this categorisation.

Conclusion

During the debate over Lance modernisation and the SNF negotiations, Mrs Thatcher and the government of Chancellor Kohl were coming at deterrence from opposite ends of the spectrum, with Mrs Thatcher arguing that the whole edifice was in danger of crumbling and Mr Genscher, in effect, contending that deterrence was so effective and robust that there was ample scope for arms control. Although this split was papered over temporarily, many of the problems have been deferred rather than solved. The danger for NATO is that they will erupt once again and that positions will be so firmly entrenched that compromise becomes impossible. There is, however, room for compromise and this lies in a force posture based on modified existentialism. Part of the reason that Mrs Thatcher has been so hostile to negotiations on short-range missiles is that she sees this as the path to complete denuclearisation. It is certainly not inconceivable that several years down the road a Bonn government could demand the removal not only of short-range missiles but also of nuclear-armed aircraft from German territory. The position based on modified existentialism offers the best opportunity to forestall this, as the allies could accept both non-deployment of Lance and the third zero in return for a strong and binding commitment that nuclear-armed aircraft deployed in West Germany would remain a crucial component of NATO's posture. One objection to this is that it would be to concede too much too soon to both Bonn and Moscow; the argument for it is that it would be sustainable in the long term, could be the basis for the re-establishment of a broad consensus in NATO, and would open up possibilities for arms control in Europe. It would also be a reflection of the underlying trends in the Soviet Union which mean that the requirements of deterrence are less stringent than in the past. At the same time, it would ensure that nuclear weapons continue to have a major role in the evolving European security system.

CHAPTER 5

The Impact of Resource Constraints

DAVID GREENWOOD

It is President George Bush's view – expressed in his (vacation) commencement address to the Untied States Coastguard Academy on 24 May, 1989 – that 'through negotiations, we can now transform the military landscape of Europe'. Moreover, the likelihood that this vision might be realised was greatly enhanced by the four-point plan which the President presented – and won the allies' support for – at the NATO Summit held in Brussels on 29–30 May, 1989. Suggesting that the talks on Conventional Forces in Europe (CFE) should (*a*) proceed rapidly to an outline agreement, and that the parties should (*b*) adopt a brisk timetable for the conclusion and implementation of a full accord *plus* proposing (*c*) equal manpower ceilings for superpower troops in Europe at a level 20 per cent below the current American strength, and (*d*) the inclusion of fixed- and rotary-wing aircraft within the scope of the exchanges; these initiatives not only fulfilled the immediate objective of finessing the short-range nuclear forces issue, which had threatened to divide the Alliance in Brussels, they also increased the extent of the common ground between the Eastern and the Western negotiators in Vienna, and hence the chances of striking a bargain there.

Thus NATO now stands prepared to contemplate, like President Gorbachev, a future in which conventional forces in Europe are significantly reduced (and more defensively oriented). For one thing it is recognised that 'defensive force density' must be a factor in the continental security equation. As elucidated in one of the elegant expository essays in the British 1989 Defence White Paper – on 'the military rationale that underlies Soviet arms control strategy' – the argument runs as follows:

Soviet military assessments acknowledge that NATO could put up a formidable conventional defence despite the Warsaw Pact's numerical superiority. But the density of forces along the front to be defended matters as much as the overall balance of forces. If large cuts in NATO forces could be secured, even at the cost of larger cuts in Warsaw Pact forces, NATO's defensive force density might be much lower, and the Warsaw Pact, with the benefit of surprise, would still be able to concentrate powerful forces to break through Western defences. By contrast, no comparable capability exists on the Western side.

More generally, it is recognised that the Alliances apparatus for deterrence and defence ought to be preserved even if troop and armament levels are cut. In another of the 1989 Defence White Papers essays the point is put succinctly:

Nothing that Mr Gorbachev has said or done is ground for imagining that he will run military risks with his country's security on suppositions about Western goodwill. We must be similarly objective, recognising that if there is indeed a Soviet re-assessment enabling us all to work together more constructively, it would be folly to dismantle, or let decay, the very structures that have helped to induce it.

'Cool and steady realism of this kind', the policy statement continues, 'is not an obstacle but the best guide to strengthening the security system.'

The significance of all this for present purposes is self-evident. Even though the United Kingdom, along with its allies, entertains high hopes for arms control in the early 1990s, the powers-that-be cannot expect and certainly should not anticipate an immediate and profound transformation of the European military scene, yielding a quick arms control 'dividend in terms of money and and power released for other uses. It follows that consideration of how resource constraints may impinge on the national defence effort in general, and on the contribution of ground and tactical air forces to NATO's order of battle in the Central Region in particular, is as relevant an analytical undertaking as it ever was. The prospect of force reductions is welcome; but arms control is not about to deliver a future where the North German plain can be protected by half-a-dozen battalions, a few interceptors, and a handful of missile batteries, simplifying programme and budget choices spectacularly and resolving allocation dilemmas at a stroke.

Resources

The obvious starting-point for an examination of imminent choices and dilemmas, with particular reference to the Central Region, is a synoptic view of the allocation of resources to defence as a whole.

In 1989–90 the United Kingdom budgeted for an overall defence expenditure of £20,143 million. There is a breakdown of this sum by *inputs* (labour, capital, real estate, and stores) in Table 5.1; and a breakdown by *outputs* – what the Ministry of Defence (MOD) used to call the 'functional costing' and now refers to as the 'analysis of the defence budget by programme' in Table 5.2.

The first of these tabulations shows that in 1989/90 outlays on *people* (including retired Service personnel) required two-fifths of the available money, almost as much as expenditure on equipment (research, development, and production). The near-equality of these proportions is in striking contrast to the position five years earlier, when the MOD's personnel bill took less than 35 per cent of the budget while spending on equipment accounted for nearly 46 per cent (see the two final columns of Table 5.1). Nor is there much likelihood that the pressure on 'people costs' will moderate in the immediate future. The cash needed for Service retirement pension and gratuities is rising steadily: it has gone up 50 per cent since 1984/85, from around £800 million to the current figure of over £1,200 million. More important, compensation for those actively serving will have to be improved in the next several years if the Services are to avoid manning and recruitment problems as, like other countries, they face the demographic 'trough' of the early 1990s. To be sure, the scale of this problem is not so great for the Untied Kingdom as for some other NATO nations (notably the Federal Republic of Germany). It is none the less significant. The number of males in the 16–19 age bracket – from which the Services draw about three-quarters of their recruits – has dropped by 10 per cent since 1983; and by 1994 it will have fallen by a further 23 per cent from current levels. On top of that, the retaining of trained manpower is already proving problematical. The proportion of personnel opting to leave on completion of engagements is increasing, as are numbers seeking premature voluntary release (PVR). At the turn of the year 1988–89 the annual rate of PVR applications from officers was running at 3.7 per cent of trained strength and that from other ranks at 4.3 per cent. Small wonder that considerable attention has been paid lately to MARILYN (the acronym for Manning and Recruitment In the Lean Years of the Nineties).

Since the medium-term outlook is that total defence spending will remain approximately constant in real terms (and more on that later), finding extra money for personnel expenses implies a continuing squeeze on *procurement* funds. The word 'continuing' is used advisedly. The sum budgeted for all equipment outlays in 1989/90 was £8,258 million (Table 5.1). That is actually less, in cash terms, than the MOD spent in 1987/88 and only a mite more than it spent in 1985/86. Thus, allowing for inflation, there has been a big drop in the allocation of resources to procurement already. This downward trend will continue: partly because ministers want it to (they are deliberately cutting cash for R&D because of a fear that defence may be pre-empting too big a share of the country's scientific and technological talent), and partly because there will be some reining-in of expenditure on production (achieved by

David Greenwood

TABLE 5.1

United Kingdom Defence Estimate for 1989/90: Analysis by Inputs

	£ million	% 89/90	% 84/85
Personal expenditure			
Armed forces	4,573	22.7	18.9
Forces retired pay	1,203	6.0	18.9
Civilian staff	2,332	11.6	11.2
Sub-total: personnel	8,108	40.3	34.9
Equipment expenditure			
Sea systems	2,722	13.5	13.0
Land systems	1,679	8.3	9.6
Air systems	3,045	15.1	20.3
Other	812	4.0	2.9
Sub-total: equipment	8,258	40.9	45.8
Other expenditure			
Works, buildings, land	1,663	8.3	7.4
Miscellaneous stores/services	2,114	10.5	11.9
Sub-total: other	3,777	18.8	19.3
Total expenditure	20,143	100.0	100.0

Source: Cm 675-II, Table 2.2.

stretching the timetables for selected acquisitions and perhaps even axeing some low-priority programmes altogether).

Turning to the functional costing – the other way of 'slicing' the £20,143 million of planned expenditure for 1989/90 – one important message of Table 5.2 is that only 55 per cent of the years money is marked down for 'teeth' activities (or 'mission' programmes), the other 45 per cent being required for the 'tail' (R&D, training, plus other logistic and administrative 'support' programmes). That is a marginally worse ratio than in 1988/89 and earlier years, casting a slight shadow of doubt over the MOD's favourite claim that it has been 'trimming the tail without blunting the teeth' of the armed forces lately. Noteworthy here also is the fact that among the 'mission' programmes the proportions of the budget going to each Service's front-line capabilities are surprisingly similar. Leaving aside reserves and auxiliary formations (mainly Army) and recognising that it is the Royal Navy which has responsibility for the nuclear strategic force, all three Service shares fall in the bracket 17.2–17.8 per cent of the total budget. This is remarkable propinquity. It suggests that, even though there has been an integrated Defence Ministry for a quarter of a century, there may still be a hidden hand at work ensuring fair shares for all.

Needless to say the official line is that this internal balance of the

TABLE 5.2

*United Kingdom Defence Estimate for 1989/90: Analysis by Outputs
(Functional Costing)*

Programme	£ million	% of total
Nuclear Strategic Forces	1,158	5.3
Navy GP Combat Forces	2,398	11.9
Navy Theatre Ground Forces	3,414	16.9
Other Army Combat Forces	191	0.9
Air Force GP Forces	3,508	17.4
Reserves/Auxiliary Formations	439	2.2
Sub-total: 'Mission' programmes	11,108	55.1
Research and development	2,350	11.7
Training	1,357	6.7
Equipment support/facilities	1,043	5.2
Other support functions	3,769	18.7
War/contingency stocks and miscellaneous expenditure (net)	516	2.6
Sub-total: 'Support' programmes	9,035	44.9
Total expenditure	20,143	100.0

Note: GP stands for 'General Purpose'.
Source: Cm 675-II, Table 2.3.

defence effort derives, not from subtle forces which ensure that budgets yield equal benefit (or prescribe equal misery) for each Service, but from the nation's security commitments and the roles of the respective arms which flow from them. In this connection a third perspective on resource allocation is illuminating, namely, an analysis of front-line expenditure – for 1989/90 the £11,108 million designated as 'mission' programmes in Table 5.2 – by precisely these *commitments* (or roles).

Such a breakdown is provided in Table 5.3. This represents an attribution of spending on front-line forces among the five 'pillars' of Britain's defences: (*1*) the strategic nuclear capacity, (*2*) protection of the United Kingdom itself, (*3*) the contribution of ground and tactical air forces to NATO's provision for defence of the Central Region (including units *in* Germany and formations *for* Germany which are home-based in peacetime), (*4*) the contribution of naval and maritime-air assets to the Alliance's forces for operations in the Eastern Atlantic and the Channel, and (*5*) capabilities for operations on NATO's flanks and outside the Atlantic Treaty area.

Inspection of this table prompts two observations. The first is that there is a certain balance here also. Despite a drop in the real value of the

TABLE 5.3

United Kingdom Defence Estimate for 1989/90: Analysis by Commitments (Mission Programmes Only)

Commitment (role)	Expenditure £m	Percentage of total
Strategic Nuclear Deterrent	1,158	10.4
Home Base	2,189	19.7
Central Front	4,349	39.2
of which		
Berlin	63	
RAF Germany + reinforcements	1,123	
BAOR + reinforcements	3,163	
Maritime	2,590	23.3
of which		
Channel	542	
Eastern Atlantic	2,048	
Other	822	7.4
Total (cf. Table 2)	11,108	100.0

Note: 'Other' includes the cost of the amphibious capability, the British contribution(s) to the Allied Command Europe (ACE) Mobile Force, the United Kingdom Mobile Force and commitments outside the NATO area.
Source: Cm 675-I, Figure 6.

United Kingdoms defence provision since the mid-1980s, the country still finds all types of force for NATO (naval, ground, and air), in each of the Alliances four major command areas, and with a full spectrum of strategic nuclear, theatre nuclear, and conventional arms. Moreover, the intention is that it should continue to do so into the 1990s.

The second observation is that the Central Region is nevertheless the crucial commitment. It accounts for *two-fifths* of all front-line expenditure as attributed in Table 5.3, more than double the spending ascribed to protection of the United Kingdom itself and nearly double that ascribed to maritime provision. But its importance in the nation's security calculations is greater than that, on a broader reckoning. After all, the resources expended on defending the 'home base' are so allotted not only because it is the homeland but also because it is a key rear area for continental operations; and the naval and maritime-air assets assigned to the Eastern Atlantic and the Channel are so assigned principally to safeguard the transatlantic and the intra-theatre sea lines of communication whose integrity is necessary, first and foremost, to permit reinforcement and resupply of the Central Front. In other words, adopting different accounting conventions – distinguishing among, say, forces-in-place, home-based contingents for roulement and reinforcement, plus force components with essentially 'derived' missions – one could plausibly attribute up to *three-fifths* of front-line spending to the continental commitment.

This commitment exercises the major claim on the United Kingdom's uniformed manpower resources too. Taking the *Army*, at 1 January, 1989 there were almost 56,000 British soldiers in the Federal Republic of Germany plus another 3,000 in Berlin, and maybe a further 20,000 Regulars in 'home-based contingents for roulement and reinforcement' (i.e., back-up for Germany). That adds up to nearly one-half of the Service's aggregate strength (regular and locally enlisted), including troops in training and other 'tail' functions. In addition, of course, there are several thousand reservists whose mission is to reinforce the British Army of the Rhine (BAOR). As for the Royal Air Force, the manpower count for RAF Germany at 1 January, 1989 came to around 12,000 (including personnel stationed in Berlin), while the numbers serving with squadrons in the United Kingdom designated for reinforcing the Central Front or flying in support of operations there probably came to 15,000 (perhaps more). That puts the proportion of the RAF's total strength of 93,000 which may be regarded as bound up with the continental commitment at between one-quarter and one-third.

Outlook

Looking ahead now, the question is: will the United Kingdom be able and willing to muster the resources to continue making this considerable contribution to NATO in the Allied Forces Central Europe (AFCENT) area, preserving the force structure *and* maintaining force levels (subject to negotiated adjustments), keeping the equipment of BAOR and RAF Germany up to date and up to, scratch *and* sustaining activity levels so that combat effectiveness is kept up to standard?

The short answer is: maybe not, or at least not unless ministers are prepared *either* to shift resources from elsewhere in the defence programme *or* to make further, and far-reaching, organisational changes to yield more efficient resource use. That is because there is virtually no prospect of additional resources being found for defence in the next several years.

As noted already, the budget for 1989/90 foreshadowed expenditure in that financial year of just over £20,000 million. In *cash* terms that was almost £1,000 million more than had been disbursed the year before. In *real* terms, though, it represented a drop in funding compared with 1988/89. In fact, as Table 5.4 shows, allowing for inflation it represented a fifth successive year of reduced provision, intended outlays for 1989/90 being some 8.5 per cent less than actual expenditure in 1984/5 when expressed at constant prices (Table 5.4 right-hand column). Nor is this trend going to be halted. Planned provision for 1990/91 is just over

TABLE 5.4

United Kingdom Defence Expenditure
1984/85–1989/90

Year	Current prices (cash) £m	Constant prices (1987/88) £m
1984/85	17,122	19,891
1985/86	17,943	19,863
1986/87	18,183	19,176
1987/88	18,856	18,856
1988/89ᵉ	19,215	18,192
1989/90ᵉ	20,143	18,162

Note: e = estimated outturn figures.
Source: Cm 675-II, Table 2.2.

£21,000 million, and the forecast estimate for 1991/92 is just over £22,000 million (both figures in cash). On official expectations regarding inflation at the time these projections were made – in the first half of 1989 – that did imply a little real growth in the short run. However, with prices generally in Britain rising at an annual rate of more than 8 per cent in 1989–90, the Government's presumption that 5 per cent more cash each year would cover inflation was (and is) absurdly optimistic. The budgetary outlook for defence is level funding at best, more likely further falls in real provision.

Given that prospect, the official claim in the *Statement on the Defence Estimates 1989* that the modest year-on-year cash increases will enable the MOD to 'sustain programmes with proper funding' is somewhat disingenuous. So too is the assertion that the projections to 1991/92 'provide a firm framework for the next three years' which 'brings valuable certainty and confidence' to forward planning. That has to be read as confidence that money will be tight, certainty that the Ministry will be hard pressed to make ends meet, and confirmation that there is neither slack in the programme nor hope of relief in the form of extra cash.

Continuing stringency must be the prospect of the medium term also. There are no grounds for believing that a fourth (or fifth) Thatcher Government would be more generous with appropriations for defence than its predecessors. Nor does anyone expect a Kinnock-led adminis- tration to come up with additional money. Hence the reasonable expectation is that, while total *cash* allocations will no doubt rise through the 1990s, perhaps passing the £25,000 million mark around the middle of the decade, the nation's commitment of *real* resources to military purposes is going to stay more or less the same, or will diminish.

That is the overall position. What the effect on particular elements of the defence programme will be is harder to fathom. If past experience is any guide, some will not feel the pinch of the budgetary straitjacket at all: the Trident acquisition is the obvious candidate for such 'protection' in the next few years. Others must suffer, however, and provision for the Central Region among them: partly because this commitment looms so large in the nation's defence finances (as has just been pointed out), partly because it is the most manpower-intensive of the five 'pillars' of the defence effort, and hence the most vulnerable to the effects of the currently adverse demographic circumstances (also noted earlier).

If past experience is any guide, the way in which resource constraints will impinge upon provision is predictable too. When funds are tight, it is *activity levels* which bear the initial burden of adjustment. Flying hours are cut for aircraft and crews, along with weapons-firing exercises, reducing proficiency. Limitations on track mileage and live firing are imposed on Army formations, with the same effect; and the flow of spares for their vehicles, guns, and missile launchers is slowed, with a consequent rise in rates of unserviceability. The pattern is familiar, not least because an indignant cavalry officer described it in a celebrated letter to the Editor of *The Times* in March 1987. Penny-pinching economies were, he wrote 'making it increasingly difficult for Commanders at all levels to train their formations and units'; and he summarised the specific problems graphically:

> Once the authorised allocation of 'track mileage' is reached, 'Exercise ends'. Vehicles breaking down often cannot be repaired for lack of spares. Crews are not able to perform their primary role. The Royal Armoured Corps has to face the additional problem of severe cuts in the allocation of ammunition for annual firing practice.

'We are neglecting our conventional defence', he concluded, ' in spite of ministerial comments to the contrary'.

The typical accompaniment of such squeezing of funds for what the Americans call operations and maintenance (O&M) is the stretching of acquisition timetables and/or the dilution of technical specifications for *equipment*. It is difficult to see how BAOR and RAF Germany can escape such irritations in the next few years. In Whitehall the hope is, of course, that the Procurement Executive will get so much better value for its money in the 1990s that having less actual cash to spend will not be a problem. Outsiders are more sceptical. The news item on the 1989 Defence White Paper in *The Economist* bore the cryptic heading 'Less Kit'. Noting that 'the uncuttable spending on Trident is near its all-time high', the paper predicted that 'conventional equipment will . . . suffer badly' with each Service having to go without 'things that are needed'. Strategic analysts broadly share this view, while in the Services themselves one regularly encounters resignation to the fact that long-awaited equipment will come into service later than expected and will not be quite up to the standard expected when it does.

Having O&M expenses and procurement timetables/specifications bear the brunt of the 'burden of adjustment' to budgetary stringency is at least preferable, in most circumstances, to the alternatives: cutting *force levels* and/or recasting the *force structure* to cover an abandoned role here, a degraded capability there. That is a course which British policy-makers and planners may have forced upon them, though, if the 'firm framework' of 1989's financial projections turns into a tightening press in the early 1990s (with MARILYN making mischief on the side). In that event, what the powers-that-be will have to do is confront the issue which has been stalking the defence arena for a decade and more: might it not be in the United Kingdom's own interest, and the Alliance's, to restructure the national contribution to NATO – including that in the Central Region – placing less emphasis on all-round competence (trying to do a bit of everything and some of it not very well), and more on special expertise (and a concentration of effort on selected tasks)?

Specialisation

This issue ought now to be addressed, not only as a response to the 'domestic' requirement for a better method of dealing with the impact of resource constraints than muddling through, but also in answer to the call which went out from NATO's Defence Planning Committee (DPC) in December 1988 for an Alliance-wide examination of opportunities for rationalisation and division of labour' in national contributions to the collective defence, 'with a view to enhancing output by better co-ordination of national efforts and optimal use of the unique capabilities and strengths of individual allies'.

The DPC's appeal was contained in the 'Conclusions and Recommendations' part of its report entitled *Enhancing Alliance Collective Security: Shared Roles, Risks and Responsibilities in the Alliance*, a document which won defence ministers' unanimous approval at their December 1988 meeting and has attracted near-universal approbation since. To be sure, that is due in large part to the report's thoughtful treatment of 'burden-sharing' matters and its key conclusion that NATO should spend less time arguing about who pays what (and how much it hurts) and on who does what (and how much it matters), and should begin exploring who can *best* do what in the Alliance interest. But the work has been praised also for its identification of 'rationalisation and division of labour' as the obvious means to that end, putting the notion of functional (and regional specialisation as a basis for national force contributions firmly on the agenda for member states' individual and collective consideration.

The Supreme Allied Commander, Europe (SACEUR) was particularly prompt (and fulsome) in voicing support for the promotion of such specialisation. In an article published soon after the appearance of the DPC's report, he wrote that 'few nations can afford the full spectrum of capabilities' in their individual force structures, but pointed out that 'the Alliance could not work if nations were to follow procurement policies of unrestrained picking and choosing: gaps would soon start appearing in our defences'. To avoid this he not only endorsed the initiation of moves 'towards a greater division of labour' but also urged 'the formulation of a collective plan that would inject some coherency into the process'.

If such a plan were to be formulated it would, without question, incorporate prescriptions for functional specialisation among the nations fielding forces in AFCENT; and the richest opportunities for a rational reallocation of roles and responsibilities would probably be found in the Northern Army Group (NORTHAG) area, where the corps of four nations – the Netherlands, the Federal Republic, the United Kingdom, and Belgium – compose the NATO layer-cake (with American reinforcement in war), and where the same countries deploy the bulk of their tactical airpower. In this area there are particularly promising options for beneficial specialisation in the provision of capabilities for Follow-On Forces Attack (FOFA) and the main defensive battle.

Under the first heading the possibilities arise in missions requiring significant investment in high technology, namely, the provision of surveillance and target acquisition assets for the FOFA task (plus associated data processing/data fusion and communications facilities, that is, related C^3I) *and* of the reconnaissance/electronic warfare capabilities required to support tactical air interdiction and the offensive counter-air mission. Under the second heading the attractive options are in the integration of ground formations along lines which have been examined recently by the Germans and the Dutch; and in the provision of an air-mobile formation to provide the Army Group Commander with a flexible operational reserve.

If the United Kingdom were to explore these opportunities with its allies it might find a way of reconciling its continuing commitment to the Central Region on the one hand and its shrinking resources on the other. In fact, it may be that there is no alternative (to coin a phrase).

Annex: Options for Role Specialisation in the NORTHAG Area*

The place where NATO's conventional defences need sustaining is the Central Region. Yet this is also where NATO's capabilities are most in

*An extract from a report entitled *Beyond Burden-sharing: A New Policy Approach*, prepared by the author (with Steven Canby) for the Office of the Assistant Secretary of Defense (International Security Policy), Washington DC, and submitted on 12 June, 1989.

danger of erosion: from a 'wasting' experience if West European defence efforts (especially the West German) diminish because of resource constraints, and/or from a rundown of American forces – over and above what may be proposed in an arms-control context – if the burden-sharing and 'role and responsibility sharing' issues are not satisfactorily resolved. Fortunately, it is also in the Allied Forces Central Europe (AFCENT) region that the scope is greatest for more efficient and effective use of the Alliance's resources through the practice of functional specialisation by the nations fielding forces there.

The richest opportunities for exploring mutual complementarities (recognising that mutual dependency is the corollary) are to be found in the Northern Army Group (NORTHAG) area. Here Dutch, German, British, and Belgian Corps make up the NATO layer-cake (with American reinforcement in war); and it is here that the same countries deploy the bulk of their tactical air power.

NORTHAG: The Opportunities

What specifically might be accomplished in this area? What particular options are there for functional specialisation? It is convenient to distinguish among opportunities in three domains, namely, (a) capabilities for Follow-on Forces Attack (FOFA) tasks, (b) capabilities for the main defensive battle, and (c) rear-area security, notably air defence. In the earlier report there were six other options; in this annex we shall consider only nos. 7–10.

Under the first heading, options for judicious specialisation occur in missions requiring significant investment in high technology:

7. Provision of surveillance and target acquisition assets for the FOFA task (plus associated data processing/data fusion and communications facilities, i.e., related C^3I) *and* of the reconnaissance/electronic-warfare capabilities required to support tactical air interdiction and the offensive counter-air mission.

Under the second heading – provision for the main defensive battle – there are a couple of options (which are in fact already under discussion):

8. 'Integration' of ground formations along lines which have been examined recently by the Germans and the Dutch.
9. Provision of an air-mobile formation to provide the Army Group Commander with a flexible operational reserve.

Under the third heading – rear-area security – there is scope for beneficial change in at least one direction:

10. Provision of air-defence capabilities (cf. Option 2).

The elementary analysis which is all that it has been possible to undertake in the present study suggests that each has considerable promise.

Option 7: Capabilities for FOFA

Among the capabilities which Commander NORTHAG must have at his disposal to perform the FOFA mission are (*a*) assets for surveillance and target acquisition plus related C^3I and (*b*) reconnaissance and electronic-warfare systems to support tactical air interdiction and offensive counter-air operations. These require costly, high technology investments. It makes neither military nor economic sense for each country which subscribes forces to NORTHAG to acquire its own national inventory of such items. It does make both military and economic sense for each to invest in specific complementary capabilities (even for one country, maybe two countries, to forswear the most technologically advanced acquisitions altogether, assigning resources instead to other elements in the Army Group's order of battle.

What 'makes neither military nor economic sense' is, however, what is happening, or about to happen. Each of the European countries which contributes to NORTHAG – and the Second Allied Tactical Air Force (or 2 ATF) – has plans to acquire, on its own account, some long-range surveillance, target acquisition and reconnaissance (STAR) capabilities plus associated equipment for signal processing, data processing and fusion, communications, etc. It is true that each has bought into the NATO force of Airborne Warning and Control System (AWACS) planes and other collective investments (in infrastructure, including C^3I, for instance); and each also intends to meet some procurement needs under joint venture arrangements. Be that as it may, each still has 'individual' acquisitions in its forward programme, typically involving a costly R&D effort and high production expense (because of the small scale of the investment in question).

This is squandering scarce resources. No one foresees the participating nations fighting separate corps battles, still less performing FOFA missions as unco-ordinated 'extensions' of such battles. It is absurd, therefore, that the Germans, the British, and the Dutch all have independent developments underway or envisaged for such things as long-range, unmanned aerial vehicles (UAVs). The rational approach to acquiring these – and all other STAR capabilities – is for (*1*) requirements to be drawn up on an Army Group/ATAF basis, and (*2*) a pattern of mutually complementary programmes to be agreed upon by the states in question.

Essentially the same argument applies with respect to reconnaissance and electronic-warfare (EW) assets for use in support of offensive operations against the adversary's follow-on forces and against Warsaw Pact airfields. Acquiring capabilities in penny packets is nonsensical, especially since these 'penny' packets turn out to have price tags running to millions of dollars, because economies of scale and learning in research, development and production go unexploited, and, for that reason, are from time to time unceremoniously axed from forward plans. (This is what the Dutch have just done with their solitary F-16 squadron equipped for tactical reconnaissance. From 1993 or thereabouts they will simply cease to perform this task.) Just as likely, of course, is that desired acquisitions never get into the forward plan in the first place. (Witness the Belgians' recent agonising over the procurement of EW systems.) Here, too, the rational approach is for (*1*) requirements to be worked out by 2 ATAF, and (*2*) mutually complementary procurement programmes to be agreed by Belgium, The Netherlands, the Federal Republic, and the United Kingdom.

This is the kind of thing expressly supported in the DPC Report of December 1988 which advocates 'enhancing output by better co-ordination of national efforts in the light . . . of the fact that there is on-going and unco-ordinated unilateral role changing (e.g., in . . . air reconnaissance) and of the requirement to face new challenges and develop new capabilities (e.g., Follow-on-Forces-Attack)'.

To this end, the DPC Report suggests that there should be 'discussions between major NATO commanders and two or three countries on . . . gradually shifting specific military capabilities' to facilitate 'optimal use of the unique capabilities and strengths of individual Allies' (para. 157a).

We think such discussions *should* be initiated; and examination of capabilities for FOFA, with particular reference to the NORTHAG/2 ATAF area, would be a good subject on which to begin. Analysis would show that neither Belgium nor The Netherlands can provide, and neither the Federal Republic nor the United Kingdom should be expected to provide the full spectrum of capabilities required. That would be self-evidently uneconomic, especially since in this area the allies must fight – and plan to fight – an Army Group battle, not a series of loosely-co-ordinated national corps battles. It would be wise, therefore, to relieve the smaller nations of all responsibility for providing capabilities in that part of the 'spectrum' which is most demanding (technologically and financially), and to encourage the medium powers also to plan on force complementarity (mission specialisation) across the spectrum. Wasteful duplication and the diseconomies of small-scale procurement, operation and maintenance can thereby be avoided.

In practical terms this means expecting no effort from the Belgians or the Dutch in surveillance and target acquisition (plus associated C^3I), electronic warfare, offensive counter-air and long-range interdiction;

they would be dependent on their allies for such provision. It means urging the British and the West Germans to make complementary rather than overlapping investments in respect of some (if not all) of these requirements. If the smaller countries were thus able to concentrate their resources on the less demanding part of the spectrum they would in fact have margin for manœuvre to increase their forward-deployed forces in Germany.

The practicalities of such matters as how Duch formations in NORTHAG might gain assured access to surveillance/reconnaissance data obtained by the Germans and utilise German communications and other facilities – these are already the subject of Working Group discussions between the two countries.

Co-ordination of national efforts in the light of *the need to seek efficiencies* is another theme in the DPC Report. Capabilities for the main defensive battle in NORTHAG offer a rich vein of opportunity in this connection, given that, as just noted, it is unlikely that the participating nations will ever be called upon to fight separate and independent corps battles. Outlined below are one general and one specific possibility.

Option 8: Integration of Ground Formations

There would be clear gains in efficiency, and perhaps even in combat effectiveness too, if Commander NORTHAG were able to define his preferred force structure and then elicit from nations the formations required for its composition, making 'optimal use of the unique capabilities and strengths of individual Allies' (rather than having to fashion an order of battle from what countries choose to offer – or earmark for assignment – which is, typically, more-or-less balanced, all-arms contingents).

The foregoing is, of course, a counsel of perfection; and 'integration ' of ground formations – conjuring up a vision of many multinational units – is something of a misnomer. However, the benefits of movement towards the ideal (a 'bottom-up' approach in the DPC's formulation) cannot be gainsaid; and the pay-offs from partial integration – German tank brigades working alongside Dutch infantry on a regular basis, or German attack helicopters employed routinely with Belgian infantry – could be considerable, matching relative capital and labour availability (see below).

This reasoning underlies the interest recently shown by West Germany and The Netherlands in moving towards *de facto* integration of Dutch ground forces with those of the Federal Republic. Among the principal matters that have been examined in conversations between the two countries are:

- the adoption by the Dutch of German tactical doctrine and equipment, thus eliminating independent doctrinal and development authorities (and, incidentally, furthering interoperability across-the-board and commonality to a large extent);
- the effective subordination of Dutch forces to 1st (German) Corps in peacetime, to permit their incorporation in the *Bundeswehr*'s C^3I system for both operational and administrative convenience (cf. Option 7 above); and
- the assumption by German territorial units of responsibility for the logistical requirements of Dutch troops in wartime (paralleling the support they provide for the *Bundeswehr* itself).

Other topics raised include the possible assumption by the *Luftwaffe* of the air-reconnaissance mission from which the Dutch plan to opt out; and of Dutch missile air-defence responsibilities in the Federal Republic (cf. Option 7).

So far as we are aware these deliberations – which have taken place in formally-convened joint working groups – have yielded nothing tangible to date. Practical problems (real and imagined) have bedevilled the exchanges. That the parties thought the possibilities worthy of detailed scrutiny does, however, augur well for the future, when resource pressures could well make today's 'problems' evaporate.

Certainly the potential gains are not trivial. In the case of the Netherlands it is estimated that, by 'meshing' their forces with those of the Federal Republic (as here envisioned) *and* avoiding uneconomic outlays on deep attack/FOFA systems (as discussed under the last Option), the Dutch could (*a*) station an additional brigade plus a divisional headquarters in the corps area and (*b*) add one or two active tank battalions plus a mobilisable tank brigade to their overall order of battle. If Belgium were likewise to 'mesh' forces with the *Bundeswehr and* forswear costly high technology investments for FOFA, a force increment of up to four brigades plus assorted divisional troops might be possible (together with a significant increase in tank strength). If an augmentation of this magnitude could be achieved in European forces-in-place and readily-mobilisable formations, the Alliance could contemplate with greater equanimity the prospect of forgoing those American troop reinforcements for NORTHAG which follow the deployment of III (US) Corps, which would mean benefit for the United States also. As for the Federal Republic itself, the attraction in promoting complementarity is – or ought to be – obvious. For the Germans concentration on capital – and technology-intensive provision offers hope of some mitigation of the demographic 'squeeze': and extra effort by the Low Countries in relatively manpower-intensive activity is a sound *quid pro quo*.

Option 9: An Air-Mobile Division

A specific possibility for beneficial functional specialisation is currently under examination in NORTHAG: the provision of an air-mobile division which would be available for employment as an Army Group operational reserve (able to undertake counter-penetration and counter-*desant* missions, releasing armour for counter-offensive operations or the decisive counter-stroke).

The requirement for more mobile operational reserves in NORTHAG has been acknowledged for a long time. Put bluntly, Commander NORTHAG has fewer resources to influence the point of main effort than an equivalent Soviet Commander; and he is less able to shift combat power quickly. Moreover, what capabilities he does have at his disposal come mainly from armoured and mechanised formations whose movement is vulnerable to delay, by (for example) air interdiction or scatterable mines, and also difficult to disguise. Hence the interest in the provision of an air-mobile division.

Since none of the countries subscribing forces to NORTHAG has the means to furnish such a formation alone, the obvious way to satisfy the need is by 'assembling' the division from functionally specialised national 'building blocks'. Among these might be:

- the German and the British airmobile brigade already committed to NORTHAG, with their transport and armed helicopters;
- Belgium's élite Para-Commando Regiment; and, possibly
- Dutch attack helicopters (when available).

Here would be an invaluable formation, capable of being committed as a division or of detaching single brigade groups to a corps; but more important for present purposes, capable of 'proving inter-allied task specialisation. The Alliance needs such an organisational and operational counterpart to the technology demonstrator of the systems world to show that there is an alternative to every nation's trying to do everything (and some of it not very well).

The wherewithal exists. Currently each *German* corps has an airborne brigade, which consists primarily of light infantry with a powerful anti-tank capability but only limited ground mobility. Each is supported by a strong aviation regiment of CH53 medium and UH-1D light helicopters, together with the Bo105 helicopter, which does reconnaissance, and when equipped with anti-tank missiles, has an anti-armour capability. Possible enhancements include an air-to-air weapon, and an improved helicopter-delivered mine system. The *United Kingdom* has converted a regular infantry brigade to the air-mobile role. It includes two air-mobile battalions strong in anti-armour weapons and a third APC-borne battalion. An Army Aviation regiment is being formed to support the brigade. This will include a helicopter anti-tank squadron, equipped with Lynx/TOW and two squadrons of Lynx light battlefield helicopters. Transport helicopters, consisting of RAF Chinooks and Pumas, are not dedicated to the airmobile task but are placed under command of COMNORTHAG for the duration of any air-mobile operation. The *Belgian* Corps currently has no air-mobile capability, though its parachute commando regiment trains regularly for air-mobile operations using allied helicopters. Similarly, the Dutch Corps does not at present have an air-mobile capability, but the purchase of 50 attack helicopters, if proceeded with, would provide a potent force.

To turn, finally, from capabilities for the main defensive battle to provision of rear-area security in the Federal Republic, we record here – but do not elaborate upon – a last policy option involving task specialisation.

Option 10: Air Defence

The provision of rear-area air defence – including the critical protection of air forces' main operating bases (MOBs) – is a job which could be made the exclusive responsibility of the *Bundeswehr*, with potentially big efficiency gains and no penalties in terms of combat effectiveness.

The provision of missile air defence in NATO's Central Region – the Patriot/Hawk belts and the close-in protection of air bases – is a responsibility shared among the different Services of several nations. On that account alone it is clearly less efficiently provided than it could be, and an obvious candidate for task specialisation. 'Multinationality' is not a political imperative here. So the options of assigning the role to one country commends itself in theory; and the obvious candidate is the Federal Republic. As it happens this is also feasible in practice, because the Germans could establish territorial units (locally-recruited and skeleton-staffed in peacetime) to perform the task.

The model here is the Air National Guard or the volunteer-manned Rapier squadrons of the United Kingdom's Royal Air Force. There is no overriding military objection to this 'model': commanders testify that, if operational effectiveness is assured, organisational arrangements are a secondary consideration; and experience with Guard and RAF units suggests that proficiency and readiness need not be degraded, may even be enhanced, and this with peacetime manning levels approaching 60 per cent below regular norms.

German assumption of Belgian and Dutch SAM responsiblities and point defence of the remaining main operating bases makes particular sense in conjunction with German assumption of the 32nd Air Defense Command's tasks. The latter requires the *Luftwaffe* to change its mode of operation from the full-up active to the partly-active but fully-ready Air Guard/RAF 'model'. In doing so, sufficient manpower remains for the Germans to assume the remaining rear-area air defence functions in Germany, namely three Belgian battalions, an eight-firing unit Dutch Patriot battalion, and four British and one Canadian point-defence batteries.

SACEUR's Commendation

As a footnote to this survey of opportunities in NORTHAG it is interesting to record that SACEUR has explicitly commended some of them (in general terms) in an article published in the April 1989 issue of *NATO Review*. Noting that 'we face increasingly the prospect that the spiralling cost of some weapons systems is such that very few nations can afford the full spectrum of capabilities', he argues that 'the Alliance could not work if nations were to follow procurement policies of unrestrained picking and choosing; gaps would soon start appearing in our defences'. He goes on to observe that some members are 'already showing a reluctance to invest in, for example, important elements of FOFA, electronic warfare, and tactical reconnaissance'. He continues with the following remarks on two complementary approaches to this problem:

> One is to build on the successful experience of the NATO Airborne Early Warning Force and widen considerably the number and type of those forces which are affordable when nations club together to field a multinational capability. . . . [It] might prove possible in the longer term to extend the concept of multinational forces . . . to suppression of enemy air defences and some elements of air defence and FOFA. One advantage of this approach is that it is generally regarded as the fairest way of ensuring that not only the burdens of defence are equitably shared, but the operational benefits are equally distributed.

And he continues:

> Multinational forces will not, however, solve all the potential difficulties of fielding increasingly costly weapon systems. A greater division of labour and co-ordination of national efforts within the Alliance may prove inevitable. Although 'role-specialisation' can conjure up images for some of constraining national sovereignty or providing excuses for others to shed unpopular tasks, it is worth recalling that some Alliance nations have already conceded many tasks to those best equipped to perform them.

This is endorsement of our suggestions on the highest military authority.

It is worth quoting at length General Galvin's wise words on the principles he believes should guide 'efforts towards a more appropriate division of labour':

> First, the overriding aim should be to use resources and skills more efficiently; dividing up roles and responsibilities between nations must never become an excuse by some for avoiding those burdens that carry the greatest political and financial burdens.
>
> Second, we should focus primarily on future, not current, tasks. Not only is it easier to plan coherently for the future, but many of the moves that one could predict to rationalise current tasks would inevitably put a greater pressure on other participants, thereby incurring accusations of unfairness.

Finally, the Supreme Commander's conclusion is further ringing endorsement of the approach advocated in this study.

> It is important to overcome the existing suspicion that surrounds the attempt to move towards a greater division of labour within the Alliance. Some nations have already served us with notice that they intend to withdraw from specific roles. If we are to avoid the picking and choosing that I regard as being so counterproductive, we need to consider urgently a collective plan that would inject some coherency into the process.

In our view such a 'collective plan' could usefully incorporate the options just discussed, focusing on the NORTHAG areas as a sort of 'laboratory' for testing functional specialisation possibilities (or multi-national provision).

CHAPTER 6

The Military Balance, Arms Control, and the Central Region

SIMON LUNN

AFTER YEARS of slumbering in the doldrums of MFBR, conventional arms control has come of age. Progress at the negotiations on Conventional Forces in Europe (CFE) in Vienna suggests that an initial agreement could be signed during the course of 1990. The remarkable momentum in Vienna reflects the dramatic improvement in East–West relations, and particularly the reorientation of Soviet security policy which has resulted in greater flexibility and openness. As a result, a substantial degree of convergence has been achieved between the proposals of the two alliances, or 'each group of parties' as they are now known in Vienna parlance. Important and complex obstacles remain to be resolved, but there is a definite sense that these can be surmounted with the appropriate dose of political will. An agreement is now in sight.

Yet many believe that the maturing of conventional arms control may have arrived a little late. The momentous political and economic changes now under way in Eastern Europe could undermine the neat formulae so carefully elaborated by both sides and effectively marginalise the negotiations. To what extent, for example, will the concept that has provided the basis for both sides' proposals – parity between the two alliances – continue to be valid? Given trends in the Warsaw Treaty Organisation (WTO), how much longer will there be two sides to make sense of these collective totals? Furthermore, to what extent will governments withstand the popular rush to disarm, rendering super-fluous carefully worked-out collective ceilings and individual alloca-tions. In other words, in today's rapidly changing environment, is the Vienna arms-control framework still valid?

The official consensus at the time of writing is that in this time of political flux the Vienna negotiations become more rather than less important. There are no illusions about the difficulty of ensuring that an inherently cumbersome multilateral process keeps pace with political change. Nor that speed, flexibility, and a willingness to compromise are now of the essence in order to reach an agreement before political events bypass the current framework. But the general feeling is that the cause of stability and security in Europe is best served by negotiated agreement rather than unilateral action, and that the military potential in Europe, so long the cause of suspicion and concern, should be reduced in a way that maximises accountability, irreversibility, and mutual reassurance. So, for the foreseeable future, conventional arms control in some shape or form will be a central element in the development of defence budgets, force programmes, and military structures.

This chapter will look at the implications of the current CFE negotiations for the Central Region and particularly the role of the British Army. It will attempt to set the context for later discussions by examining the military background within which the Western Alliance CFE proposals has been developed, including the vexed question of the conventional balance, assess the current proposal and its potential contribution to stability, and finally look at the implications of the CFE framework for future Alliance defence requirements.

The Military Context

The Alliance approach to conventional arms control was developed in a military context dominated by an extremely pessimistic view of the relationship between the conventional forces of NATO and the Warsaw Pact. The official view was that the WTO enjoyed substantial numerical superiority over NATO, particularly in the forces and key weapon systems that could be brought to bear rapidly in a time of crisis. It was argued that, in the event of conflict, this numerical superiority, together with the advantages of geography and initiative that naturally accrue to the WTO, would result in the rapid demise of NATO's conventional forces, and the inevitable reliance by the Alliance on the early use of nuclear weapons. While deeply ingrained in official thinking, this pessimistic view of the conventional situation in Europe did not go unchallenged. Attempts were made from time to time within the formal policy process to demonstrate that the conventional situation was not as bad as orthodox thinking would have it. Such efforts were normally undertaken by the United States' trying to pursuade its Allies that a credible conventional capability was within reach with just a little extra effort in the right place. The orthodox view came under more sustained attack, however, from the outside world. A wide range of institutes and individual analysts disputed both the numbers and what they mean.[1]

The reason for this divergence of view lay in the politics and the methodology of comparing the conventional forces of the two sides. Despite the graphic certainty of official publications – the familiar red bars towering over the smaller blue ones – there is no easy way of assessing and presenting the conventional balance. No single assessment can do justice to what is a highly complex picture. Two methods are traditionally used to assess the balance. First, an essentially static count is made of the men and weapons that would be available to either side. Secondly, there is a more sophisticated 'dynamic' assessment of how these forces would interact in combat. Both methods depend on a number of criteria or counting rules which are highly variable – for example, what forces are measured, in which area and according to which timeframe. Furthermore, dynamic assessments involve judgements about the readiness and availability of forces, the effectiveness of opposing weapon systems, and factors such as training, reliability, and morale, and so forth. The conclusion of any force comparison depends on assumptions and judgements which are open to very different interpretations. Hence the inherent difficulty in presenting a definitive assessment. It follows that, in terms of public presentation, the nature of the process facilitates the selection of criteria which support particular policies or attitudes – politics are never far from the surface of any force comparison.

These methodological problems have been compounded by the limited knowledge, until recently, of WTO forces. Because in the past the WTO did not publish data on its own forces, Alliance assessments depended on fragmented evidence gleaned from a variety of intelligence sources and then on a substantial degree of extrapolation.[2] This methodology leaves much to be desired in the accuracy of the final count. Consequently the confidence of the intelligence community in their estimates of WTO forces has varied considerably, depending on the area and type of system under consideration. For example, confidence in the estimates of Soviet tanks in Eastern Europe would be relatively high, in the Western military districts much less so. By contrast, estimates of Soviet armed forces manpower throughout the Soviet Union would be very low. This is because it is extremely hard to account for the substantial numbers of Soviet military personnel who are outside recognised units and occupied in administration and training, or with units such as construction or railway troops.

The obvious limitations of force assessments and the frequent over-simplification of official publications has stimulated vigorous public discussion, much of it highly critical, of the prevailing pessimism. However, the official message has been largely undented by this external debate and the orthodox view of the imbalance and its potential consequences has held sway. Given the evident complexity of force analysis, such uncomplicated certainty appears somewhat surprising. But there are a number of fairly obvious explanations. First, the fact is that in several key categories and on a reasonable assumption of 'readily available' forces, the WTO forces were numerically superior to those of NATO[3] – by how much and whether this disparity mattered were different questions. Secondly, the military authorities saw it as their role to jog reluctant governments and parliaments into making the necessary defence expenditure available, which inevitably meant a continual emphasis on the enormity of the task facing them. Finally, military assessments of how a potential conflict would go were inevitably based, if not on a 'worst', then on a 'less than best case' scenario, which again provided an appropriate basis for 'doom and gloom' predictions.

During the 1980s the message from NATO's military authorities became even more dire. WTO, and particularly Soviet military capabilities were said to be growing both quantitatively and qualitatively while Alliance capabilities were at best standing still. The result was General Rogers's persistent warnings of a 'widening gap' and the attendant low nuclear threshold which he assessed to be measured in days not weeks.[4]

Yet despite the persistence of these military warnings and their apparent endorsement by NATO's political leadership via ministerial communiques, neither the resources nor the capabilities to redress this situation were forthcoming. A persistent gap stretched between what the military authorities insisted was necessary for a credible strategy and the forces nations were actually willing to provide. The reason for this discrepancy lay in the politics and the strategy of the Alliance – the emphasis on deterrence rather than on defence, the ambiguous relationship between nuclear and conventional forces, and the unwill-ingness of Europeans to contemplate conventional war – which pro-duced an implicit acceptance of conventional 'insufficiency'. The Alliance formally acknowledged that, as a defensive alliance, NATO did not need to match the WTO 'man for man and weapon for weapon'. Moreover, there was a general feeling that, whatever the military situation, the East–West relationship itself was relatively stable and the chances of war remote. In these circumstances most of the Allies were willing to live with the existing situation, the commitment to do more was rhetorical and was largely for the purposes of the burden-sharing debate.[5]

Finally, it is worth remembering that, while the Alliance was convinced that it was badly off, it was never very precise about how badly off. There was no real blueprint of Alliance conventional requirements. Again, for political and strategic reasons, NATO has never defined the levels and types of nuclear and conventional forces required for deterrence and defence,[6] nor for how long it would be prepared to fight a conventional war. It is true that the Alliance Force Planning Process (FPP) offers a framework of coordination within which NATO's military authorities can develop proposals for improvements and hence attempt to influence national plans. But these military recommendations work on the basis of what nations are willing to provide rather than on what is actually needed, the possible rather than the ideal. The answer to the question 'how much is enough?' has always been 'more than we have now', normally accompanied by a list of deficiencies and requirements that embraces all areas: everything is needed and everything is equally important.[7] However, the advent of conventional arms control promised a new and more disciplined planning environment.

Enter Arms Control

The willingness of both sides to move ahead in a serious fashion with conventional arms control was signalled during the early months of 1986. Hardly surprisingly, the Alliance's approach to negotiations was strongly influenced by the prevailing military views on the nature of the balance. However, at the same time, the emergence of arms control as a serious actor had a number of consequences for the world of force-planning itself. For a start, it demanded the closest possible harmonisation between the arms-control and the defence-planning process. Such co-ordination would appear to be self-evident. However, for practical and organisational reasons force-planning and arms-control policies have tended to develop along parallel but separate paths, at times almost in splendid isolation from each other. Harmonisation is difficult enough at the national level. It is compounded at the Alliance level by the artificial separation of the defence-planning side of the Alliance from the political, as a result of the non-participation of France in the Integrated Military Structure. Awareness of this institutional obstacle is important in assessing how the Alliance has developed its CFE proposal and, more importantly, how it has handled its implementation.

However, there is another more conceptual problem. Arms control has to confront issues that defence planning has been content to leave unanswered – what levels of forces are required in Europe? By seeking to establish equal levels of similar systems in a particular region arms control begins to provide the answers to such questions. As a result force planners are faced with the novel prospect of parity and finite levels of forces, rather than the insatiable appetite of an ambiguous Alliance strategy. The prospect of equal levels has in turn focused attention on the concept of stability. What is it, and, in particular, how can arms control help to achieve it? One problem in this respect is that, in an effort to make negotiations easier, arms-control proposals tend to deal with relatively simple formulae which do not easily accommodate the complex demands of the world of military stability.

Stability is an elusive concept on which to reach agreement. An objective definition would be 'a condition that is not prone to rapid or violent change'. The problem is in translating that definition into the European security environment, and specifically into the military relationship between the two alliances. In this context a situation could be said to be stable when there is mutual reassurance of the absence of immediate threat and mutual confidence in the capacity to defend one's territory. These, however, are high subjective judgements involving political and military factors – intentions and capabilities. In terms of military stability, forces are considered stable in the degree to which they minimise the potential for pre-emption, surprise attack, or rapid force generation, and by contrast emphasise defence. Stability is therefore not a function of numbers and certainly not of parity, but rather depends on the location, configuration, and the orientation of the forces concerned.

The term 'stability' figured prominently in the definition of Alliance CFE objectives and principles. For the Alliance the starting point was the instability inherent in the existing situation owing to the massive preponderance of WTO forces, and particularly of the size, configuration and offensive orientation of Soviet forces deployed forward in Eastern Europe. The characteristics determine the principles and objectives of the CFE proposal, namely: the need to reduce WTO numerical superiority, particularly Soviet 'invasion' and reinforcement capabilities; to establish parity in key categories via highly asymmetrical reductions, on the principle of 'he who has most reduces most'; and to do so in a way that affects Alliance capabilities as little as possible, again on the principle that existing inadequacies and inherent disadvantages meant that the Alliance itself had little spare capacity to reduce.

Hence the decision to concentrate on key 'terrain seizing' capabilities (tanks, artillery, and armoured troop carriers), to seek parity at levels only slightly lower than existing NATO totals, with stationing and sufficiency rules directed principally at constraining Soviet forces, and a distinction between active and stored equipment with the aim of protecting American reinforcement assets stored in POMCUS sites. In addition, the Alliance developed a package of stabilisation measures designed to complement the reductions by imposing constraints on the residual forces. Reciprocity was a persistent complication in the development of these proposals. The Alliance knew which constraints it wished to impose on WTO forces. The problem was always the reciprocal effects of these same measures on the flexibility of Alliance forces.

For its part, the WTO accepted many of the Western objectives and principles; but its insistence on the inclusion of air power and the persistent reference to naval forces and to tactical nuclear weapons indicated serious differences over the concept of stability.[8]

Current Status[9]

Any assessment of the current status of the negotiations must take full account of their highly political nature. For the Alliance this political dimension has involved the diverse range of concerns, interests, and sensibilities of the 16 member nations. These range from the sensitivity of flank nations to what they perceive as 'Central Regionitis' and the neglect of their interests, to the initial determination sometimes bordering on paranoia of some nations to exclude systems remotely connected with nuclear weapons lest this lead to denuclearisation. It is no exaggeration to say that disputes within the Alliance have been as much of a problem as those between the two alliances. From the very beginning the most intractable question has concerned the nature of the negotiations – whether they were between 23 independent states or between the two alliances.

The predominantly French view, that the negotiations were not bloc to bloc, has meant that the role of NATO as a collective entity in the development of the Alliance position has been kept to a minimum. The creation of the High Level Task Force (HLTF) – to co-ordinate the initial Alliance negotiating position – and as a body that is 'NATO and yet not NATO' represents a classic compromise on the nature of the negotiations.

The issue of collectivity has continually dogged the development of the Alliance position. It has re-emerged recently in the drafting of treaty text. Although force ceilings are expressed collectively, it has been decided for legal and political reasons that treaty signature and all subsequent obligations and responsibilities must be taken by nations. However, each alliance will be responsible for ensuring before signature that its individual allocations do not exceed the appropriate ceilings; hence signature of the treaty will require prior co-operation and agreement with the Alliance on entitlements.

The Alliance is not alone in having to reconcile internal differences. The WTO, once the haven of uniformity, has become increasingly pluralistic. Consistent with the changing political order in Eastern Europe certain East European members have become increasingly assertive in developing and presenting national positions. Whilst from a political perspective this has been a welcome development, the fact that consensus is now required from 23 as well as from 16 has had an adverse impact on the speed of the negotiations.

Despite these political problems, a surprising degree of progress has been achieved. Much of this is due to Eastern acceptance of Western concepts and proposals. These shifts in position by the East have included: a move from the principle of equal percentage reductions to that of equality of outcomes; acknowledgement of WTO superiority in certain weapon systems; acceptance of the principle of asymmetrical reductions; and a new enthusiasm for on-site inspection and the detailed provision of data. Moreover, during the mandate discussions the WTO accepted, albeit reluctantly, the Western insistence on the exclusion of naval forces and tactical nuclear weapons.

However, the Alliance has also made concessions. The Bush initiative in May 1989 reversed a previously determined Alliance position to exclude aircraft and helicopters, and by suggesting ceilings on American and Soviet-stationed manpower went some way to meet Soviet requirements for overall ceilings on manpower. As a result of these concessions, agreement now exists on the five weapon categories to be limited (known as treaty-limited items, TLI) with partial agreement on manpower. The ceilings for tanks and APCs have been agreed, the stationed and sufficiency limits are close, as are the regional sub-ceilings. There is also considerable convergence in the respective packages on stabilisation and verification measures.

However, substantial differences still remain to be resolved. Of the five TLIs only artillery has an agreed definition, the gap on the others is narrowing slowly. Multi-purpose platforms, such as armoured vehicles and helicopters, pose a particular problem. A tightly-focused definition to catch the most relevant systems risks the postential for circumvention, but an all-embracing definition loses the specific focus and means that relevant systems are traded against the less relevant. The WTO is also unhappy with the West's distinction between active and stored equipment, which it argues allows for the retention of substantial amounts of equipment in central Europe.

The two most serious areas of disagreement concern aircraft, where the East insists on excluding five different categories, of which the so-called strategic assets, including interceptors, are the most difficult; and manpower, where the WTO proposal calls for overall ceilings on all forces in the ATU zone, and particularly on the inclusion of all stationed forces, not just American- and Soviet-stationed forces.[10]

Apart from these issues of definition, two rather more substantial and enduring ones lurk in the background: implementation and verification. Implementation will be a time-consuming and costly operation, particularly for the WTO, and due allowance will need to be made for the inherent complications of the process. Likewise, verification of treaty implementation could be a massive operation. The technical problems of verifying the entitlements established under the treaty are self-evident. But two qualifications are in order; first, the margin for error in conventional arms control is obviously of a different order from that for nuclear systems; secondly, as the climate between East and West improves and as mutual confidence and reassurance grow, verification standards may become less demanding. The demand to verify and the degree of reassurance sought will vary from country to country, and, as it will be a national responsibility, it will be a question of 'he who doubts, checks'. Both the level of concern and the capacity to react will depend on the country concerned. In this respect Alliance co-ordination of national efforts will be important, though what form this co-ordination will take remains to be seen.

Implications for NATO

For NATO the reductions imposed by a CFE I agreement as it is emerging are rather modest compared with those to be taken by the WTO.[11] The CFE limits will require some adjustment to Alliance forces, and will impose some additional tasks, such as verification, but will require no substantial change to existing defence arrangements. In this sense it could be said that CFE will offer defence planners some relief from budgetary pressures and will impose a degree of order on a potentially anarchic process of unilateral reductions. But the real significance of a phase one agreement for NATO lies in the short term in the politics of implementation, and in the longer term as a warning of things to come, and of the need to contemplate defence requirements in a security environment very different from that which has governed thinking for the past 40 years.

From the Alliance's view-point the overriding priority will be to ensure a collective approach to the implementation of reductions and also to the provision of future defence needs. This means ensuring to the greatest degree possible that the reductions and entitlements are implemented in a way that is both equitable and cost-effective, and makes the best use of NATO's collective assets. The long-established planning machinery of the Alliance would appear to be the natural mechanism for achieving this. Ideally Alliance implementation would work on the basis of a centrally-designed blueprint. However, the position of France will limit the involvement of NATO's political and planning authorities, and, anyway, even the planning process itself tends to work from the bottom up, that is from capitals, rather than from the top down.

Some thought has already been given to the possibility of rationalising the reduction process to allow for the transfer of relatively modern equipment from the Central Region to the less wealthy Allies, a concept known as 'cascading'. However, apart from the practical problems of shuffling equipment from one Ally to another, such a concept is unlikely to be politically tenable. Alliance proposals call for the destruction of withdrawn equipment, and, although it can be argued that this applies to the net reduction and does not prohibit internal redistribution, such a move is likely to be seen as suspiciously like circumvention.

The formula likely to be adopted to co-ordinate CFE implementation will be a reinforced HLTF in which defence planners will sit alongside arms controllers in order to discuss the distribution of reductions and entitlements. While the collective needs of the Alliance will be an important criterion, each nation will have special concerns that it wishes to safeguard – regional requirements, modernisation programmes, and, for smaller nations, the need to avoid the reduction of force structure. Above all, there will be the domestic imperative of seeking to maximise economic benefits, although at this initial stage these will not be particularly substantial. It remains to be seen whether the Alliance will succeed in co-ordinating the entitlements established by CFE I in a fashion that is satisfactory to all; obviously there is considerable scope for internal dissension. Moreover, it is a fair bet that in the co-ordination and allocation of entitlements political factors, whether regional concerns or considerations of burden-sharing, will be as important as military judgements.

However, assuming that phase one implementation can avoid internal disruption, the really serious questions for the Alliance go beyond a phase one agreement. They concern considerations of Alliance defence requirements under the conditions of parity, and the question of a further agreement involving deeper reductions. Both considerations raise a number of fundamental questions concerning Alliance strategy. Is there a finite level of Alliance forces based on force-to-space ratios required to maintain the commitment to forward defence and below which NATO may not go? Or will substantial changes in WTO forces through reductions, restructuring, redeployment, and reconfiguration permit the Alliance to change its own defence concepts and capabilities? Will they permit lower levels of readiness and higher reliance on reserves, different structures, locations, and operational concepts? Does the future 'lie with the swift' in the form of highly mobile platforms, air-mobile and amphibious groups? What priority for missions such as FOFA? What flexibility will now be possible in the interpretation and implementation of forward defence? To what degree can current Alliance defence arrangements be configured differently? And, finally, what types and levels of nuclear force will be required and will be politically sustainable?

How the Alliance will deal with these questions will depend on a number of factors – developments within the Alliance itself, the changes in WTO and Soviet military forces, and changes in Eastern Europe.

First, with regard to internal Alliance developments: despite the talk of change, it is not axiomatic that parity in the major systems defined in the CFE agreement will lead automatically to major changes in the near term to current NATO defence arrangements and dispositions, nor indeed that deeper reductions will necessarily follow. Apart from the inate conservatism that generally pervades most defence establishments and policies, there is a strong sense of caution in a number of capitals that, given the current political instability, now is not the time to be making fundamental changes in defence arrangements. Furthermore, concerning further and deeper negotiations, it is argued that the scale of CFE I implementation for the WTO, both in terms of manpower demobilised and equipment destroyed, will of necessity demand a healthy breaking space before a second negotiation begins. Finally, of course, there are those who argue that in view of NATO's inherent disadvantages and existing deficiencies and of fixed requirements, the Alliance has no room nor need for dramatic change to existing arrangements.

However, such caution appears to be running in the face of political, economic, and military realities. There is already a strong constituency building that seeks a more radical approach to future defence arrangements. Governments and parliaments in many countries are indicating that they believe the current climate no longer justifies defence expenditures and capabilities at existing levels. Most defence budgets have been frozen pending the results of Vienna. Current political trends in the Federal Republic, including environmental concerns, suggest that the presence of Alliance forces stationed in existing numbers will certainly diminish substantially with or without a further Vienna agreement. Moreover, a number of authoritative voices have gone on record with suggestions that NATO should be looking at reductions of at least 50 per cent of existing levels. Whatever the military logic of fixed force-to-space ratios, circumstances would suggest that Alliance and national planners alike should start looking at different ways of doing things, particularly in view of the changes now under way in the WTO force structure.

There can be little doubt that fundamental changes are taking place in Soviet military policy. The new defensive doctrine formally adopted by the WTO in May 1987 reaffirmed the non-aggressive intentions of the WTO. More significantly, however, it declared that at the military technical level or what in Western terminology is the military strategic, operational, and tactical level, WTO forces would be organised on the principle of defence and reasonable sufficiency. Soviet spokesmen have acknowledged that this development is in direct contrast to the previous emphasis on the need for decisive offensive operations. Now they argue that the Soviet Union is prepared to receive the first blow and will respond with sufficient force only to restore the status quo. As examples of this defensive doctrine WTO spokesmen point to the unilateral reductions now under way in all WTO states, to the restructuring of residual forces on defensive lines, and to the defensive character of operational planning and training.

What do these changes signify for Western planners? First, in the near term the unilateral withdrawals and the reductions under a CFE I will have a substantial impact. Above all, these developments will increase warning time and facilitate predictability, and should permit the Alliance to adopt more relaxed defence arrangements in terms of force readiness and the mix between active and reserve forces.

However, a number of Western analysts warn against complacency. They argue that current trends towards smaller, and more mobile and effective forces will lower force densities on both sides and will suit Soviet military commanders very nicely. Moreover, these analysts point out that 'restoring the status quo' will require counter-offensive capabilities, and that these will not look so very different from existing offensive capabilities – albeit, it should be added, that these capabilities will be deployed in a more reassuring location.

Much of the problem in ascertaining the degree of 'threat' posed by Soviet military forces lies in the distinction between offensive and defensive capabilities. It is important to distinguish where this distinction is meaningful and where it is not. At the declaratory level it is clearly essential that a nation confirms its non-aggressive or defensive intentions. However, as the saying goes 'intentions change, capabilities remain the same'. Hence it is force capabilities and doctrine that are traditionally assumed to provide the acid test of an offensive or defensive disposition. However, the utility of such a distinction depends on the level of command to which it is applied. At the tactical level it is exceedingly difficult to impute specifically offensive or defensive characteristics to individual weapons systems or particular units.[12] At this level forces and systems must be able to deliver firepower over a certain distance, to go forwards or backwards, to take as well as to hold terrain. Of course, taken in isolation some systems would appear better suited to defence than to offence. But within the overall context of the balanced armed forces of today the distinction becomes blurred.

The offence/defence distinction has more meaning, however, at higher levels of command organisation where the size, location, and orientation of forces can be said to take on distinctly defensive or offensive connotations. Again, there is room for ambiguity and subjective interpretation, for example, over Soviet arguments concerning the offensive nature of NATO's deep-strike systems. However, even if it is difficult to make a clear distinction between offence and defence, it is possible to identify aspects of force stuctures that are less threatening than others, and therefore contribute to rather than undermine stability. In the current environment the important question is how much counter-offensive potential is consistent with a defensive doctrine.

Two final points are in order. Whatever the changes, Soviet military forces will not suddenly become totally benign overnight. Their military will continue to perform their tasks as effectively as possible, including the modernisation of their armed forces and the utilisation of new technology. The degree to which their forces will be seen as threatening will depend on where they are and what they look like, but even more on the political context in which they operate. The 'capabilities not intentions' argument has always been a misleading distortion of threat assessment. Capabilities have never been seen in a vacuum, but always through the prism of political intentions. The challenge posed by Soviet military power will not vanish but will be of a very different order than in the past and will allow the Alliance considerable leeway for new arrangements.

In this respect the final factor is the most crucial – the political agenda in Eastern Europe. Political change in Eastern Europe will change the character, and undoubtedly undermine the existence of the WTO. There is talk of making the WTO more political, although what this entails is never spelt out. As East European countries go their own way, the future of the WTO is doubtful – an alliance only makes sense if it comprises countries with similar values and interests. It is conceivable that the WTO could continue on the basis of regional interests or as a framework to continue to make sense of conventional arms control agreements – but both possibilities would seem highly artificial and very short term. Whatever political arrangements materialise, the military forces of the non-Soviet WTO members are ceasing to be relevant to Western security calculations.

Conclusions

For defence planners and military men alike, the future European environment offers many possibilities but few certainties. The paradox is that political developments suggest a fundamental reappraisal by the Alliance of existing concepts and structures. Yet the very uncertainties inherent in the political changes taking place tend to put a brake on innovative thinking or dramatic readjustment. In looking to the future, however, several general observations may be made.

Barring a dramatic regression in East–West relations, current trends, particularly in WTO military power, should stimulate a re-evaluation of the basic principles underlying Alliance strategy: flexible response, how flexible, with which systems and aimed where? Forward defence, of whose territory and with what forces? Such an evaluation will lead to substantial adjustments in the numbers, types, and disposition of the military forces deployed in Europe and available for Alliance defence.

Arms control will continue to play an important role in the reshaping of defence arrangements so that residual forces contribute to stability. While the precise shape and form of further Vienna CFE negotiations remain unclear, the need for co-ordinated reduction and verification procedures is now well established. However, in looking to arms control to strengthen stability it is important not to overburden the process. Arms control by its very nature deals in relatively simple formulae which do not always withstand the exacting scrutiny of operational analysts or stability purists. Moreover, in thinking about stability it is important to remember that there is no single condition that is not vulnerable to technological innovation or to the ever-suspicious mind.

Despite the significant political changes in the strategic environment, there is no reason to believe that the concept of collective security as embodied by the Atlantic Alliance will become any less relevant to its current membership. Indeed, notwithstanding the prospect of closer European integration, the transatlantic relationship, including some form of American presence in Europe, will have an even more essential role in preserving stability in a new European security order. NATO therefore will retain its relevance as a framework within which like-minded nations will continue to co-ordinate their security policies. However, as security itself becomes a less urgent issue, so the Alliance will become less important in the normal order of things. This will be particularly true of its military dimension. The integrated structure will continue, but on a different scale as each nation looks to reorganise and reduce defence expenditure and capability.

Whatever the security environment of the future, nations will continue to require armed forces. In sustaining these forces they will be forced to address the same sorts of questions – what sorts of force, for what types of role and mission? In this context each individual member will reassess its current contribution to the Alliance. It is difficult at this stage to second-guess the results of these deliberations. However, one thing is certain, given the uncertainty that will continue to prevail in Europe these questions are better answered within the collective framework of the Alliance than apart from it.

Part II
THE OPERATIONAL LEVEL

CHAPTER 7

The Future of FOFA

PETER SHARFMAN

Introduction

THE DEBATES of the last few years have demonstrated that Follow-on Forces Attack, or FOFA, can be understood – and misunderstood – from a wide variety of perspectives. This chapter addresses FOFA from the perspective of decisions about the future structure of military forces: the task of setting priorities among desired force capabilities and possible procurements of military systems. There are other perspectives – not addressed here – which are equally important. FOFA represents an interesting study of how harmony within the Atlantic Alliance can be shaken and then restored, but that story could be better told by those who lived through it. FOFA also raises some interesting technical issues regarding the translation from the laboratory to the field of certain highly innovative technologies, especially in the face of credible countermeasures; but these issues could hardly be discussed in an unclassified setting. Finally, FOFA raises some significant issues for military strategy and operational art, since senior field commanders would have to make critical decisions under enormous pressures if NATO ever faced the possibility of carrying out FOFA during an actual war, but again these issues would be better left to the military professionals.

This chapter is largely based on an analysis carried out for the United States Congress, which has the constitutional responsibility 'to raise and equip armies', but not to direct them in battle nor to carry out diplomacy. In this particular case, Congress did not ask whether FOFA was a good idea; instead it asked what FOFA as a mission for NATO meant for Congress's mission to equip the US Army and Air Force. The analytical effort focused therefore upon a relationship – that between FOFA as a military mission and decisions regarding the procurement of military systems. Similarly, the subject matter of this chapter is neither FOFA as such nor the issues of what military systems are most needed or most cost-effective. Rather the chapter addresses the significance of FOFA for future procurement decisions.

There are two systems in particular that the United States is currently developing which are justified to a large extent by their role in FOFA: the Joint STARS radar surveillance aircraft with its associated ground stations, and the ATACMS short-range ballistic missile. The United Kingdom is engaged in an active R&D programme in the area of airborne stand-off radar for ground surveillance, with considerable attention being paid to NATO interoperability. However, to the best of the author's knowledge, Britain has no firm plans at this point to procure Joint STARS, ATACMS nor any British-designed equivalents. If the British defence budget were large enough, the country would probably procure both capabilities, or would at least give the most serious consideration to doing so. It is not the purpose here to suggest either how large the British defence budget ought to be, or how whatever money is available ought to be spent. The purpose is to say something about how those who are making such decisions should think about FOFA.

Specifically, this paper addresses three issues:

● FOFA as a case in point of how to assess military systems which have multiple missions, when each mission requires that multiple military systems work together.
● The role of Joint STARS systems (comprising an aircraft carrying a ground-imaging radar and extensive processing equipment, a series of ground stations, and communications linking them) in FOFA, as an illustration of how to assess the level of performance needed to justify the development of a new and expensive system.
● The impact of conventional arms reductions in Europe on NATO's need for FOFA capabilities.

Thinking about a Package

The FOFA mission carries the complexity of the battlefield to new heights, or perhaps to new depths.

For most of the history of warfare, the complexity lay in strategy and in logistics: the art of knowing what numbers and types of fighting force and supplies should be in what place at what time, and the perhaps more difficult art of getting them there. Actual combat consisted of using one's weapons against an enemy who was close by, and hoping to kill him before he could kill you. While being successful in battle often called for extraordinary leadership, courage, and skill, *thinking* about such combat was very easy. Responsible officials (or Congressmen) who may not have any ability at all to fight in a tank nor to design one have no difficulty at all in understanding that a good tank requires firepower, mobility, and protection – and that tank design involves trade-offs among these three desiderata and cost.

In contrast, a FOFA mission involves a chain of systems. To carry out FOFA, we must do the following: (*1*) carry out surveillance of a wide area in order to obtain information about the location and activities of potential targets; (*2*) process the surveillance data into usable information, and transfer this information about where potential targets are to the appropriate commanders; (*3*) decide which targets to attack, and transmit this decision along with location information to those carrying out the attack; (*4*) carry out a more detailed reconnaissance in order to detect, locate, and track the specific targets to be attacked; (*5*) carry a weapon to the target, either on an aircraft or by means of a missile; (*6*) control the trajectory of the platform (aircraft or missile) as last-minute updates on the target's location become available; (*7*) attack the target with a weapon, such as a bomb or a terminally-guided submunition; (*8*) put the target out of action with the munition at the 'business-end' of the weapon, which is easy if the target is a truck but quite difficult if the target is a modern Soviet tank; and (*9*) assess the results of this attack. Each of these nine functions will be performed by a different system. (The US Army discusses such a mission in terms of three phases: decide (items *1–3* above), detect (item *4*), and deliver (items *5–8*).) I have broken the problem down into nine phases to emphasise the number of different systems that are required, although in some cases the same system could perform items *1*, *2*, *4*, and *9*.)

So whereas it is simple to decide to buy a tank, it is complicated to decide to buy a FOFA capability. For each of the nine functions, there is a choice among systems that could be procured. Moreover, most of these systems would be used for other missions as well. For example, an F-15E aircraft (the ground-attack version of the familiar F-15) could be used as a platform for FOFA. Alternatively, the ATACMS short-range ballistic missile could be used as a platform, carrying essentially the same munitions against the same targets as an F-15E. On the other hand, the F-15E could also be used in the offensive counter-air mission, and indeed the US Air Force tends to consider offensive counter-air as a higher priority mission than FOFA. In principle, the ATACMS missile could also be used for offensive counter-air, but ATACMS is an Army system and offensive counter-air is an Air Force mission. A FOFA mission would require very timely targeting information, but arguably the ATACMS needs a more recent update than the F-15E. An F-15E is much more expensive than an ATACMS, but it can be re-used, provided it is not shot down.

Pity the poor Congressman, or for that matter the poor Secretary of Defense, who has to decide whether to procure the F-15E, ATACMS, or both, or neither, and how many of what to procure.

The problem gets worse. A FOFA mission requires RSTA (reconnaissance, surveillance, and target acquisition) systems, and numerous C^3 systems to process and transmit the necessary information from the RSTA systems to those who target the weapons. How many of such RSTA and C^3 systems are needed? It depends, to the first order, on how many FOFA missions would be required each day, which is to say on how the theatre commander would decide during an actual war to allocate his assets among FOFA and other missions (such as offensive counter-air or fighting the close battle). Decision-makers make the best guesses they can. Unfortunately, the politics of procurement do not always lead to sensible decisions; a notable problem in the past has been the reluctance of all concerned to acquire sufficient quantities of munitions to balance the numbers of platforms, and it remains to be seen whether the same imbalances will occur in the FOFA context.

A final aspect of the problem is the question of technical risk. If several different systems must work together in battle, and all are the objects of development programmes, it is perfectly possible that one of the new systems will not work as well as the others. Indeed, it is not merely possible, but probable. The risk here is that a weak link in the chain will render the other links ineffective. For example, a wonderful set of systems to find enemy tanks, identify them, provide up-to-the-minute information about their locations, and then deliver a weapon that hits a tank would all be useless if we had failed to develop and buy a munition capable of defeating the tank's armour.

Faced with these dilemmas, the standard ways of thinking about procurement issues are not much help. Must we then simply fall back upon the trained intuition of experienced military leaders?

The author suggests that there is an analytical method that could help, although in isolation it can hardly solve the problem of making hard choices. It is not known who invented it, but it should be acknowledged that the author was persuaded of its value by Glenn Kent, a retired Lieutenant General in the US Air Force, and now a senior member of the RAND Corporation. This analytical method is to focus one's attention on alternative operational concepts.

The analyst would imagine a number of scenarios for carying out a FOFA mission. For each scenario he would specify which military system caried out each of the functions necessary; in other words, specific sensors, specific communications systems to carry the sensor data, specific systems to process the sensor data and present it in usable form to commanders, specific systems to carry the firing orders to specific platforms (including all the systems need to support them), with specific weapons and specific munitions. Where possible and it was sensible to do so, existing systems would be specified, ideally systems already deployed, unless they were already fully tasked with missions likely to be even more critical and urgent than FOFA. Where necessary and sensible, new developmental systems would be specified. If no sensible system seems to be available to perform a critical function, drop that scenario.

Each scenario that passes the tests of plausibility would become a tentative operational concept. There might be several dozen tentative operational concepts for FOFA: some concepts might be well suited for certain targets and poorly suited for others, some might depend on the successful solution of a technical problem which is still being worked, and other concepts might simply represent alternative means of doing the same thing. Each tentative operational concept would be analysed to estimate its likely cost, effectiveness, and degree of technical risk.

Then the senior military planners would select a subset of these operational concepts. They would attempt to select the most cost-effective, but the more resources that were available, and the higher the priority given to having a FOFA capability, the larger the number of operational concepts likely to be selected. For each selected concept, a decision would also be made about how many such operations we would want to be able to perform per day.

Each selected operational concept would then become a guide to procurement: we would develop and procure *all* the systems necessary to carry out the selected concept at the selected rate. If a budgetary restriction or a technical shortfall made it impossible to procure a system which was critical to the implementation of a certain concept, then that concept could be dropped from the plan – and the other systems required by that concept would remain in our plans only to the extent that they are part of other operational concepts (including, of course those with no connection to FOFA.

Of course, in actual war the commanders would depart from the plans, as wartime commanders must always depart from peacetime plans. Some operational concepts which looked promising in peacetime analysis would fail to work and would be dropped. Some critical assets would be destroyed by the enemy. New concepts to use whatever assets were available would be improvised on the spot. But procurement by operational concept would at least ensure that systems which had been brought to support FOFA, or at least in part to support FOFA, would not be prevented from doing so by peacetime failures to purchase all the links in a chain.

Thinking about Requirements

The Joint STARS development programme is moving ahead in a generally successful way, and in all probability the United States will procure and deploy it; indeed, in 1988 the Defense Acquisition Board increased the planned procurement from 10 aircraft to 22. However, several years ago there was an intense debate over whether to develop this system at all. It is instructive to examine one aspect of that debate, which illustrates the dangers of taking too rigid an approach to military modernisation.

The Joint STARS aircraft will be modified Boeing 707 airframe equipped with a very capable radar and with extensive, on-board, processing equipment. The radar will scan the ground at ranges out to several hundred kilometres, with a capability to survey broad areas with low resolution or to examine small areas with high resolution. The radar can also be operated to pick up either moving targets or fixed targets. When the system was being designed, a formal requirement was established that specified what targets the radar should be able to image, at what range, with what resolution, and how often the radar should be able to scan a particular area of interest, all of which are certainly relevant to the system's military utility.

However, this requirement, as stated, has led to criticisms of the Joint STARS system which are quite plausible at first glance, and yet on closer inspection highly misleading. To illustrate the difficulties of thinking clearly about FOFA, it is necessary to outline this misguided criticism and then refute it.

Like most radars, the Joint STARS system can only image targets which are in a line of sight from the aircraft. This means that it gets its maximum coverage of enemy territory when it is flying at a high altitude as close as possible to the enemy territory. (The currently-accepted acronym for the dividing line between territory held by friendly forces and that held by hostile forces is FLOT, which stands for Forward Line Own Troops, and which has replaced FEBA, which stood for Forward Edge of the Battle Area. For the purpose of thinking about Joint STARS, which is concerned with hostile, ground-based air defence, it would be more relevant to think of something like FEEAD, for 'Forward Edge of Enemy Air Defence, but in this chapter we shall use the current acronym FLOT.) If the Joint STARS aircraft can fly back and forth parallel to the FLOT, at a high altitude and only a short distance behind it, then it can obtain the maximum coverage of enemy forces. Even then, as attention shifts further into the enemy's rear, an increasing number of interesting areas (such as stretches of road) become invisible for a period of time because they fall into the shadow of hills. As the aircraft flies lower, or as the aircraft flies further back from the FLOT, the number of interesting targets in rough terrain that are hidden increases, for exactly the same geometrical reason that more and more things become shaded from the sun as the afternoon wears on and the sun moves lower in the sky.

Unfortunately, a Joint STARS aircraft flying at a high altitude very close to the FLOT is a relatively attractive target for enemy air-to-air attack and enemy ground-based air defence. This vulnerability is enhanced because the system cannot do its job of radar surveillance without emitting. As the Joint STARS aircraft moves further back from the FLOT and/or reduces its altitude, it moves out of the range of an increasing proportion of enemy ground-based air defences, and it becomes increasingly difficult for enemy fighter aircraft to fly close enough to attack Joint STARS without themselves being shot down. But this increased survivability comes at the expense of decreased coverage for the Joint STARS radar, which is its whole reason for being there in the first place. In addition, the Joint STARS aircraft could manœuvre if it were under attack, but the radar would not be very useful while the aircraft was manœuvring, and possibly for several minutes thereafter.

These considerations led critics to formulate the following plausible, but fallacious, charge: 'If the Joint STARS is operated so that it can meet its radar coverage requirements, it will be shot down. If it is operated so that it is survivable, it can't meet its radar coverage requirements. Therefore it could never actually accomplish its mission.' At one time this line of reasoning led the House of Representatives to vote to cancel the Joint Stars programme although the Senate eventually saved it. However, it is suggested that this argument is founded on misunderstandings both of military requirements and of survivability.

To begin with, any competent enemy activity in any war will have the effect of degrading our military capabilities. The infantryman's rifle is less effective when the infantry is subjected to hostile fire; the artillery is less effective when subjected to counterfire; tactical aircraft are less effective when subjected to enemy fighters or air defences; and even C^3 is less effective when subjected to jamming. Moreover, the extent of this degradation always depends on how hard the enemy tries – any individual military system or organisation can be rendered ineffective by an enemy attack that is sufficiently large and determined. The designers of military systems and organisations do not pursue the impossible goal of rendering them invulnerable to attack; rather, they pursue the challenging but realistic goal of making them *resistant* to enemy attack. More precisely, the goal is to make them so resistant that the enemy must pay an unacceptably high price to seriously degrade or to eliminate their capabilities.

So it is with Joint STARS. The requirements for coverage never meant, and never could mean, that a given level of coverage by each and every airborne radar should be preserved against any imaginable level of enemy attack, any more than we would expect an isolated infantry platoon to withstand unaided the assult of a combined arms battalion. Rather the requirements for coverage should be interpreted as three parallel requirements:

- a specified level of coverage during a peacetime period of crisis, or in wartime when not actually under attack, this is a technical problem, which the ongoing development programme gives every indication of solving completely;
- if subjected to heavy levels of enemy attack, a level of coverage that would be so useful as to be worth the cost of the system; this is partly a technical problem, and partly a question of operational tactics;
- an enemy determined to render the system ineffective should have to pay an unacceptably high price; this is not only a question of technical achievement and of tactics, but also a question of NATO's having an overall tactical air capability so strong that the Soviets would be courting defeat if they devoted a major fraction of their fighter aircraft and SAMs to pursuing Joint STARS (note that exactly the same argument applies to AWACS, and attacking both Joint STARS and AWACS would require more enemy resources than attacking either).

The requirements for Joint STARS were written by estimating what radar coverage could be provided at the existing state of the art for a reasonable cost with reasonable reliability, maintainability, etc., and then from this envelope of possibilities choosing the kinds and amounts of coverage that military commanders would most want to have. Then a judgement was made that the benefits of this level of coverage were well worth the estimated costs of providing it.

This does *not* mean there would be no military benefits obtained if only 90, or 80, or even 50 per cent of the desired coverage were provided. It presumably does mean that as coverage diminishes, the military benefits also diminish. Therefore, the system should be resistant to enemy efforts to diminish its coverage; we can accept a diminution of the military benefits of Joint STARS if and only if the enemy must pay a sufficiently high price to deprive us of some degree of benefit.

Therefore the officially stated requirement should be viewed as a goal for the development programme, but not as a level of capability which must be sustained against any possible enemy attack if the developed system is to have any value at all. It is an unfortunate fact that public opinion stands ready to believe that the military and military contractors have 'failed', and that any newly-developed system which enemy action could degrade to the point where its capabilities fell short of the nominal requirements in any respect is a complete waste of money. But public opinion is often wrong on this issue.

It is, of course, the case that if an enemy can degrade a system's capabilities, then the cost should be weighed not against the benefits from the system we originally planned, but rather against the level of benefits we actually expect to obtain, including as a benefit the cost to the enemy of attacking it.

Again, we ask that military systems be survivable enough to accomplish their missions, but 'survivable' does not mean 'invulnerable'. Wars inherently cause not only casualties but the attrition of military systems. Moreover, the rate of attrition depends in part on the choices made by the enemy; in particular, Joint STARS aircraft will suffer attrition faster if the enemy is willing to lose a substantial number of fighter aircraft in the process.

It seems, therefore, that we should think about Joint STARS in terms of two alternative operational concepts. These are merely illustrative. (The US Air Force and Army are working out more detailed operational concepts which promise to be more effective, but which are also classified.)

• The first concept is for use during a crisis when mobilisation is taking place but the two sides are not shooting at each other. In this case the Joint STARS aircraft would 'orbit' back and forth at high altitude along the inner-German border, providing detailed information about Warsaw Pact mobilisation and movement to pre-battle positions. Because there would be no immediate threat of their being shot down, the aircraft could position themselves so as to obtain maximum coverage, which would meet or exceed the formal requirements laid down at the outset of the programme. There could be a problem caused by enemy jamming, since in peacetime the Soviets could use powerful jammers without being concerned that NATO missiles could home on them and destroy them. However, being free to fly as they wished and emit at full power would help the aircraft in overcoming jamming.

• The second concept is for use during a battle. In this case the Joint STARS aircraft would spend most of their flying hours some distance behind the FLOT, possibly at lower than optimum altitudes, so as to reduce their vulnerability to enemy attack. They would still obtain some coverage of enemy activity, but coverage would be less (less comprehensive and less timely, but not *much* less) than in a pre-battle situation. They might also operate on irregular schedules and fly irregular paths, which would further enhance their survivability. However, at critical points during the battle when up-to-the-minute information about enemy activity was most needed, or when a command decision had been made to attack a given Warsaw Pact follow-on force at a given time and detailed targeting information was needed at that time, Joint STARS aircraft would fly into position to make the necessary observations. For these brief periods the Joint STARS could be escorted by NATO fighter aircraft and ECM aircraft, but even so they would have to accept additional vulnerability because their mission was so important. Once the critical need for information had passed, the Joint STARS would 'retreat' to a safer location to await the next moment when enhanced radar coverage was really necessary.

Used according to this wartime concept, Joint STARS coverage might be less than the coverage envisaged in the original requirements, but the military utility of this coverage would be almost as great as the utility of the coverage that could be provided if we did not have to worry about enemy attacks on Joint STARS.

It would also be necessary to have some Joint STARS aircraft in reserve. After all, the requirements for Joint STARS coverage are most critical, and it is therefore worth the risk of flying in locations where the enemy can attack. The enemy has the greatest incentive to use up his own SAMs and risk his own fighter aircraft in an effort to shoot the Joint STARS down. In short, the more we need to have one Joint STARS aircraft in position, the more we need to have several aircraft that could be in position. Thus the recent decision to increase the number of aircraft planned for procurement inherently diminishes the concern we should have for the survivability of the aircraft.

In short, the simple questions, 'Can Joint STARS meet its requirements?' and, 'Could Joint STARS survive to provide the envisaged military benefits?' are too simple to be useful. The correct question is this, 'If the Joint STARS aircraft are flown and the Joint STARS data are used in battle in a militarily sensible way, what is the relationship between the coverage we can expect and the attrition we must expect?' Furthermore, what is the relationship between the coverage we would obtain and the military benefit we would expect to derive? Based on the answers to these two questions, 'What is the relationship between the number of aircraft we buy (and therefore the amount of attrition we can endure) and the military benefit we can expect?' One possible answer is that we should not buy the plane at all, if the expected attrition looks high and the expected military benefit looks low. The answer actually given by the Defense Acquisition Board was to go ahead to develop and deploy Joint STARS, and to plan to procure 22 aircraft. This suggests that with enough aircraft, we can obtain the coverage we need at critical points in the battle, even taking account of the risks of attrition, and that this coverage offers so much military benefit that it is worth the costs of the expanded Joint STARS system.

Thinking about Arms Control

It may seem somewhat perverse to be talking about the purchase of expensive new military systems, when the attention of both the taxpayers and their elected representatives is focused firmly on the prospect of arms reductions in Central Europe. Despite the enormous complexity of any viable CFE (Conventional Forces in Europe) agreement, the Soviet Union has now moved so close to the NATO position that one can actually believe that a worthwhile agreement will be reached within a reasonably short period. The huge reductions in Soviet forces which NATO had demanded and which Gorbachev seems willing to undertake will, of course, greatly reduce the military threat on the Central Front. The taxpayers will surely see such a reduction in the threat as an opportunity to reduce the burden of defence spending, and will be sceptical, to say the least, about major programmes for force modernisation.

When the FOFA concept was first developed, NATO's problem was how to respond to the seemingly inexorable build-up of Soviet conventional forces in Europe. FOFA was a response to the problem of the staggering numbers of Warsaw Pact tanks, armoured fighting vehicles, and artillery tubes in two ways: first, by attacking these before they were in a position to shoot back, and secondly, by 'metering' the flow of enemy forces into the battle, disrupting Soviet plans and delaying Soviet reinforcements to the point where NATO, fighting from defensive positions, could deal with the attackers.

If the Soviet Union actually reduces its forces, as Gorbachev says it will, then arms control will have dealt with the endless numbers of Soviet tanks artillery, and mechanised infantry far more effectively than FOFA could have. What then would be the need for FOFA?

It can be argued that, in fact, a major conventional arms reduction in Europe along the lines now under negotiation would make FOFA capabilities even more relevant and valuable than they would have been if the Soviets had continued to follow Brezhnev's military policies. In a world in which a CFE agreement has been signed and implemented, we could look to FOFA capabilities to enhance our security in three separate ways:

First a major concern, once arms reductions had been implemented, would be to make certain that NATO had adequate warning if a serious Soviet military threat were to reappear. Thinking about NATO's requirements for intelligence, warning, and treaty verification requires us to distinguish several possible cases:

- one threat is a surreptitious Soviet build-up ot forces in violation of the treaty. This is a major problem for treaty verification. It is possible that the Joint STARS aircraft could play a useful role in such verification, but the author is not aware of any analysis of the nature and value of such a contribution.
- a second threat is a massive Soviet build-up, in blatant violation of

the treaty, with extensive mobilisation of reserves and a major movement of forces forward. This would certainly be easy for NATO to observe, but it would constitute a major challenge for NATO's ability to mobilise, and the ability of the United States in particular to move forces quickly across the Atlantic. Here, too, FOFA capabilities are not especially relevant.

- a third threat is a sudden movement of forward-deployed forces into positions from which they could attack, preparatory either to a short warning attack or to a political ultimatum backed by the threat of a short-warning attack. (This threat would be enhanced if it had been preceded by a successful attempt surreptitiously to build up forces in the forward area.) Any thinning-out of NATO's own forward-deployed forces would make NATO more vulnerable to such a threat. This threat, which is arguably the most difficult for NATO to counter, is the one to which FOFA is most relevant, and which therefore requires more detailed discussion.

The FOFA sensors, including but certainly not limited to Joint STARS, are designed to do more than simply locate and identify forces in the enemy's rear; they are designed as well to give our commanders a picture of what the enemy is doing. The objective in wartime would be to identify the main axes of enemy advance, the forces which were concentrating to attempt a breakthrough, and the forces which were being readied to exploit the breakthrough once it was accomplished. In the days or even hours preceding the outbreak of war, the same sensors, data-processing equipment, and staff organisations could provide information that would help NATO to discover what Soviet forces were doing, and what their probable objectives were. The FOFA capabilities could not only detect Soviet force movements preparatory to an attack (though they could not, of course, tell us whether the Soviets intended to attack or merely to intimidate), they could also offer detailed, credible, and timely information about the attack preparations.

One of NATO's major problems, if the Soviets suddenly prepared for a short-warning attack, would be to make the internal decision processes of the Allies as well as the multinational decision process at SHAPE work rapidly enough to respond in time. The Soviets could be expected to try to exacerbate this problem by a judicious combination of *maskirovka* (the combination of camouflage and spoofing for which Soviet doctrine appears to be more advanced than our own), disinformation, and misleading political signals. A timely NATO response would be far more probable if Joint STARS and other sensors, together with an in-place organisation for processing the data, gave the NATO Allies a highly reliable and detailed database which could be fully shared among the

Allies and which was resistant to *maskirovka*. Merely agreeing at the outset on what Soviet troop movements were taking place would enormously simplify the task of agreeing on a response.

An even greater problem for NATO would be an acute scarcity of resources that could be mobilised in time. Even if a CFE agreement produced a reasonably even balance both in the forward areas and in the ATTU (Atlantic to the Urals) region, and even if NATO were able to co-ordinate a vigorous and prompt response, the Soviets would have an excellent chance to conduct a surprise preparation for an attack in such a way as to achieve numerical superiority in selected locations along the inner-German border for at least a few hours. In this situation, the FOFA capabilities could give NATO commanders invaluable clues about precisely where the Soviet forces were heading, so that NATO could concentrate its temporarily inadequate resources in the most critical areas.

Secondly, if a war did break out in the future between a Warsaw Pact and a NATO which had both reduced their forces under a CFE agreement, it is not at all unlikely that the war would be one of movement, manœuvre breakthroughs, flank attacks, and meeting engagements. The simple fact that the density of forces on both sides would have been reduced would make this more likely, and if a war broke out before either side was fully mobilised, prepared, and in position it would be still more likely that the Soviets could achieve the war of manœuvre which their doctrine calls for. But if this is to be prevented – if NATO could, in fact, succeed in carrying out its strategy of forward defence – it would be possible only if NATO forces succeeded in holding defensive positions against attackers who (at least temporarily) far outnumbered them.

This suggests that NATO commanders would have an urgent and critical need for cross-corps support. If a breakthrough is to be averted, then the outnumbered defenders must receive help from other sectors quickly. If a breakthrough takes place, then resources must be concentrated for a counter-attack, whether it takes for form of a meeting engagement or a flanking attack.

In all of these cases, FOFA capabilities could be critical, provided that NATO designs its FOFA capabilities to work just as well 'sideways' as they would in striking at the enemy's rear. The aircraft or missiles can fly as easily – perhaps more easily – from one NATO corps sector to another as they can into the Soviet rear. However, the C^3 capabilities would have to be designed to permit cross-corps support something that is being done within 2 ATAF and 4 ATAF, but less so for 'cross-ATAF' operations and hardly at all for the ground forces. It would make sense to design the processing and C^3 capabilities associated with the FOFA-capable sensors so that they would work just as well to identify targets within a Soviet operational manœuvre group (OMG) that was attempting to move through NATO territory as they would to permit an attack on the OMG while it was still behind Soviet lines. If this were done, FOFA capabilities could provide a means for NATO forces in one corps sector to support NATO forces in another without taking the time to move there.

In general, the less fire support (whether from air forces or ground forces) NATO has available, the more desirable it would be to be able to apply that fire support where it is needed most. If this is true, it follows that the deeper the reductions in a CFE, the more desirable it is for the remaining forces to be capable of FOFA.

Thirdly, a third consequence of conventional force reductions in Europe is that the forward-deployed forces will constitute smaller proportions of the total military potentials of the two alliances. Therefore if a war should break out, the Soviet Union is likely to perceive a great need to move those active forces which it still maintains on Soviet territory forward into the central European battle. NATO, for its part, will also be mobilising and moving the mobilised forces forward. If the outcome of the conventional battle is not decided in the first day or two, then it may hinge upon the relative abilities of the two sides to mobilise and reinforce.

If such a contest in reinforcement develops, then each side will have some built-in advantages. NATO is favoured by having, in the last analysis, more resources, and also a denser and more developed transportation net. The Soviet Union is favoured by a geography that enables it to bring forces forward more rapidly. The largest member of NATO is separated from the theatre by the Atlantic Ocean, and the second largest member – the Federal Republic of Germany – would have its mobilisation complicated by its being a battlefield.

In such a contest it would be critical for NATO to disrupt and delay Soviet reinforcement. Huge Soviet forces would be moving on relatively few rail lines and then along a limited number of goods roads. If NATO could force the Soviet reinforcements either to wait behind or to move cross-country, then it would have done much to even the contest in reinforcement, or even to win it. This, of course, is what FOFA is all about.

It does suggest, however, that if and when substantial CFE reductions take place, NATO may wish to re-examine its decision to concentrate on relatively short-range FOFA. It remains perfectly true that it is more difficult and more expensive to attack Soviet forces moving through Poland than to attack them 100 km or less from the FLOT and moving up to the attack. However, the more the forward forces were reduced, and the more the Soviets would have to depend upon troops moving from Soviet territory through Poland in order to pursue a conventional vistory, the greater the value to NATO of deep FOFA.

Thinking about Deterrence

From the very beginning, the purpose of NATO has not been to fight a war, but to deter a war by being conspicuously able to fight one if necessary. This remains the case today while Gorbachev talks of his newly defensive intentions, and it will remain the case in the future even after a CFE agreement. In particular, while NATO can well hope that the concentration of the Soviet Union on internal economic problems may diminish even further the likelihood of war, and that a CFE agreement may diminish the imbalance of conventional forces that has been a source of concern ever since 1945, NATO must still maintain a posture of deterrence for the indefinite future.

From the viewpoint of post-CFE deterrence, FOFA capabilities appear particularly useful. The principal reasons for this are those outlined above – FOFA capabilities would be very useful in responding to precisely those military threats that a CFE agreement would make most plausible – or perhaps the least implausible.

However, there is a secondary but still significant point. The FOFA mission calls for capabilities that draw on the leading edge of Western military technology. These are technologies which, as far as we know, the Soviets have not yet mastered. Moreover, if Gorbachev is serious about redirecting Soviet resources from the military to internal economic development, the resources (especially the technical people and the precision manufacturing capabilities) which would be needed for developing a Soviet FOFA capability are precisely the resources which should be redirected first, for they correspond to the greatest deficiencies in the Soviet civilian economy. Therefore there is some reason to hope that in a post-CFE world, NATO's ability to carry out FOFA could be a capability that the Soviets would not match for a long time. If this proved to be the case, it would surely enhance deterrence in a very significant way. Not only would NATO's FOFA capabilities help NATO to respond to the most threatening things the Soviets could do, but the very fact that they were unable to match these NATO capabilities would probably lead the Soviets to exaggerate their military value.

It therefore behoves NATO to be careful when the Soviets talk about restructuring forces in Europe into defensive postures not to give up readily the ability to deter so well that defence remains unnecessary.

The views expressed in this paper do not necessarily represent those of the Office of Technology Assessment Board, the MITRE Corporation, nor of any of the latter's sponsors.

CHAPTER 8

Future Defence of the Central Region

MAJOR-GENERAL A. J. G. POLLARD

WHEN CONSIDERING a controversial subject like passive defence, it is as well to remember Field Marshal von Manstein's warning that it is 'a policy that usually leads to the defeat of the weaker party'.

It is difficult to anticipate options for defence a decade or more in advance. Dramatic political change in Eastern Europe has altered all our calculations and technology continues to advance rapidly. These two factors are not in themselves unusual in recent history. Perhaps more unusual are the current arms negotiations on significant military issues covering both nuclear and conventional forces. These three issues (political change, technological advance, and the imperative of arms negotiations) face East and West alike. They inevitably cloud the future and make prediction difficult. It is the combination of these factors, in concert with others, which will be addressed in this chapter. It aims to identify future options for defence, to propose which option should be adopted and examine the forces required to execute the option selected.

The Spectrum of Defence Concepts

To provide a structure against which the range of options can be assessed, this chapter develops a spectrum ranging from a wholly defensive concept, which can be termed passive defence, to a mainly offensive concept, which can be termed active defence. Figure 8.1 illustrates the spectrum.

Introducing the words 'passive' and 'active' does not render the words 'defensive' and 'offensive' redundant, but merely establishes the general nature of the defence posture adopted, and within each posture both offensive and defensive elements will exist. It is the balance between these extremes which identifies the position of any concept on the spectrum. Though the spectrum is not strictly a measure of mobility

111

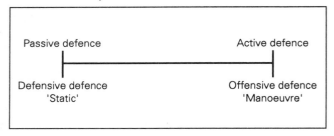

FIG. 8.1

The Spectrum.

there is a tendency to relate 'static' with 'passive' and 'manœuvre' with 'active'.

Within the defined spectrum of defence it is possible to establish a number of markers. These are shown in Figure 8.2.

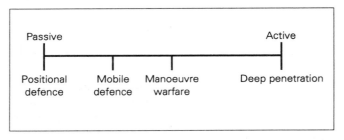

FIG. 8.2

Defence Concepts.

On the passive side is positional defence; this may be appropriate when the frontage and depth to be covered are within the capability of the force adopting this concept; progressively to the right, are mobile defence, manœuvre warfare and deep penetration. It must be emphasised that these terms are associated most closely with the operational and the tactical level of war rather than with the strategic, although the distinction is not always precise. Within these levels, too, there are distinctions, since manœuvre warfare is an overall concept to be pursued at the operational level, while mobile defence is essentially tactical. The real point however is that, in a celebrated definition,

'The defensive battle must not be allowed to drift into a negative opposition in which the commander at bay merely reacts to enemy moves.'

The converse is similarly true; defensive capabilities will exist within an offensive strategy. Most, if not all, great military thinkers have considered how both offence and defence contribute to military success and the winning of wars. It is not the intention here to enter into a debate on the effectiveness of either form of defence, merely to identify the options available.

History provides examples of each of the differing modes of defence, and, although it is dangerous to generalise, there are some common threads. For example, from late 1914 in the First World War, the positional defence of trench warfare led to a strategic stalemate at enormous cost to human life. To break the stalemate the Germans adopted a tactical solution, namely deep infiltration by foot infantry, as in the March 1918 offensive. The Allies adopted a technological solution, the tank, as shown in Figure 8.3.

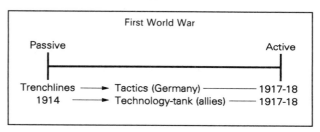

FIG. 8.3

The Elements of First World War Operations.

As long as the will to fight on remained, then neither side could have broken the stalemate until such changes, tactical or technological, were made. To win, an offensive or active capability had to be created.

At the start of the Second World War the Maginot Line was a manifestation by the French of a positional defence mentality. French armoured forces added an offensive capability from the outset of the war and, thus, France's position on the spectrum was further to the right than it had been during the First World War. Against this the Germans adopted the concept of deep penetration, or *blitzkrieg*. The *Wehrmacht* was mostly a 'foot and cart' army which was able to fix the enemy whilst the manœuvre formations struck in depth, as shown in Figure 8.4. It is worth remembering here the vital part that air power was to play in the German concept of operations for deep penetration.

More recently, in the Arab–Israeli wars, particularly the Yom Kippur War of 1973, the Israeli concept can also be identified on the spectrum. The Suez Canal and the Bar Lev line provided positional defence centred on strongpoints, with the intervening areas dominated by patrols. The offensive element was formed from manœuvre brigades and it was as a result of their skill at manœuvre that the Israelis were ultimately successful. The Arab armies failed because they were unable

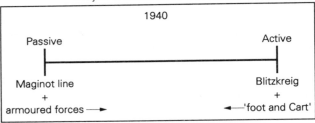

FIG. 8.4

The Elements of Operations in 1940.

to maintain this manœuvre despite the early success that came from achieving strategic surprise. The need to achieve strategic surprise is also a fundamental aspect of Soviet military doctrine.

These examples have not been provided to establish the spectrum as the only way of assessing concepts of defence but rather to demonstrate three points. First, basic postures, representing a main theme of passive or active defence, can be identified in many of the concepts of defence in history. Secondly, within the basic postures there is generally a combination of both offensive and defensive elements. Thirdly, manœuvre tactics or manœuvre elements have nearly always been a prerequisite for victory or success in defending territory.

The modern battlefield will be both blurred and confused. Nevertheless, those forces involved in the fighting can be bracketed into four distinct types:

- Forces whose task it will be to prosecute the battle forward of the main forces. Technology today (and more so in the future) gives the ability to attack and to destroy the enemy at great ranges using modern long-range precision guided munitions (PGMs) and land-based aircraft. This phase of the battle has been variously named as Follow on Forces Attack (FOFA), but also as the deep attack (DA) battle.
- Forces allocated to the main defensive area (MDA) or the contact battle, whose task it will be to channel, disrupt and prevent enemy manœuvre.
- Manœuvre forces held back usually under army group (AG) command for use as reserves or, in the case of air-mobile forces, in the DA or FOFA battle.
- Forces allocated for the security of the rear areas, whose task it will be to ensure that the battle is not lost for want of logistic support.

Each of these elements (and they will be referred to frequently within this paper) can clearly be identified within current concepts of defence, and it is the priorities given to each of them which identify the passive or active nature of the defence. Sustainability is a vital ingredient in any allocation of resources to defence and its importance is considered later in the chapter.

Whilst it would be a largely unproductive exercise to identify the position of current concepts on the spectrum described, it is nevertheless important to identify those factors which bear upon the choice of the defensive concepts that are available. This is essential, since once the concept has been selected decisions must be taken on the balance between equipment, manpower, and sustainability to execute that concept; this will then determine the size and shape of the armed forces. The factors are themselves mainly variables and this fact compounds the problem of forecasting.

Factors Affecting the Size and Shape of the Armed Services

The Threat and How It Might Develop

The political and social initiatives announced by President Gorbachev have clear implications for the threat and how it might develop. Change is inevitable. The Soviet economy, to be restructured, requires additional resources which must in part reduce defence spending. However, as the Soviet General Staff will fight to retain some offensive capability, it is difficult to forecast the result of these changes. The Soviets accept the desirability of achieving parity in numbers of forces on both sides, identifying, in the reduction in the density of forces, the opportunity, in the event of war, to make use of their advantage over the West in their ability to mobilise greater numbers more quickly. However, the Soviets will maintain a force which they calculate to be strong enough to win a war in the conventional phase. In short, parity in both numbers and quality, in both manpower and technology, would seem to be the aim in disarmament proposals. Should parity be established, a quality versus quantity competition may result between NATO and the Soviet Union. In that case the alliance which produces the equipment, develops the better concepts, force structure, and training, and establishes the higher state of readiness will have a significant advantage.

Conventional Arms Reduction Talks (CFE)

Clearly, any consideration of options for defence must make some assumptions about force levels at the turn of the century, though such quantification today is problematic to say the least. It is, however, reasonable to expect three significant changes. First, that some agreement on conventional armed forces will be reached by 1991.

Secondly, that implementation will take between four and six years to complete. Finally, that within the systems currently being considered – tanks, artillery, armoured troop carriers, and air forces (fixed and rotary wing) – cuts in current levels of at least 10 to 15 per cent will be made to NATO forces. NATO has consistently used a qualitative advantage to counter Soviet numerical superiority. With fewer weapons and parity of numbers between East and West, weapon system effectiveness and equipment reliability will become the measure of not only operational readiness but also operational capability. Manpower will also have been reduced at least commensurate with the cuts in weapons systems, and similarly each man will have to be as effective as possible, favouring the retention of professional soldiers in the order of battle.

There are many hurdles to be overcome in order to produce a robust treaty that will ensure security and stability at reduced force levels. This is important because the interpretation of force reductions and the actions needed to achieve the new balances can be destabilising. It is therefore imperative that the decisions made are correct in the first instance. It is evident, however, that the political imperative of forward defence will remain in being albeit less forward; that NATO strategy will be one in which nuclear weapons still have a part to play (even though negotiations on strategic nuclear forces will aim to achieve parity at lower levels), and that a chemical threat is likely to remain. National contingents and allied tactical air forces (ATAF) will still be deployed in West Germany, albeit with fewer systems in their inventory and with possibly some changes of role. In the broad area of systems and manpower a change in the balance of investment is likely, and this will reflect changes in the balance between the four force elements described above and sustainability. And, finally – but most significant for the subject of this chapter – the balance that is being sought between East and West is parity in terms of capability and numbers, with each side adopting a defensive strategy.

Technology

Technological advances continue apace and we have progressed, in all aspects except perhaps in costs, from a corner shop of choice to a supermarket. It is thus more important than ever that an agreed doctrine guides research and development and procurement, if mistakes are not to be repeated and resources wasted. Technology can provide significant improvements in defence capabilities and particularly in surveillance and target acquisition (STA) sensors, as well as in the amount of information available and the ability to fuse data into a useful form, in command and information systems (CIS) and in the range, lethality and autonomy of weapons.

These advances are likely to affect the battlefield in a number of ways. First, the whole battle area will become more transparent. Forces, including those in rear areas, will be easier to locate, more timely decisions to engage can be taken and improved chances of a hit at longer ranges will make deep-attack systems much more potent. As a result, concentrations of armour will be more difficult to hide, and, accordingly, easier to disrupt once they start to move. Covered approaches, such as urban and forested areas and routes in radar shadow, will become more attractive, with dispersion in assembly areas and concentration only at the point of action being the preferred means of operation. Secondly, far higher kinetic energy muzzle velocities will mean that tanks will remain an important element of the manœuvre battle at the tactical level. Thirdly, there will be an increasing need for mobility to concentrate forces rapidly for counter-action to restore the initiative. The deployment of helicopter formations in conjunction with army tactical missile systems (ATACMS), multi-launch rocket systems (MLRS) and, if possible, air, at the operational level will exploit the speed, reach, reaction time and hitting power of the helicopter. Fourthly, the viability of manned aircraft for DA can only be maintained by considerable expenditure in stealth, new high technology weapons and electronic countermeasure (ECM) technologies. With counter-air technologies currently not subject to CFE limitations, the task of manned aircraft can only become more daunting and their offensive capability is likely to be reduced as the balance of effectiveness moves towards counter-air technologies.

Socio-political Change

There are perhaps two key areas of change that must be considered, while noting that socio-political developments may differ between the United Kingdom, Germany, the United States, and the USSR. Within the time frame one area, demography, is reasonably precise. The number of young men and women in this country is in decline, as shown in Figure 8.5.

The other area, less precise, is the change in British society and the effects which this may have on recruiting. Aspirations and attitudes to military service are indeed changing as is, currently, the public's perception of the threat. The Services will clearly need to be more competitive in the job market. In planning, the assumption must be made that, short of major policy changes regarding conscription, fewer men will be found in the recruitment pool for the regular Army. Any such reduction in manpower must be compensated for in a number of ways, the most important of which will be equipment design and technology, the further employment of women, and better use of reservists.

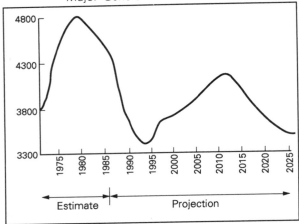

FIG. 8.5

UK Population Aged 15–19 years, 1971–2025.

Budget

A nation's financial contribution to defence is driven by a combination of the perception of the threats to which it is subject, the wealth of the country, and, in Britain's case, commitment to NATO, the Commonwealth, the United Nations, and internal security. All of these are subject to change. In the last ten years defence has been allocated between 4.3 per cent and 5.4 per cent of GDP (Figure 8.6).

As a nation prospers a stable percentage of GDP provides an increased budget. Within the defence budget the allocation of resources to manpower and equipment changes to reflect changing priorities, as is clear from Figure 8.7, which illustrates the relative costs of manpower and equipment within the Army budget in three years within the last decade.

What is not clear from Figure 8.7 is that defence inflation, the costs of both manpower and equipment, has outpaced general inflation, and hence the squeeze on the equipment programme. If the socio-political predictions prove accurate, manpower costs are likely to rise even faster in the future, purely on the basis of supply and demand in the free market of a capitalist society, and so the proportion spent on equipment will continue to fall. At the same time equipments are likely to continue to cost more relative to the rise in the defence budget. It would therefore be prudent to plan on a defence budget which, in real terms, is static.

If these assumptions prove correct and they seem realistic, then either manpower or equipment, or both, will have to be reduced. When the factor of demography is also taken into account then a plan to reduce

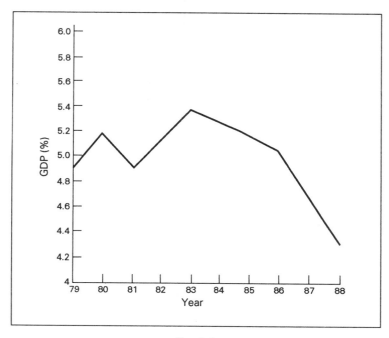

FIG. 8.6

British Defence Budget Relative to GDP.

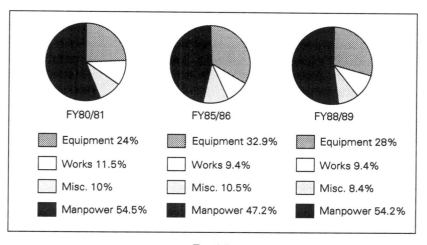

FIG. 8.7

Army Expenditure.

manpower makes sense. If combat power is not to be reduced, then technology will have to compensate for the reduction in manpower. There is nothing new in this, as Figures 8.8 and 8.9 show, and the next two decades are likely to see a continuation in the trend. A small part of this compensation might be achieved by the increased use of simulators in training to maximise both the individual and the collective contribution to the effective use of ever more sophisticated equipment.

Equipment Programme

While seeking to strike the future balance between manpower and equipment it must be noted that much of the Army's current and planned equipment still is likely to be in use in the Central Region well beyond the year 2000, including: in the armour/anti-armour role, Challenger, Chieftain replacement, attack helicopter (AH), TRIGAT and Warrior, in the indirect fire role, MLRS, AS 90, in the AD role, Rapier, Javelin, HVM, in the STA role, Phoenix, counter-battery airborne stand-off radars, communications, command, control and information systems, including trunk communications, artillery target-engagement and air-defence command and information systems, and combat net radio.[1]

The options for future modes of defence will have to take account of the capabilities and demands of these existing weapons and systems. Unless current planned expenditure is radically altered, then the room for change is limited. The equipment programme is slow to react, certainly far slower than that in the Warsaw Pact, emphasising the need for a clear long-term view of the land/air concept which equipment and organisations are designed to support.

Planning Factors

It is not within the scope of this chapter, which seeks to point toward the most cost-effective mode of defence, to examine in detail other factors which would require detailed planning for war. These include: warning time, readiness, sustainability, and the predicted duration of any future conflict. It is, however, important to address the nature of the NATO Alliance and the need for consensus and the effect this will have on the United Kingdom's contribution to the Central Region.

The Allies Factor

Clouding the issue in the Central Region are the differing views within the Alliance on concepts of operations, on the higher command structure required to direct operations, and on equipment and organisation to

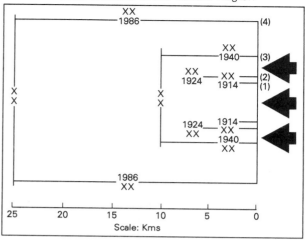

FIG. 8.8

The Changing Divisional Area

Notes:
1. 1914: 4.5 km wide; depth not specified
2. 1924: 6 km wide; depth not specified
3. 1940: 10 km wide × 7–12 km deep
4. 1986: 20 km wide × 25 km deep

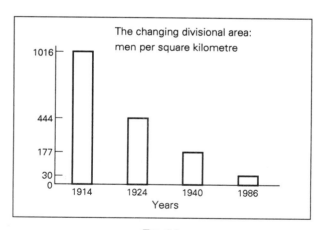

FIG. 8.9

Battlefield Density.

match future changes. Discussion is essential but arguments are counterproductive and will become dangerous if CFE results in smaller forces and thus even smaller reserves. It is important to understand that any concept of defence must address central Europe in general terms and not the problems of individual national corps. This point has been made by Field Marshal Bagnall and more recently by General von Sandrart. It is of critical importance that the debate should lead to a common concept of land/air operations which is accepted by all the national contingents.

CFE and manpower shortages, not to mention budget constraints and the reduced perception of the threat, are all likely to reduce force levels. Already NATO is stretched under the strategy of forward defence to produce an adequate shield, while reserves, to provide the sword, will become smaller. Given this expected reduction in forces, the successful employment of reserves is essential. A common operational policy is vital if individual national corps are not to seek to fight their individual tactical battles, fought with nationally acquired equipment, which do not fully contribute to the common NATO goal. Consequently the operational level of command will become increasingly important.

This division between national defence interests and national industrial/procurement interests continues to create serious difficulties in interoperability of equipment for NATO commanders. Worse, scarce resources are currently wasted in the duplication of reasearch and development and in small-scale equipment production runs. More specifically the provision of adequate command, control, communications, surveillance, and target-acquisition systems at NATO's operational level are required to enhance interoperability and to maximise the combat effectiveness of operational reserves. (Also the issue of forward defence needs to be re-explored, the question of whether equipment can replace men in forward defence must be answered; technology may offer the opportunity to use 'smart' sensors and weapons forward in place of men, but whether this is politically acceptable is open to doubt.) Finally, West German environmental concerns are also manifested in the increasingly vocal opposition to field training exercises and low flying in Germany. Perhaps again, technology, in the form of enhanced simulation systems, may provide a measure of relief.

Evolution: NATO Strategy and Concepts

Strategy

It is important to highlight that NATO strategy is, and has since 1949, been based on both nuclear and conventional forces, and nowhere is this more apparent than in the Central Region. It is to deny the Soviets the opportunity to achieve strategic surprise that non-German NATO forces are garrisoned in the Federal Republic to prevent the need for an early use of nuclear weapons; and so, like Israel, NATO must have sufficient manœuvre forces to compel any attacker to comply with the defensive plan. This dual capability is fundamental to deterrence: too great an emphasis on nuclear weapons, signalling a return to the tripwire strategy, could undermine the credibility of NATO's strategy; too great an emphasis on conventional forces alone could appear to offer the prospect of a purely conventional – and therefore 'thinkable' – war. The general trend, however, in this balance of nuclear and conventional forces from the end of the tripwire strategy, through the variations of flexible response to the NATO London Declaration of 1990, has been away from early reliance on nuclear weapons towards improved conventional capabilities. Within this trend, and owing to the constraints of CFE in particular, the balance of resources within the conventional force structure continues to be re-examined. In future the re-examination must include consideration of the ratio of armour to anti-armour weapons and of fixed-wing aircraft to rotary wing aircraft and missiles.

NATO Concepts

The purpose of NATO is the prevention of war and this depends upon deterring the enemy from attacking. Deterrence can only remain effective whilst the Alliance's deterrent is credible. Notwithstanding nuclear deterence, conventional forces must remain credible in order to deter, and it is the offensive capability of conventional forces which deters. NATO commanders today generally accept that in a war of attrition NATO could not win. Against this background, three recent NATO commanders have developed operational concepts which are now transforming NATO strategy in the Central Region. As Supreme Allied Commander Europe (SACEUR), General Bernard Rogers set out the concept of operations for the attack of follow-on forces (FOFA), in order to provide the additional depth NATO needs without compromising the policy of forward defence. DA extends the battlefield forward into enemy territory by using greatly improved STA systems and smart, long-range weapons to locate, disrupt, delay, and destroy enemy forces on their move forward to the battle area. The intention of FOFA is that these disrupted enemy forces should then arrive at NATO's forward line of own troops (FLOT) in more manageable force ratios.

As commander of the Northern Army Group (NORTHAG), Field Marshal Sir Nigel Bagnall developed a concept which allowed the reserve divisions of the German and the British corps to be used in conjunction with the AG reserve, for operational manœuvre under AG control, either to counter penetrations of the main defensive area or to exploit opportunities for offensive action which would gain the initiative for the defender. The flexibility shifted the emphasis away from a main defensive-area battle of attrition, towards a more balanced defence, a combination of positional and mobile defence: the shield and the sword.

Meanwhile, as Commander-in-Chief Allied Forces Central Europe, General Leopold Chalupa developed a concept for rear-area operations designed to hasten the flow of reinforcements, and improve sustainment and freedom of action for forces in the forward defence. There is a common thread in all these concepts, in that each of the four force elements described earlier can be identified.

The factors considered in this chapter will clearly affect not only how the United Kingdom will in future contribute to NATO's common defence, but also raise some fundamental issues for NATO as an alliance. The most fundamental will be how NATO's concept of defence develops in response to the changes these factors illustrate. To put into context the options for how NATO's future concept of operations might develop, the spectrum can be subdivided into three areas: passive defence (embracing the concept of defensive defence), mobile defence, and manœuvre warfare. It is within these three broad areas that the future options will be considered.

Future Options

Passive Defence (Left of the Spectrum)

Passive defence, truly defensive in nature, is characteristically both non-provocative and non-offensive. A NATO defence based on improved barriers, strong-point and indirect fire would pose no political or military threat to the Soviet Union, while denying it the prospect of rapid, successful, offensive action.

Proponents of the concept point to the benefits it could bring; it would increase stability in central Europe; change the nature of the arms race in that the Soviets would need to respond only to NATO 'defensive' arms enhancements; and could lead to a reduction in conventional forces on both sides. This form of defence has received serious consideration in NATO.

Its weaknesses are that, in the event of war, most damage would be on NATO territory, while Soviet territory would be largely exempt from the consequences of military action. Military commanders also mistrust static defences because, historically, they have often engendered complacency in those relying on them. A further significant criticism is that some elements of passive defence are unduly reliant on emerging technologies, particularly PGMs, STA, and command and control. If technological developments fail to match expectations, or are matched by Soviet counter-measures, the effectiveness of the defence must be in doubt.

But it is the philosophy of defensive defence that is most dangerous.

Defensive defence denies the conventional offensive force elements and thus questions the validity of deterrence. Ideally the conventional offensive capability would be non-provocative, but the blurring of the distinction between the defensive and offensive ultility of modern weapons systems makes this hard to achieve. And finally defensive defence can only lead to a war of attrition, in which Alliance commanders generally accept that NATO could not defeat the Soviet Union. In short, the passive defence option does not provide adequate deterrence and a more robust operational concept is required.

Mobile Defence (Mid Spectrum)

The current NORTHAG concept lies to the left of the spectrum, although its reserve divisions give an offensive ground capability and, of course, at the operational level of command, air, and at the strategic level of command, nuclear weapons, give further offensive or active elements to this concept. It is these offensive elements, at the strategic and the operational levels that have helped to secure stability in Europe, posing, as they do, significant risks to the USSR.

However, it is precisely these offensive ingredients that are becoming less potent, in part because the battlefield is becoming more transparent. Commanders will find it increasingly difficult to get ground forces to the right place at the right time. On top of this manned aircraft, a point made above, will require greater investment in ECM, stealth, and new high technology weapons if they are to retain a credible offensive capability. Finally, while the strategic nuclear offensive capability is, of course, politically sensitive, it is in fact peripheral to NATO's warfighting capabilities in the Central Region.

The point is that more will have to be invested in the offensive capability of both ground and air forces to compensate for this technological and political degradation, if the offensive and deterrent elements of the concept are to remain potent. The balance between deep-strike systems, that is, aircraft, and missiles, will be a matter for operational analysis, but an increase in resource allocation to deep strike and manœuvre elements (the attack helicopter, for example) is necessary even if it is at the expense of elements currently committed to the MDA or rear-area security.

This concept can be developed to retain its current position in the spectrum by compensating for reductions in one area by increasing investment in another. But unless there is a radical reassessment of the man/equipment ratio, including aspects of equipment maintainability, reliability, and the sustainment of the force, the savings in manpower necessary to be able to afford the equipment may not be possible. Taking other factors, such as CFE, budget, and demography, into account this might not be the best use of the new weapon systems available as far as an overall concept is concerned.

Before moving to manœuvre warfare, it is worth clarifying our distinction between manœuvre and mobile warfare. Manœuvre warfare designates the control, at the operational level of command, of manœuvre formations either in the depth battle (the battle fought in the enemy's depth, which keeps his echelons apart), in reserve action, or in the MDA. Mobile warfare involves mobility around a degree of positional defence with manœuvre controlled at the corps or the tactical level of command.

Manœuvre Warfare (Right of the Spectrum)

The concept of manœuvre warfare is essentially a progression from the current deep-battle concept. However, for active defence there must be a larger slice of offensive capability, with emphasis on the air, FOFA and manœuvre resources. In this concept FOFA resources, manœuvre forces in the MDA, and operational reserves must be capable of destroying the enemy simultaneously throughout the depth of the battle area.

A number of studies have suggested two divergent means of employing manœuvre and deep-battle forces. First, chop back the FLOT 100 km and use the space created to destroy the enemy with deep-battle and manœuvre forces across the front, and particularly on main thrust lines. In-place forces provide a web or sponge effect and armoured divisions then have time to react, get into position, and mop up anything that gets through. Second, use deep battle and manœuvre forces simultaneously both beyond and within the FLOT. The former will aim to paralyse the enemy's depth formations, command and control, and logistic base to ensure that only 'manageable' formations arrive in the MDA. The latter will support the deep battle and/or will manœuvre to destroy enemy penetrations of the MDA, as part either of the tactical battle or in further offensive operations at the higher level. It is this emphasis on manœuvre and deep-attack forces which provides the necessary offensive and deterrent capabilities and, by reducing the reliance on men to produce firepower, allow equipment costs to be offset against manpower costs.

Before finally addressing the future in specific rather than in general terms, three fundamental points must be re-emphasised: first, the forward defence of mainland Europe and flexible response are likely to remain NATO strategy; secondly, any change to the strategy or concept must be accepted by NATO as a whole; and thirdly, the concept will have to match current and planned equipment which will still be in service. There is no blank sheet of paper on which to set down an entirely original concept.

The Future

Doctrine for the Land/Air Battle in the Central Region

Without prejudging the outcome of CFE, the British contribution to the defence of Europe must remain an integral part of CINCENT's land/air campaign within an overall concept of manœuvre. A dual land-and air-based FOFA element will be needed to conduct deep attack forward of the FLOT. The MDA Battle will continue to be fought by a combination of positional and mobile defence to shape and destroy the leading enemy formations, but with fewer resources, particularly manpower. The control of the major manœuvre elements, which must be given a greater proportion of resources and which must be configured to react to the unexpected with the swiftest possible concentration of combat power, should be held at the operational level. This operational level of command must be given the surveillance, target acquisition, and command and control resources to prosecute operations at AG and ATAF.

Forces Required to Execute the Doctrine

To achieve significant disruption and destruction of enemy follow-on forces in depth, a ground-and air-based FOFA capability is essential. For the United Kingdom a system such as ATACMS will be needed. The surveillance, target acquisition, command, control and communications infrastructure to provide the necessary targeting and communications capability must be a priority, so that the system can be controlled at AG/ATAF, whilst being fired by units within the Corps.

The *main defensive force* must be robust; a mix of armour, long-range, anti-armour weapons and attack helicopters with a combination of both kinetic- and chemical-energy weapons, supported by heavy indirect-fire forces, able to manœuvre in contact. This will place a premium on both mobility and countermobility capabilities. The trend that formations, manpower and equipment will have to cover yet larger areas will continue. Weapons will need longer ranges, better STA, and a day and night capability.

The *manœuvre force*, again controlled at Army Group or corps, should comprise a mix of close air-support aircraft, attack helicopters, air-mobile forces and armour. These will be supported by long-range artillery. The role of these forces will be to concentrate firepower quickly at the critical point to exploit tactical and operational advantage.

To pay for the equipment these forces require there must be fewer men. Revised unit structures should be incorporated; these should provide the same number of units, but either smaller in numbers of men or a combination of regular, reservists and TA soldiers with a greater emphasis on combat power provided by equipment rather than manpower. For example, *rear-area security forces* will not achieve the same priority in resource allocation. As the threat of enemy penetration should be reduced by the enhanced effectiveness of the deep, contact, and manœuvre battles, the relative lack of forces in the rear area is unlikely to be critical.

In the context of manpower, other fundamental questions must be answered. The balance of regular and reserve soldiers needs to be studied. Whilst individual reservists with essentially individual skills can be easily assimilated into a unit or formation, team and crew skills can only be developed in the team or crew environment and need longer training and practice to achieve the necessary skill levels. At the extreme, units and formations of reservists cannot be expected to achieve more than a fraction of the competence and flexibility of regulars. With the expected reduction in the pool from which manpower is drawn, an answer is needed now. Training effectiveness must similarly be maximised. The introduction of simulation must proceed rapidly and embrace all levels of training; it should be used by formation commanders and staffs, battlegroups, crews and individuals.

Notwithstanding the need for resource allocation to specific types of system, the question of sustainability must be addressed simultaneously. NATO must decide how long it needs to be prepared to fight, if it is not to be pressured into consideration of the early use of nuclear weapons. Operational analysis has a part to play in this. Sustainability impinges on the manpower/equipment ratio and also on the size of the force affordable. Consequently, each future equipment must be appraised in terms of reliability and the manpower bill both to operate and maintain it; whenever possible technology and machinery must replace the man. If parity in numbers eventually results from CFE it will be the quality of equipment and training, the state of readiness and the existence of a well-developed and understood concept which will dictate the military balance of power.

Course of Action

NATO is a defence alliance and accordingly its strategy must be defensive in nature. It is not a contradiction to suggest that within the strategic defensive posture there should be a deterrent capability at the strategic level and an offensive capability at the operational and the tactical level. The balance is a fine one, but an agreed NATO concept towards the right of the scale is required. To achieve this the erosion of the current British tactical and operational offensive elements will need to be corrected. For Britain this will involve greater investment in DA and manœuvre forces, and will result in a shift in emphasis from mobile warfare towards manœuvre warfare. Again, irrespective of the outcome of CFE, to achieve this shift a number of actions are required: a radical reappraisal of the man/equipment ratio with emphasis towards replacing manpower with compensating increases in equipment-based combat power; a positive approach to establishing the true manpower cost of future equipment, taking reliability, maintainability, and sustainability into account; and a drive towards achieving significant interoperability of equipment based on shared costs, shared research and development, and shared production runs; and command of formations at the operational level. Future equipment design, organisations, and manpower must be matched to the proposed concepts if the whole is to be effective.

Future concepts of operations themselves must hinge on the West's ability to conduct offensive operations in the context of defensive strategy. The trends identified in this paper must be acknowledged now and incorporated deliberately into long-term organisational and equipment plans. The field Army needs to be smaller, more agile, far-seeing, and to have a longer reach if it is to fulfil its dual tasks of deterrence and fighting in the future.

CHAPTER 9

Modes of Defence: Aspects of the West German Debate

HANS D. LEMKE

Introduction

IT IS widely agreed that prospects are good for successful progress in the Vienna talks on Conventional Forces in Europe (CFE) and for a substantial transformation of the Central European military scene within a few years. Modifications of the Western defence posture may be appropriate under the condition of numerical parities for the most offensively-oriented weapons systems somewhere between 10 and 15 per cent below given NATO levels. Drastic changes will be unavoidable if further force reductions are to be negotiated in subsequent stages, as has been already carefully provided for in official documents from both sides. This raises a topic which has not until recently been on the agenda of NATO's military planners: how to combine forward-defence requirements and arms-control potentialities.

This is the problem: on the one side, results of arms-control accords will limit force strengths of both sides, thereby leading to alterations of traditional threat perceptions and of existing defence concepts as well. On the other hand, arms reductions alone will not necessarily improve the military situation in the Central Region; they may even produce intolerable instabilities. Therefore, there is an urgent need to make sure that the CFE process will not jeopardise NATO's security, which relies on nuclear deterrence and forward defence. 'Security first' must continue to be the governing principle. This calls for the development of future defence concepts as deliberate inputs for, rather than as accidental outputs of the Vienna arms-control negotiations. In other words, future defence planning must comprehend defence requirements as well as arms-control objectives – of course, in this order of priority – and any future arms-control planning must be based on reliable defence concepts.

After phase I of the CFE talks the debate on the defence of central

Europe will continue or even revive. For this it may be profitable to recall some of the proposals developed in support of 'alternative defence' concepts, which have had a long tradition in the Federal Republic of Germany. This is one purpose of this chapter. Furthermore, some tentative ideas on a future comprehensive defence and arms-control concept will be developed.

Early Ideas

The West German debate on how to organise the defence of NATO's central European front is older than the *Bundeswehr*. In substance, it is the discussion of the merits of a non-provocative, more or less static defence posture versus a more active or entirely mobile defence. This is by no means an intellectual problem restricted to our time. For example, Carl von Clausewitz distinguished four options for a defender: (1) to attack the enemy immediately at the outset of his penetration into the theatre of war; (2) to occupy defence positions close to the border and attack the invader upon his arrival in front of these positions; (3) to conduct defence operations from close to border positions, including counter-attack actions; and (4) to withdraw from the border and initiate final resistance in the central parts of the country.[1] For Clausewitz, it should be added, offence and defence were nothing else but two forms of combat equally aiming at victory through annihilation of the invading enemy force. But since for him defence was the stronger of the two forms, he favoured option (4) in which the aggressor would be subjected to losses before encountering the maximum resistance of the defender.

Initiators of the modern debate may be found in civilian, ex-military and military circles, and more on the left than on the right of the political spectrum. Although the subject of the debate is a matter of tactical and operational concern, points of departure usually were political and as such controversial as regards governmental positions. As a rule, alternative defence proposals ran into almost unanimous rejection by German military planners and more conservative experts, either or both for political and professional military reasons.

The origins are found at the beginning of the 1950s, as the first planning steps for the establishment of the new German armed forces were being undertaken. Colonel Bogislav von Bonin, a chief military planner of the Amt Blank (the predecessor of the later German defence ministry) came up with a proposal for the defence of the German borders to be organised in a 50-km static defence belt, emphasing light infantry equipped with anti-tank weapons and means. This covering force was to consist of up to 200,000 German soliders with approximately 8,000 anti-tank guns, and provide the protection and time necessary for allied mobile forces to launch their (decisive) counter-attack.

The military rationale of this plan was based on the experience gained by the Wehrmacht during its operation ZITADELLE in the 1943 Battle of Kursk where German tank armies had not succeeded in penetrating well-prepared Soviet defence systems. Bonin's political idea behind the plan was *inter alia*, to initiate a non-provocative, forward-defence concept not at that time envisaged by NATO planning, and to avoid the need to keep American nuclear weapons deployed on German soil.

Bonin was dismissed and his plan never carried out. The official decision taken provided for German Army divisions emphasising armour and mobility, and that is what we still have. This was primarily for political reasons, which are still relevant today: (1) Chancellor Adenauer wanted to move the FRG swiftly into the role of an equal Alliance partner; (2) for the sake of full involvement of NATO partners in the defence of Europe, German forces must be able to operate side by side with allied formations. Similar organisation, equipment, and tactics of all armed forces involved were therefore mandatory.

Explicitly or not, Bonin's ideas survive in the contemporary strategic debate. His concept stood in severe contrast to the offensive concept put forward by the SPD leader Kurt Schumacher, who declared its adoption by NATO as a condition for his party's agreement to the rearming of the FRG. According to Schumacher's claim, allied forces were to be deployed well into the eastern part of West Germany, and be prepared to counter any aggression by deep offensive strikes into Warsaw Pact territory at the very beginning of war. Such ideas are not reflected in the present debate.

Recent Proposals

Fundamentals

The alternative defence concepts which have been under discussion in the last few years and which may have some significance for the future debate, were developed after the mid-1970s. For their proper understanding it is useful to consider some of the telling conditions given at the time of their genesis. These are principally the following: predominance of the military aspects in the East–West conflict; lack of progress at the MBFR talks; continuous decline of the social consensus on defence-related issues, in particular nuclear matters, which became obvious during the INF debate and in the rise of the *Friedensbewegung* (peace movement); and diminishing financial capacities owing to the increasing costs of modern military equipment.

There are numerous designations for the various proposals, which more or less give an impression of the objectives. They prove that alternative defence is a different thing to different authors. Jonathan Dean has established a list of descriptive labels used in the international discussion,[2] most of which may be found in the German debate. Among these, 'stuctural incapacity for attack' (*'Strukturelle Nichtangriffsfähigkeit'*) has achieved some prominence over others and even gained the status of a leading notion, although there is no standard understanding of this term.[3]

Generally speaking, 'alternative' means: different from NATO's strategy of flexible response, but not necessarily different from the forward defence principle, which is favoured by most proponents who accept military defence at all.

On the one side, alternative defence concepts widely concur in political fundamentals:

● The objection to nuclear deterrence and retaliation is the most common starting point for alternative defence proposals. This would call for the reduction or elimination of NATO's dependence upon nuclear weapons through the strengthening of conventional defence capabilities. The background is political: credibility of nuclear deterrence is denied, theatre nuclear forces (TNF) would devastate primarily German territory; and ethical: nuclear deterrence is perceived to be immoral. However, related proposals are far from uniform; in fact, they cover the entire spectrum from total rejection of Western nuclear weapons to acceptance in principle of a mutual minimum deterrence based on 'European' systems. In any case, the primary intention of alternative defence proponents is to develop new conventional defence concepts, which are suited to the avoidance of the use of TNF as a last resort in war. Thus far they are quite in line with NATO's traditional aim of strengthening conventional defence which, of course, has never been sufficiently achieved.

● The objective of emphasising the defensive intentions of the West by eliminating or at least reducing the alleged provocative character of the Western military build-up: this would be achieved by renouncing FOFA and related deep-interdiction options, and by reducing predominantly offensive weapons systems like mechanised ground forces and attack aircraft. Rejection of conventional strike options against targets on Soviet territory is not uniformly shared by alternative defence proponents either. Again, the justification may be found in political or ethical apprehensions, or in both, with the political argument being that far-reaching conventional weapons and mechanised ground forces must *a priori* be perceived as threatening to both sides. Thus, they are valued as important sources of military instability and of the on-going arms race. Renunciation of defence concepts relying primarily on offensive counter-aggression elements is therefore declared mandatory. Related proposals range from total rejection of any such means to gradual reductions.

On the other hand, the various concepts differ in details of tactical and operational use of the remaining conventional elements. But the best way to explain the distinct ideas is by briefly describing some of the proposals. In doing so, 'social defence' concepts (propounded by Theodore Ebert and Wilhelm Nolte) will not be dealt with. These are defined as 'non-military, non-violent self-preservation' concepts and would certainly not support the case of future defence planning in the Central Region. What remains may be arranged in to groupings.

'Classical' Approaches

This group contains rather radical concepts characterised by the emphasis placed on static or area defences, and by the rejection of mobile elements in the defence posture.

Horst Afheldt's reactive and static '*Technokommando*' model (1976) is one of the most discussed radical concepts. Admittedly, it had been based on previous proposals developed by Guy Brossolet and Emil Spannocchi. Afheldt's concept relies on a network of autonomously fighting, small groups of German light infantry, equipped with a large number of conventional rockets and deployed over the whole of West German territory. Each of the platton sized *Technokommando* operates in an area of 10 to 15 square km, with some concentration provided for in the eastern portions of the country. They are meant not to present targets for the aggressor's nuclear weapons. Invading forces will be brought to a stop by continuous attrition. There are no mobile, armoured units, and no attack aircraft.

Criticism of Afheldt's concept must be primarily directed at three features: exclusively German manning of the network; deliberate inclusion of the entire West German territory in an area defence concept, in contrast to NATO's forward defence; and total lack of any counter-attack capacities.

Later on, Afheldt developed a modified concept (1983) by adding a network of heavy rocket artillery ('*Netz der Raketenartillerie*') and an 'information and control network' ('*Informations- und Führungsnetz*') to what he now called the '*Jäger* commando network' ('*Netz de Jägerkommandos*'). This, however, did not substantially reply to the aforementioned criticism.

Norbert Hannig's 'defence wall' concept (1984) forgoes heavy mobile elements in the defensive posture, including battle tanks and fighter bombers. The terrain at the political borders will be blocked by modern mine systems and other passive means, deployed in a four-kilometre barrier belt. Mobility of forces will be replaced by fire, to be brought to effect within and behind the belt. Fire will be delivered by infantry weapons, ranging from 50 to 6,000 m, by PGMs launched from dug-in combat vehicles, and by artillery rocket-launchers of various ranges up to 200 km. Mobile light units and anti-tank helicopters are to counter breakthroughs. NATO allies in place will participate.

Criticism of the Hannig model comes under three headings: renouncing any counter-attack capabilities deprives NATO of the possibility to push back invading forces out of NATO territory; relying on a purely static defence posture prevents NATO from reacting flexibility to the fast changing situations on the battlefield; and for implementation of the concept, high technology weapons and means may be required which are not yet available.

To resolve the last point may be a matter of time and funds. The first two objections, however, are a matter of military art based on wartime experience. They will be valid as long as the potential aggressor has the capacity to concentrate mechanised forces and to achieve breakthroughs at selected locations in a linear defence line.

'Moderate' Approaches

A series of moderate approaches relying on 'mixed' defence concepts were initiated at the beginning of the 1980s. Common to all of them is the fundamental objective of deploying non-provocative, defensively-oriented forces close to the borders, and of keeping armoured counter-attack elements well in depth. There are numerous differences between individual models in details of implementation, mainly with reference to numbers and depths of deployment belts or zones, and to the problem of border-crossing action. The following are the most important proposals:

Manfred Bertele's early comprehensive arms-control concept (1980/ 82) providing for 30 line infantry divisions and 10 reserve mechanised brigades on either side within the very centre of Europe, composed of West and East Germany and western Czechoslovakia.

Jochen Löser's proposal (1981) discriminating between 'shield' forces (*'Shildkräfte'*) of light infantry deployed in a 40 to 60-km attrition belt at the borders, and 'sword' forces (*'Schwertkräfte'*) of traditional armoured counter-attack units deployed in a mobile defence zone (*'Raumverteidigungszone'*) behind the shield forces belt. Löser's model provided for counter-measures against targets on enemy territory, including long-range fire and counter-attacks by ground forces.

Echart Afheldt's 'transitional concept' (*'Übergangskonzept'*, 1983) which combined a 70 to 100-km light-infantry zone at the borders and traditional mechanised units deployed behind it.

The Study Group on Alternative Security Policy (SAS) approach (1984) combining an 80-km light-infantry 'containment belt' (*Fang-netz*') and armoured 'rapid commitment' forces ('*Feuerwehr*') within the rear parts of and behind the infantry belt. The SAS concept renounces any action against the aggressor's territory.

Albrecht A. C. von Müller's 'integrated defence model' ('*Inte-grierte Vorneverteidigung*', 1985) which comprised four elements: a 5-km 'fire and barrier belt' ('*Feuer- und Sperrgürtel*') with a sensor net, mines of various types, and fire power from modern artillery; a 25-km light-infantry 'containment belt' ('*Fangnetz*'); a 60-km manœuvre zone with heavy armoured units; and a rear defence zone with light mobile forces. Von Müller accepts counter-actions against targets beyond the borders, including counter-attacks by ground forces.

Andreas von Bülow's proposal of a German Army structure of the 1990s ('*Bundeswehrstruktur der 90er Jahre*', 1987) combining a 40 to 60-km light-infantry defence zone at the borders and traditional armoured units deployed primarily behind the forward zone.

Most recently Egon Bahr, Andreas von Bülow and Karsten Voigt published their common proposal from a 'social democratic point of view' of future European security ('*Europäische Sicherheit 2000*', July 1989). This concept calls for, *inter alia*, 13 infantry-heavy army corps deployed in a 'forward security belt' ('*Grenznaher Sicherheitsbereich*') free of offensively-oriented weapons, for reserve forces of one armour and one artillery brigade for each corps to be deployed behind the forward security belt, and for step-by-step elimination of fighter bombers.

Fundamental objection has been put forward against moderate models by those experts and military planners adhering to the conviction that the most suitable means to counter a superior aggressor are large mobile, armoured units which allow for maximum operational flexibi-lity, and for regaining the initiative in battle. Perceived advantages such as qualitative leads in weaponry on NATO's side, superior morale of Western soldiers, and better leadership qualities of Western military ranks, particularly on the lower levels of command, are frequently used as supporting arguments for highly mobile defence concepts. Such criticism may or may not be correct under the prevailing military conditions in central Europe. Even a future situation of numerical parity at lower levels will not make the decision for either an entirely mobile or a mixed defence concept easier; from a purely military point of view, both options will gain more benefit than they hitherto may have had. However, what NATO needs is a concept of war prevention, not of warfare. This is the crucial criterion for developing the future defence model.

A Future Concept

The author's proposal for a future concept will now be briefly outlined. It emphasises the necessity to reconcile defence and arms-control requirements, as indicated in the introduction.

Fundamentals

The aim of preventing war demands appropriate deterrent capabilities; the best form of deterrence is still nuclear deterrence. Therefore, from a Western point of view, NATO's strategy of flexible response should not be abandoned unless the political and ideological origins of the East–West conflict are first eliminated. Further development of nuclear weapons, including TNF, is therefore necessary. Common ceilings for warheads permitted to both sides may be appropriate. In any case, conventional forces should be organised in a way as to render unnecessary any resort to tactical nuclear weapons as a military means for operational purposes.

Forward defence is mandatory, particularly from a West German point of view. This principle aims at denying early success to the attacker, at avoiding other but temporary losses of terrain, and at reducing damage to the territory and the population. It requires means and procedures suitable for initiating stable, cohesive and defensive operations close to the border, immediately at the outset of aggression. This prohibits the adoption of area-defence concepts using the entirety or large parts of the country for continuous attrition, and of static, belt-type defence postures which may be perforated by concentrated forces or overcome by air landings. Forward defence also demands counter-attack elements of sufficient strength to regain lost territory.

NATO's defence must continue to be demonstrably multinational. This forbids the acceptance of any concepts providing for German national defence of the Federal Republic as long as NATO allies are present. Public consent is important for NATO's defence. This will in any case be difficult to achieve in regard to the nuclear component of flexible response, and really deep cuts in both alliances' conventional postures may increase the difficulties of maintaining public recognition of defence requirements. A lot of persuasion will have to be done. However, the prospects for achieving greater public support of NATO defence would be enhanced if decisions were taken for a low-cost, low-manpower, and obviously non-provocative defence concept.

For the sake of stability in the Central Region, non-threatening but reliable effective defence postures are essential within both alliances. The key condition to be aimed at is therefore *mutual superiority of defence*[4] which, following the principles of logic, cannot be achieved by simply reducing the prevailing offensive capabilities. In addition to arms reductions, the restructuring of forces will be indispensable. Thus what NATO should try to attain in Vienna is an agreement on mutual reductions of offensively-orientated potentials to the lowest reasonable levels, and the introduction of strong, non-offensive, defensively-orientated light forces into both sides' military organisations, which are best suited for holding the line and, to the extent possible, unsuitable for large-scale offensive action.

General Features of the Concept

The proposed concept will be a 'mixed' one, relying primarily on the attrition of the aggressor by fire and, secondarily, on mobility.

Land, air and sea-based TNF will be kept for deterring conventional attack and the use of nuclear weapons by the aggressor. Land-based TNF should exclusively or predominantly consist of relatively long-range SNF, thus requiring modernisation of the available Lance systems.

Modern area surveillance, target acquisition, data transmission and fire-control techniques will allow the transfer of traditional close air support (CAS) and battlefield air-interdiction missions (BAI) from air to ground forces. Air interdiction (AI) may become superfluous if really deep cuts in WTO armoured ground forces are made. In other words, depending on the size of negotiated force reductions, the future defence concept may substantially renounce the combat air support of ground forces and FOFA, and the means necessary for implementation, but with the exception of anti-tank helicopters.

Consequently the defence of Central Europe will be accomplished predominantly by ground forces. These may be organised in traditional army corps or field armies comprising two distinct components: 'light divisions' and operational reserves. According to previous NATO experience, a total of nine army corps or field armies should be sufficient for covering the entire 900 km central European front line between the Baltic and the Danube.

The core of light divisions should combine barrier engineer, anti-tank, and light infantry units, in this order of priority. For combat support, artillery and anti-tank helicopter units will be needed, and some mechanised elements on each of the command levels above battalion. Tentatively a maximum of 150 to 200 armoured combat vehicles could suffice for equipping these counter-attack forces. Light divisions may be tailored for defending 50-km wide defence sectors; accordingly, each army corps or field army would dispose of two such units.

The major component of operational reserves will be one 'heavy division' for each army corps or field army, which by type would correspond to presently available mechanised forces. Its combat strength should be determined below presently given levels of armoured divisions, and by approximation should comprise, as a reasonable limit, a maximum of 200 main battle tanks (MBT) and 160 mechanised infantry combat vehicles (MICV). Additionally, operational reserves will dispose of artillery and anti-tank helicopter units for support of combat by the light divisions.

Presumed Course of Battle

Any enemy attack will probably be supported by massed artillery and preparatory fire from the air. Avoiding or at least minimising subsequent losses calls for the forward location of defensive positions beyond the ranges of most of the aggressor's artillery. Nevertheless, the first task in war will be suppression of the enemy artillery. This will involve the entire artillery of corps and divisions, and fighter bombers if available.

It goes without saying that the terrain between the forward defensive positions and the borders cannot be left to the aggressor. Instead, his forces must be subjected to maximum attrition at the outset of the invasion. This is the purpose of the 'attrition-zone' to be prepared immediately at the borders. The depth of the zone will depend on both the ranges of the aggressor's artillery and the terrain characteristics. Attrition will be achieved by anti-tank and anti-personnel mine systems, by artillery and mortar fire using passive and active ammunitions, by anti-tank helicopters, and by flat-trajectory fire from guns and light rockets. The emphasis placed on means in the order of priority given above also aims at reducing the numbers of personnel needed in combat, and at increasing the prospects of survival of our own personnel deployed on the battlefield. In favourable situations, early counter-attacks by mechanised units may be appropriate in this second phase of battle, aiming at the final destruction of previously reduced enemy formations.

The third phase of battle will be conducted in defence sectors behind the attrition-zone. Anti-tank and infantry elements will prepare and man defence positions only in selected portions of the sectors. Operations of the attrition-zone type will be conducted in the unoccupied parts of the sectors, immediately in front of and between defensive positions. The crucial objective is to definitely stop the aggression within the defence sectors.

Divisional and corps counter-attack operations will be conducted to destroy remaining enemy forces, or to force them to withdraw, and to regain lost territory. This would be the last phase of battle. Needless to say, we may speak of separated tasks and phases only for the purpose of analysis. In reality, the tasks mentioned will have to be executed more or less simultaneously, and continuously involve all components of the defending force.

Conclusion

Social-defence and static- or area-defence concepts should be rejected because their war-prevention potential must be considered as unacceptably low, and because they do not correspond to the principle of forward defence. Thus only two fundamental possibilities for defending Central Europe may be regarded as potential candidates for a future defence concept – 'mixed' models and mobile defence. Besides the need to support the conventional arms-control process, there are other arguments favouring mixed rather than entirely mobile defence concepts. Three of them will be briefly discussed.

The first is the commonplace experience pointing to the fact that it is usually unwise to rely in a fight for survival on weapons and methods used by a superior opponent. This should be particularly true under the prevailing conditions characterised by the antithesis of offensive versus defensive doctrines in East and West.

Another argument says that mobile-defence concepts and a forward defence strategy may not be harmonised easily. The first requires sufficient depth of the defence sectors for highly mobile, far-reaching operations, and the deliberate acceptance of more or less temporary losses of large portions of territory to the aggressor. The principle of forward defence, however, striving *inter alia* for damage limitation, denies extensive use of the territory to be defended and any major surrender of terrain. So what NATO had been doing in its General Deployment Plan (GDP) is more or less to restrict classical mobile defence operations to the tactical commands below divisional level. This appears to be a compromise, complying neither with mobile defence nor with forward defence principles in a satisfactory manner.

The third objection to a strictly mobile defence concept is based on the amazing progress which has been achieved recently in the fields of area surveillance, target acquisition, data transmission, fire control, and hit-and-kill probabilities of modern ammunition. Modern technologies support both the aggressor and the defender; however, the defender should be able to gain more from them. This would call for the extensive use of attrition by modern mines and indirect artillery and mortar fire. Eventually combat support forces, such as engineers and artillery, may become the principle elements in the future defence posture, and thus take over much of the prominent role which has traditionally been assigned to mechanised combat forces. However, for the final success of forward defence one must rely on counter-attack capabilities.

From a theoretical point of view, modification of NATO's defence posture and planning would be appropriate, even disregarding the current conventional arms-control process. However, the Vienna negotiations are taking place and future defence planning cannot be carried out without considering the implications of the CFE talks.

CHAPTER 10

The Counter-offensive: a Theoretical and Historical Perspective

BRIAN HOLDEN REID

THE NATURE of the counter-offensive is fundamental to an understanding of the art of war. In reiterating the old cliché that the best form of defence is attack, the historian should realise that all he is doing is reducing to an hoary old formula a strategem which is time-honoured. If Napoleon was correct in his advice that if the commanders of the future wish to prepare themselves for war, then the best method is to study (and re-read) the campaigns of the great soliders of the past, Alexander the Great, Hannibal, Caesar, Gustavus Adolphus, Turenne, Frederick the Great, and so on, it is remarkable how frequently such men were able to turn an initial misfortune to their advantage and strike once the enemy had committed himself. For the counter-offensive permits a commander to seize the initiative once he has been able to divine the enemy's intentions by a premature move, and then impose his will on the course of subsequent military operations. To strike first is to risk the wastage of resources before the object of the campaign is gained. The offensive demands above all surprise and mobility. Mobility implies making the best use of the available time required to attain the object. If surprise is sacrificed, movement tardy and time wasted, then the best prepared offensive will fail. In wars fought before the Industrial Revolution, it was time and space that were essential in resisting an attack. In the Seven Years War, Frederick the Great sacrificed his entire kingdom before launching his counter-attack. Since the immense social and techno-logical upheavals of the nineteenth century, it has been weapon-power that is the crucial factor, because the speed of technological change has reduced space, increased our capacity to do more in less time, and both increased and diminished our ability to move in war. And it is these factors that will be analysed in this chapter in relation to the theory and conduct of war.

It is as well at the outset to be clear about our terms. We need look no further for a clear definition of counter-attack and counter-offensive than the works of Major-General J. F. C. Fuller, who provides the most authoritative discussion of the art of war in the English language. 'A counter-attack is a driving back operation', he wrote in 1931, 'and a counter-offensive a driving forward one; the object of the first is to restore a position, to gain back something lost, and of the second to change a situation, definitely to abandon the defensive and assume the offensive'. There are two types of counter-attack – the immediate and the deliberate – the first 'forcing back an enemy who has penetrated the foremost line of defended localities', the second a prepared operation which follows the enemy's attack. The term 'counter-stroke' may be construed as the function of the operational level – a counter-attack which determines the course of a single battle.[1]

The great outpouring of theoretical writing on war that followed the Napoleonic Wars, which is still the essential starting point in any consideration of war as a social phenomenon, was greatly concerned with the relationship between the offensive and the defensive. Any analysis of this subject must, inevitably, start with Clausewitz's monumental study, *On War*. Clausewitz was of the opinion that 'pure defence' was 'contrary to the idea of war', for the simple reason that passivity 'should be applied to the basic concept, not to all of its components'. This somewhat ambiguous, Teutonic philosophising does embrace a fundamental truth which has been frequently neglected by the British Army and deserves extended study: that the defensive and the offensive cannot be separated. Clausewitz goes on:

> ... if we are really waging war, we must return the enemy's blows; and these offensive acts in a defensive war come under the heading of 'defence' – in other words, our offensive takes place within our own position or theatre of operations. Thus a defensive campaign can be fought with offensive battles, and in a defensive battle, we can employ our divisions offensively.

This argument was part of an overall thesis that the defence was the *stronger form* of war. Although this argument has been the subject of considerable criticism, Clausewitz did hedge it with qualifications that were often overlooked by his critics. 'If defence is the stronger form of war, yet has a negative object', he wrote, 'it follows that it should be used only so long as weakness compels, and be abandoned as soon as we are strong enough to pursue a positive object'. The conduct of military operations was determined by the object of the war. This consideration would become more weighty as policy assumed a greater importance. Furthermore, the decision had to be sought in battle and not by manœuvre. The object, Clausewitz averred, was the destruction of the enemy's forces and this should be attained mainly by the engagement – though this was a means to an end and not an end in itself.

In other words, a war in which victories were used only defensively without the intention of counter-attacking would be as absurd as a battle in which the principle of absolute defence – passivity, that is – were to dictate every action.[2]

In developing this argument, Clausewitz analysed with considerable clarity the major characteristics of the counter-offensive. The first important point he made was that, 'The tactical initiative can rarely be expanded into a major victory, but a strategic one has often brought the whole war to an end at a stroke.' Though such a stroke assumed major blunders on the enemy's part, remaining on the defensive itself was risky. 'The defender cannot, as he can in tactics, surround the surrounder in turn, for he cannot deploy his troops in the relative depth required, nor keep them sufficiently concealed.' But the nature of the theatre of operations will work in his favour, especially if his troops are familiar with the area of operations while the attacker's are not. 'The larger the area of operations', Clausewitz went on, 'that it [the attacking army] must traverse, the more it is weakened – by the effect of marches and by the detachment of garrisons. The defending army, on the other hand, remains intact. It benefits from its fortresses, nothing depletes its strength, and it is closer to its sources of supply.' Given this correlation of advantages, Clausewitz came to the conclusion that attack and defence 'balance one another'.[3]

Having assessed the advantages that accrue to these forms of war, Clausewitz moved on to emphasise the role that policy had in shaping the imperatives that drive military operations. He was contemptuous of passive defence for 'merely parrying a blow goes against the essential nature of war, which certainly does not consist merely in enduring'.

Once the defender has gained an important advantage, defence has done its work. While he is enjoying this advantage, he must srike back, or he will court destruction. Prudence bids him strike while the iron is hot and use the advantage to prevent a second onslaught . . . this transition to the counter-attack must be accepted as a tendency inherent in defence – indeed one of its essential features.[4]

It is this line of argument, that the offensive must follow the successful defensive if the object is to be attained, that inspired Clausewitz's famous and oft-quoted observation that 'a sudden powerful transition to the offensive – the flashing sword of vengeance – is the greatest moment for the defence'. He places this movement under the overall heading of defence, and not the attack, and this should be borne in mind when assessing the validity of Clausewitz's overall thesis that the defence is the stronger form of war. Certainly the place of the counter-attack in sustaining defensive deadlock will be analysed shortly. The counter-attack required precise timing and firm initiative and, moreover, an appreciation of its essentially defensive form.

If it is not in the commander's mind from the start, or rather if it is not an integral part of his idea of defence, he will never be persuaded of the superiority of the defensive form; all he will see is how much of the enemy's resources he can destroy or capture.

This ambiguous passage, so typical of some of the philosophising that clutters up Clausewitz's otherwise acute analysis, does contain an important implicit assumption. If the defensive is seriously thought out, then 'defence will no longer cut so sorry a figure when applied to the attack' and, therefore, the offensive 'will not look so easy and infallible as it does in the gloomy imagination of those who seek courage, determination and movement in the attack alone, and in defence only impotence and paralysis'. In making this prediction, Clausewitz was to be proved correct.[5]

Before proceeding to a discussion of the developments which resulted in the ascendancy of the defence over the offence, we should consider those elements that Clausewitz deemed fundamental to the conduct of the defensive-offensive. He was at some pains to restate the importance of economy of force; that the object of battle for the defender was '*to inflict heavy losses on the enemy at low cost to himself* '; thus all the arts of the attack-assault, surprise, and flanking advances – would be brought to bear on 'the attacker's centre of gravity while the outcome still hangs in the balance, in order to produce a total reversal'. The battle would be decided by the maintenance of a turning movement, which should be countered by the reserve – amounting to one-quarter or even one-third of the defender's entire force – which is thrown into the attack in a counter-turning movement which should destroy the attacker's penetration of the rear of the defensive position. Clausewitz was quite clear that this subordinate turning movement could not be expected to act as a general envelopment of the attacker's now ill-organised and beaten forces. 'So', he concluded, 'the difference between the forms of victory will lie in the fact that in an offensive battle the attacker does the turning and then converges on the centre, while in a defensive battle the movement is more likely to fan out from the centre towards the periphery'.

Although Clausewitz conceded that the historical record demonstrated that victories were more likely to spring from offensive rather than defensive operations, he was highly critical of the prevailing view that indecisiveness was implicit in the defensive form.

> In this absurd manner it has become a basic assumption that defensive battles are meant merely to repulse the enemy and not destroy him. We consider this a most damaging error, in fact a confusion between form and substance. We maintain unequivocally that the form of warfare that we call defence not only offers greater probability of victory than attack but that its victories can attain the same proportions and results.

There was, in addition, an important corrollary to this contention, namely, that it applied not only to each single battle, but to the *aggregate* success of battles fought in a given campaign.[6]

To sum up Clausewitz's profound analysis: he held that the defence was the stronger form of war. But this should not be interpreted as passive defence but the defensive-offensive. This was the key to economy of force and success in war, especially if the defender was numerically inferior to the attacker. The counter-attack should be mounted employing all the artful devices of the offence: counter-envelopment, surprise, mobility, and the use of reserves. But when should this counter-attack be launched? The strength of the attacker is rarely increased during an offensive, it is more likely to be eroded. 'The attacker is purchasing advantages that may become valuable at the peace-table, but he must pay for them on the spot with his fighting forces.' Some past offensives had led to decisive success and forced the defender to the peace-table, but these had been rare. Consequently, Clausewitz developed a concept that is crucial to an understanding of the counter-offensive, namely, *the culminating point of the attack*. The majority of offensives – for instance, the protracted offensives undertaken by the Spanish in the years 1580–1609 in a vain atempt to quell the Revolt of The Netherlands, or Charles XII's invasion of Russia in 1709 – 'only lead up to the point where their remaining strength is just enough to maintain a defence and wait for peace. Beyond that point the scale turns and the reaction follows with a force that is usually much stronger than that of the original attack'. Detecting this point of material and moral exhaustion, when the full tide of the enemy's assault has spent itself, required 'discriminative judgement' on the part of the commander.[7]

Once this point had been identified, then the counter-offensive should be driven home with all the strength that could be mustered from the reserves, and the pursuit must clinch success. 'If the enemy is thrown off balance', Clausewitz writes with feeling, perhaps with a strong recollection of the Prussian pursuit of the French after Waterloo, 'he must not be given time to recover. Blow after blow must be struck in the same direction; the victor, in other words, must strike with all his strength, and not just against a fraction of the enemy's'. Only 'by daring all to win all, will one really defeat the enemy'. But Clausewitz was writing before the technological developments of the Industrial Revolution had made an impact on the battlefield. The question from 1859 onwards was whether it was possible to attain this kind of victory with shock action against improved weaponry. It is to the question of the objective that we should now turn: 'daring all to win all'.[8]

The emphasis on the offensive during the French Revolutionary War and the Napoleonic Wars was just as much a reflection of social and political imperatives as of audacious generalship: an enthusiasm for exporting the Revolution beyond France; the realisation that once armies had been mobilised it would have caused greater economic dislocation to have demobilised them; and to make the war pay for itself. Speed of action was determined by a lack of supply lines, and thus mobility was in part a product of the desire to keep an army moving to find food so that some semblance of order could be maintained.[9] The result was a dashing series of offensive victories relying on shock action which hypnotised future generations of commanders. The Clausewitzian defensive-offensive was not an important element in Napoleonic warfare. The Emperor argued that 'it is a very great mistake to allow oneself to be attacked'. A general 'must not be afraid to deliver battle, and should seek out the enemy everywhere to fight him'. It was the Duke of Wellington that accorded the clearer model of an army waging war by means of the defensive-offensive. In the Peninsular War, defensive battles like Busaco (1810) had a tactically offensive element, and in conjunction with the Lines of Torres Vedras, eventually drove the French out of Portugal. Rather, it was Napoleon's grasp of the factors of time and space which was such a vital element in his success. Space should be used to mislead and mystify the enemy, then traversed with great rapidity. 'The loss of time', he once wrote, 'is irreparable in war; reasons alleged for it were always bad; because operations only fail through delays'.[10]

But after Waterloo technological developments operated in such a way as to reduce the importance of the offensive element. In 1836 Baron Jomini observed that, 'The new inventions of the last 20 years seem to threaten a great revolution in army organisation, armament and tactics . . . The means of destruction are approaching perfection with frightful rapidity.' The inventions which Jomini alluded to (mostly appearing over the previous half century), shrapnel, the percussion cap and the cylindro-conoidal bullet did increase the amount of firepower that could be brought to bear on the battlefield. The last two, in Major-General Fuller's opinion, rendered the rifle 'the most deadly weapon of the century'.[11] In addition, the expansion of the railways permitted the movement of larger numbers of men to the battlefield; this became an important element in strategic planning. The upshot of these developments was that more men were carried to – and could be supplied on – the battlefield. Armies grew in size and were more difficult to command and control. A combination of numerical strength and greatly supplemented firepower led inevitably towards wars of attrition. In the crowded confines of Europe, but also in the wider spaces of North America, expansive Napoleonic manœuvres became more difficult, if not impossible, to mount. Entrenchments were required to protect more human targets from an avalanche of projectiles. Under these circumstances the counter-offensive, as Clausewitz had anticipated, became more important. But it sustained the attritional process rather than, as Clausewitz had hoped, evolve into a more decisive form of war.[12]

This first became evident during the American Civil War (1861–65) rather than in Europe. The Civil War is an important example because, despite the influence of geography, the great spaces of North America could not outweigh technological factors. In the German Wars of Unification, partly through good luck and partly through better preparation, Moltke and the Prussian General Staff had seized the initiative and secured great victories in the first phase. France in 1870, for example, had been decisively defeated before attrition could be brought to bear; the French were not given time to mount a counter-offensive, though Moltke's armies advanced and were supplied in a manner reminiscent of Napoleon.[13]

In North America, however, where a similar decisive victory was not secured in the first phase of the Civil War at Bull Run in 1861, the great spaces could not compensate for the increase in defensive firepower.[14] The Civil War was marked by an increased intensity of combat compared with the Napoleonic Wars – up to 10,000 engagements can be listed, of which 50–100 may be considered general. Griffith, in a provocative study, has suggested that the handling of large numbers of ill-trained volunteers and conscripts and the inadequate standards of staff training exhibited in the Civil War contributed to the failure of a number of offensive operations. He is surely correct in suggesting that, 'Running a successful defensive battle imposed simply less of a strain on an army headquarters than maintaining a successful offensive.'[15] This had important implications for the numerically and technologically inferior side. The Confederates had staved off defeat in the first phase of the war by a counter-stroke at Bull Run. They were able, when organisational and material factors permitted, to launch counter-attacks which lengthened the duration of the war. By forcing the Union armies to occupy Confederate territory and crush all its armies, the tenacity of Southern resistance ensured that, when defeat came, it was total. Counter-attacks, both at the operational and the strategic level, contributed to the indecisiveness of the war.

It should be underlined that this move towards the ascendancy of positional warfare and the counter-attack was not acknowledged by many senior commanders. These continued to wage war by Napoleonic standards, emphasising rapid manœuvre and shock action. Before the Battle of Murfreesboro in 1862 General William S. Rosecrans issued the following general order, and it would be multiplied may times over before 1914:

> Keep ranks. Do not throw away your fire . . . Close steadily in upon the enemy, and, when you get within charging distance, rush on him with the bayonet. Recollect that there are hardly any troops in the world that will stand a bayonet charge, and that those who make it, therefore are sure to win.[16]

But American generals were forced to employ entrenchments, often against their better judgement, to protect their men from increased firepower. Both Grant and Sherman had failed to entrench before

Shiloh. Yet a year later Sherman was employing entrenchments in the *offence*. These developments had important implications for the numerically weaker side. There can be little doubt that entrenchments rendered it far more difficult to envelope and annihilate the defender. The mobility of the attacking army was reduced, and space and time factors were constricted by defensive works which permitted the defender to economise his force. Attrition, in fact, offered relative security.[17] This thesis is upheld by a study of the great battles in May–July 1864 in northern Virginia. On two occasions, during the Wilderness and again at the 'Bloody Angle' at Spotsylvania, Lee delivered counter-strokes which, though they did not decisively defeat Grant and throw him back over the Rapidan, permitted Lee to maintain the cohesion of his army and retire to ever stronger defensive positions. Hagerman sums up Lee's achievement: he 'had shown that an army fighting on interior lines, even under nearly overwhelming conditions of deprivation and against vastly superior numbers, could sustain a prolonged existence by the use of field fortifications and defensive manoeuvre'. The Army of Northern Virginia inflicted 64,000 casualties on the Union forces in the first three months of the campaign, and a further 50,000 in the following eight months of the war; it suffered losses of about one-third of these figures. Given that Lee had cancelled out time and space factors by keeping Grant bottled up between the Potomac and the James River, these figures bore a chilling portent, and underlined the importance of the defensive-offensive in any future war between the European great powers.[18]

Colonel Henderson, writing in 1898, summed up these lessons elegantly in his study of Stonewall Jackson, 'That a concentrated attack on a vital point is a better measure of security than dissemination along a frontier, that the counter-stroke is the soul of defence, and that the true policy of the state which is compelled to take up arms against a superior foe is to allow that foe no breathing space . . .'[19] But, on the whole, it was the scale of the American Civil War that was ignored by European soldiers, not least the importance of the counter-attack in the later phases. Such observers were engaged primarily by a selective reading of the Franco-Prussian War, especially its opening phase (not the protracted siege of Paris that followed), one of lightning manoeuvres and decisive, overwhelming victories. It is easy to draw a caricature of pre-1914 thinking. Although it may be represented as blimpish and blindly ignorant of increases in firepower, thoughtful soldiers did discuss the implications of technological change. A French official report of 1875, for instance, observed that, 'Troops massed in column, or in line in close order, can no longer manoeuvre, fight, or even remain in position under fire.'[20] Yet by the end of the nineteenth century a greater attachment to moral factors can be detected. Firepower was acknowledged as important in determining the character of the future battlefield. Colonel

Foch, for example, noted in his lectures to the *École de Guerre*, that 'Fire is the supreme argument. The most ardent troops, those whose morale has been the most excited, will always wish to seize ground by successive rushes. But they will encounter great difficulties, and suffer heavy casualities, whenever their partial offensive has not been prepared by heavy fire.'[21]

Indeed tactical commentary was frequently accurate in its predictions. Count Schlieffen, the author of the famous plan, in a memorandum completed in 1905 observed of the battlefield of the future, that 'All along the line the corps will try, as in siege warfare, to come to grips with the enemy from position to position, day and night, advancing, digging in, advancing again, digging in again, etc., using every means of modern science to dislodge the enemy behind this cover.' It was not necessarily at the tactical level that thinking was wishful or inaccurate, but higher up. It was agreed that casualties would be heavy. The Directorate of Training in the British Army estimated that casualties would run as high as 65–75 per cent per annum.[22] But no army expected the fighting to last that long. If the offensive could be sustained by moral factors over short periods of time, if the striking forces could be kept overwhelmingly strong, and launch a pre-emptive strike, then the war could be brought to an end quickly. As General Sir Ian Hamilton observed in 1911 in one of his characteristically lyrical moods:

> War is essentially the triumph, not of a *chassepot* over a needle-gun, not of a line of men entrenched behind wire entanglements and fire-swept zones over men exposing themselves in the open, but of one will over a weaker will . . . the best defence to a country is an army formed, trained, inspired by the idea of attack.[23]

Armies, therefore, should not hold back. To do so would detract from the initial overwhelming blow that all commentators agreed could bring the war to a short, sharp conclusion. The fabric of civilisation, they also agreed, could not endure a long war. Foch, who had a talent for drawing together commonplace sentiments in an exuberant and persuasive form, held that successful strategy required that it was vital '*to bring to the point of shock all* available troops . . . Movement governs strategy. May we not stand and await that shock? Of course not. If we did not seek it, it might well not occur at all, or occur under bad conditions; we might then fail to destroy the forces of the adversary . . .' This offensive act required mass and velocity, and it was expected that ultimately firepower would support, and not detract from, the offensive. 'Firepower does not weaken the offensive spirit', observed General Bazaine-Hayter, commander of the XIII Corps, in October 1906. 'Never forget that a defensive battle will seldom bring victory. However powerful weapons become, the victory will go to the offensive which stimulates moral force, disconcerts the enemy and deprives him of his freedom of action.' Thus a tendency to divorce the offensive from the defensive was apparent before the First

World War. Attack (or, for that matter, mobility or firepower) was not considered with reference to security. This was the great blunder of the pre-1914 generation of military pundits, not any failure to predict the dominance of entrenchments.[24]

It is striking how rarely pre-1914 plans had taken seriously the possibility of a counter-stroke of some kind. Yet the First World War on the Western Front was very largely governed by one, namely, the First Battle of the Marne, which drove the Germans back from Paris in 1914 and intiated the trench deadlock. Thereafter the stranglehold of trench warfare was tightened by counter-offensive action. It is not possible here to examine this conflict in detail. It must suffice to take two detailed case studies: to examine how and why counter-attacks prolonged the trench deadlock, and then proceed to discuss how they brought the war to an unexpected conclusion in 1918, and what was learnt from their conduct.

The great entrenched systems which spread like spider's webs over northern France in 1915–16 presented a major problem which had faced Grant under very similar conditions in 1864, namely how to pass an army through intricate defensive positions. Before 1914 military commentators had assumed that such defences could be by-passed and enveloped. But the cramped and crowded regions of Western Europe, with flanks resting on the Alps or the sea, had rendered this impossible. Thus armies were forced to move from the tactics of envelopment to the tactics of penetration. The strategic problem was shaped largely by the salient which the Germans had retained in 1915, Nieuport–Noyon–Verdun. But the penetration of this area required protracted artillery bombardments and close co-operation with the infantry, which was not always forthcoming. The infantry could advance only under the cover of an artillery bombardment. This raised the question of exploiting a possible breakthrough. The distribution of reserves was vital, for these would secure the victory. Yet if they were placed too near the front line, they could be attacked by the enemy's artillery, and if they were held too far back, then opportunities would be wasted while they advanced to the battlefront, as Haig found to his cost at Loos in September 1915. Finally, the battles of 1915 taught 'that it is not possible to carry two defensive systems in one bound, and that directly the first is captured a methodical attack must be mounted against the second'. The battles of 1916 were even more costly because their enormous artillery bombardments sacrificed surprise and thus the Germans were prepared to resist them. Yet given the great length of the German defensive position and its comparatively small depth, only a relatively small penetration was required to dislocate it.[25]

The German defensive techniques that evolved in 1916–17, in an attempt to resist the increasing weight of Allied offensives, gradually moved away from a doctrine that emphasised the defence of every single inch of ground, irrespective of its value, towards a doctrine that enshrined mobile defence, using infantry, who would be thrown into the attack under the cover of artillery fire, to protect or reclaim those areas which were vital to the maintenance of the German defensive system, and it was a *system*. Thus defensive battles assumed an offensive form, as the infantry would have to leave their second lines in order to retake the first line. In General Ludendorff's opinion, 'the immediate counter-attack acquires decisive importance . . . It is the most effective and the most economical method, both of human lives and of ammunition, of restoring the situation quickly and decisively'. The front would be divided into three zones, the first (lightly held), the second (the artillery protective line), and the main defensive line. The importance of placing reserves correctly was grasped as fundamental to the success of the defensive experiment. But this was rendered less difficult through the Allied sacrifice of surprise by long bombardments; or if wrongly gauged, reserves could be rushed to a threatened sector of the front in the time that elapsed between the initial assault and the time that it took to bring up the artillery to assault the second line; much time was lost hauling heavy guns over communications shattered by artillery fire. As Captain Wynne concluded, the new German defensive methods 'brought up to date the teachings of Clausewitz' with 'a flashing sword of retaliation'.[26]

Such were the ingredients that contributed to the bitter reality of trench stalemate, in which technological factors had so cancelled out time and space factors, that the launching of a counter-attack would prove vital in frustrating an Allied offensive; and conversely, if any army could be passed through these defences, only a short advance would suffice to rupture the German defences. The offensive and the defensive had to be brought back into a closer relationship with one another. The problem was solved for the Allies by Ludendorff's gamble in attempting to secure a decision on the Western Front in 1918. He was forced to do this for political and strategic reasons, but it presented the Allies with an unexpected opportunity. 'Whilst it becomes ever more difficult to overcome an opponent who is standing on the defensive', Captain Liddell Hart has commented, 'offensive action may decisively upset an opponent who is not ready for the defence'. He continued:

> The most effective strategy is thus to leave or to induce an opponent to throw himself against one's defences, and then, when he is shaken by the abortive effort, to deliver a riposte before he can assume a defensive attitude and to press the riposte home.[27]

As the campaign of 1918 had such an impact on the inter-war reformers, its main themes require some analysis.

The German spring offensive launched in March 1918 reached its 'culminating point' in July in Champagne in the Marne salient. On 13 July Marshal Foch decided to mount a counter-stroke which would deprive the Germans of offensive power by striking at their communications in the rear of the salient. The offensive, Foch wrote,

> while not seeking a decision – should consist of a series of movements to be undertaken immediately . . . They will also serve to keep the fighting initiative on the side of the Allies. These movements should be executed with such rapidity as to inflict a succession of blows.

Surprise was reinstated as a vital factor in the operation, and great pains were taken to conceal preparations for the attack. Foch managed to concentrate a local superiority of 2:1. Both these elements were important because they played on German preconceptions. The Germans persisted in thinking in terms of preparing to continue their own offensive rather than resisting a French counter-stroke. The human mind 'sees what it wants to see; and what it wants to see is what accords either with existing beliefs or its desires'. The French successfully persuaded Ludendorff that nothing was amiss which required a reassessment of the German position. The French counter-stroke not only coincided with the German 'culminating point' (Prince Rupprecht, an army group commander, commented to the Chancellor that 'we should have nothing to gain but everything to lose if we prolonged the fighting'), but Ludendorff was paralysed psychologically by this unexpected blow. Still, after four days the counter-stroke had progressed no more than 10 km. The French failure to exploit pointed to the future importance of armoured forces in sustaining this kind of operation.[28]

A major difference between the 1918 counter-stroke and the offensives of 1916–17 was that, whereas the French and the British had mounted separate and poorly coordinated offensives, that of 1918 was a *simultaneous* effort at penetration. The British mounted a counter-stroke of their own at Amiens in August 1918. Nonetheless, although these two counter-strokes were successful compared with the great battles of the Somme and Third Ypres, their advances were small, despite the use of tanks – compared with Ludendorff's. The most important development since 1917 was that the Allies had forged a coherent 'weapons system' which was the equal of the Germans', that brought the weapons fielded into a close relationship with one another – infantry, artillery, machine guns, aircraft, and wireless telegraphy. Thus before the pursuit opened in September, with the breaching of the Hindenburg Line, 'the great advantages that, formerly, defence had possessed over offence', writes Professor Wilson, 'had been whittled away to a crucial extent. As a result, the Allies could impose upon a now inferior adversary a series of reverses, none decisive in itself but mounting irresistibly to a conclusive control of the battlefield'. From confirming the stalemate, technological development by 1918 had brought about conditions that permitted the defensive-offensive to break it.[29]

The campaign of 1918 had a profound influence on the two most influential British writers on war, Major-General Fuller and Captain Liddell Hart. Both drew inspiration not so much from aspects of the specific conduct of the campaign as from certain of its embryonic features. Liddell Hart, for instance, had drawn on Ludendorff's methods in March 1918 to expound his 'expanding torrent' concept of offensive operations; Fuller's own experience during the March retreat had triggered off his notion of psychological paralysis as the strategic object of the attack. The similarity of the actual experience of 1918 with the nature of their ideas has led a number of writers to doubt their essential originality. This is a complex question which has been obscured by a fundamental misunderstanding as to the role of military thinkers to which Fuller and Liddell Hart themselves contributed. It is not the function of such writers to cast themselves in the role of the clairvoyant, predicting the future by adopting some agonised stance with brows firmly gasped in the right hand. The originality of Fuller and Liddell Hart should be gauged mainly in relation to their ability to rationalise existing military experience and project its implications both backwards and forwards in time; and this Liddell Hart and Fuller tried to do with varying degrees of success. But their adumbration of certain core concepts inherent in the study of warfare as a whole does not stand or fall by their ability to predict successfully future events. It was in estimating their own success in the predictive field which led them, Liddell Hart especially, to make excessive claims for themselves. In the final part of this chapter, I wish to examine Fuller's and Liddell Hart's writings on the counter-offensive with this assumption in mind and test them against the realities of the practice of war in two different types of military operation, the counter-stroke at Arras in 1940, and the Ardennes counter-offensive of 1944.[30]

The defensive-offensive lies at the core of the theoretical writings of Fuller and Liddell Hart. Fuller had begun his career by expounding the tactics of penetration as a way of avoiding the full blast of war – the increased weight of firepower on the battlefield. By the end of 1918 he was convinced that envelopment would not be reinstated as a decisive act at the operational level until all armies were mechanised. Once armoured forces could enjoy the simultaneous advantages of mobility *and* protection, then they could operate dynamically from a firm base. With complete mechanisation the elements of the counter-stroke to which both writers gave varying degrees of emphasis (psychological paralysis of the enemy's command which knocked his entire force 'off balance', the importance of surprise, and the questions of timing and decision which would test the abilities of future commanders in both controlling their attacking forces and deploying their reserves) could be developed to a much more sophisticated level than had been possible with the crudely mechanised armies of July and August 1918. In October 1918 it was necessary for the Allies to advance but 40 miles beyond the Hindenburg Line before Ludendorff's armies collapsed.[31] Mechanisation would render envelopment (and the assault on the enemy's rear) more practicable than in 1914. Then, the Schlieffen Plan had lacked the mobility to attain its ambitious objectives. Armoured vehicles allowed troops to fight *and* move across the battlefield. Earlier improvements in military transport, such as the railway, had enhanced only strategic not operational mobility.[32]

But the notion of the defensive element as complementing the offensive thrust was fundamental to a proper appreciation of this concept, as it still is. It is reiterated endlessly in Fuller's and Liddell Hart's writings. 'Protection', wrote Fuller, 'is the foundation of all action, offensive and defensive'. Thus

> To assume the offensive simply for the sake of attacking is a poor argument . . . Should the defensive nature of the ground be in your favour, it is frequently advantageous to let the enemy attack and use up his reserves, and then to counter-attack him in flank and rear. The time to change over from the defensive to the offensive is when the enemy is thoroughly involved and approaching exhaustion.

From this base the decisive attack could be launched once the process of 'stabilisation' – depriving the enemy of striking power (movement) – had been completed. That is, 'overwhelm the enemy at a point which when captured will threaten the security of his entire army, and which on account of the clinch he is unable to reinforce'.[33]

Liddell Hart's thinking was broadly similar, with some changes of emphasis. Thus 'the true time for a counter-attack is not when an attacking enemy has gained his objectives, but when he has failed to gain it, for his disorder will be accentuated by the lack of a clear position and will be multiplied by depression'. Liddell Hart thought counter-attacks under other circumstances were rarely justified, especially if by a cry for defence for its own sake, which Ludendorff had wisely disregarded. He continued:

> In confining the aim of the counter-attack to the mere ejection of the enemy from a point that he has captured, its true meaning and purpose have been narrowed. It should have full scope as a form of 'attack'. Any force . . . which launches a counter-attack should be prepared to press it home and go on pressing so long as the enemy gives way.

He then developed a specific point with which Fuller would have agreed wholeheartedly:

> To that end any force should have its defensive plan adapted, and its reserves ready, to back up the success of a counter-attack launched . . . just as it is ready to use them in exploiting any penetration made by its forward units in the ordinary attack.
>   To take advantage of such opportunities, however, we need to give the counter-stroke a wider horizon and a larger place in our training.[34]

Thus, technological change, or rather a vision of the impact of technology, had altered the scope of the counter-attack from sustaining the defensive to maintaining the velocity of the offensive. In attempting to grapple with these complex problems, Fuller and Liddell Hart, by understanding that the defensive and the offensive were integral parts of the art of war, had modified Clausewitz's basic concept to meet the demands of drastically changed conditions.

The contrasting examples of Arras (21/22 May, 1940) and the Ardennes show how these arguments need to be related to the weapons and the resources available to the forces seeking to mount a counter-offensive. Both operations were failures at different levels. The attack at Arras was a hurriedly improvised counter-stroke to gain 'elbow room' south of the town. It struck an exposed German flank and created near panic both among the fighting troops and at Rommel's headquarters. An eye witness moving forward with 4 RTR reported:

> To our great surprise we found that we had come straight into the flank of a German mechanised column which was moving across our front. They were just as surprised as us and we were right in amongst them . . . and for some quarter of an hour . . . there was a glorious 'free for all'. We knocked out quite a lot of their lorries; the Germans running all over the place.

But surprise cannot in itself compensate for other deficiencies. As Colonel Granville-Chapman observes in his recent profound analysis of the subject, 'surprise is not an end in itself. It cannot be effective on its own as it is a condition of success not success itself'. The momentum of the advance was slowed down primarily because, as Brigadier Vyvyan Pope wrote critically, 'the commanders generally were too far back. In an armoured action it is essential that commanders should be well up to take immediate advantage of fleeting opportunities and to deal with sudden changes in the situation'. Intelligence was mishandled and not passed down the chain of command. Consequently the advance was stalled. Given the tiny force available, a hurriedly thrown together composite of something like two brigades, the exact nature of the operation had to be made clear. This was not done. Operational requirements in themselves are not sufficient justification for launching a counter-stroke; they must be related to the strategic requirements. Yet though Liddell Hart's stress on the need to exploit fleeting opportunities and train for them is justified, attaining surprise cannot compensate for a numerical deficiency if the strategic initiative is already lost.[35]

The point is that at Arras the all-important defensive base was too weak to launch a successful counter-stroke. Not only did the operation lack air cover, but the base behind it was crumbling dramatically. Although Matilda Mk II tanks achieved a local superiority over German tanks, this did not produce a psychological paralysis of the German command, and Rommel countered them by using 88-mm guns in an anti-tank role for the first time with lethal effect. Thus the technological and material basis on which the counter-stroke had rested was too fragile to sustain its initial edge, and it was driven back. It had gained two vital days for the withdrawal of the BEF to Dunkirk, and contributed to the bout of nerves which led to the issue of the German order to halt on 24 May, which enabled the evacuation to take place, but it could not reverse decisively the adverse strategic situation which culminated in the fall of France.[36]

These considerations bear even more heavily on the Ardennes counter-offensive because of its greater scale. The Germans intended to launch a force of 30 divisions in a counter-offensive whose aim was to destroy 25–30 Allied divisions operating north of the Ardennes and seize the port of Antwerp. The Allies lacked any strategic reserve; in Fuller's opinion, Eisenhower's distribution of his forces was so faulty that it defied the principles of war. Nonetheless, the German aim was wholly unrealistic, and their forces too weak to attain them. The German forces, for instance, lacked air cover and relied on the weather to conceal them. As in July 1918, a skilful deception operation convinced the Americans that the Ardennes front was thinly held and quiet. Yet, though achieving surprise, the momentum of operations stalled disastrously. Initial objectives did not fall as rapidly as calculated, and when reinforcements were brought up these no longer enjoyed surprise. The Germans lacked cross-country vehicles to by-pass obstacles effectively. Consequently the opening blow was too weak to maintain the initial advantages, and once the weather cleared, Allied air power proved decisive. Once again the defender was not psychologically paralysed, and Eisenhower, after the initial shock, reorganised his forces. As at Arras, resources and the quantity of equipment proved a decisive counterweight to an offensive that had gained an initial advantage.[37]

This chapter has sought to show that in both the theory and the practice of war, the counter-offensive, a developed form of the defensive-offensive, has had a decisive influence on military operations. Whether armies have maintained a predominantly offensive or defensive form has largely been a function of military technology which frustrates or accentuates movement. This is a concept termed by Fuller the *constant tactical factor*, which postulates that 'every improvement in weapons has been met by a counter-improvement which has rendered the improvement obsolete; the evolutionary pendulum of weapon-power slowly or rapidly, swinging from the offensive to the protective and back again'; so which aspect of the defensive-offensive is ascendant will depend on a cyclical, technological phase. Although each historical event is a product of unique historical circumstances which cannot be replicated exactly, it is not beyond the bounds of reason to predict that technology will work in the future to reduce mobility but increase offensive power in the defence, as prevailed in 1916–18. Likewise, it might be suggested that conditions of deadlock not dissimilar to those of 1917 will prevail in a future war, with one major difference: that the range of weapons entrodying the 'emerging technologies' is so much greater than the artillery of 1916–17 that 'no man's land' will have a much greater depth, say 50 miles. It is hazardous for historians to predict but whether this notion has any merit or not, it may be deduced from the above that manœuvre warfare and attrition are also complementary elements, which contain both offensive and defensive forms whether forces are on the move or at the halt. Thus the elements of manœuvre warfare apply under both defensive and offensive conditions. These elements include:

- That the tank is still the only weapon on the battlefield which combines offensive power and defensive strength.
- That seizing and holding the initiative demands *manœuvre* even in the defence.
- That manœuvre implies psychological paralysis just as much as physical destruction. The prime function of this is to reduce the enemy's power of movement, and thus the velocity of his attack.
- That this demands an attack on the enemy's command system, irrespective of whether he is deployed offensively or defensively.
- That this may be achieved by dislocating the enemy in such a way that he should be persuaded that the battle is not how he *expected* it should be; that his doctrine and methods have failed.
- That the defensive-offensive should be conceived of as *one* operation, with both tactical thinking and training methods adapted accordingly.

But I would like to conclude on a cautionary note. The historical examples explored here in some detail all indicate that, no matter how skilful the defence or how cunning the counter-stroke, the weaker side has invariably lost. That, whether it be Lee and the Army of Northern Virginia or the Germans in the Ardennes, counter-offensives, even if they prolong a tenacious defence, will not for long delay the collapse of the materially inferior side. It is here that the Arras counter-stroke provides us with a case study that deserves far greater study by serving soldiers in the British Army, for it illustrates small-scale conditions of beleagured, under-equipped units fighting against overwhelming odds. At Arras in 1940, the counter-stroke was launched in virtual ignorance of what the French Army was doing. In any future war we must ensure that counter-strokes are co-ordinated with our allies and not studied or trained for in splendid isolation. Neither should we delude ourselves, by a detailed study of the past, that launching a counter-offensive at any level is an easy matter. As Field Marshal von Manstein warns us, 'I doubt if there is anything harder to learn than gauging the moment when a slackening of the enemy's resistance offers the attacker his decisive chance.'[38]

CHAPTER 11

The Counter-offensive

MAJOR-GENERAL J. J. G. MACKENZIE

'He who stays on the defensive does not make war – he endures it.'
(Colmar von der Goltz)

WARFARE IN the modern era has been characterised by a preoccupation with counter-offensive operations. Clausewitz described the resumption of the offensive as 'the flashing sword of vengeance – the most brilliant point of the defence' and went on to suggest that any commander who did not 'include this transition in his idea of the defensive would never understand the superiority of the defensive as a form of war'.[1] Somewhat earlier Sun Tzu observed that 'invincibility lies in the defence; the possibility of victory in the attack' while noting that the 'skilled commander seeks this victory from the situation rather than demands it from his subordinates'.[2] Most recently in a draft of the new American doctrine, '*AirLand Battle – Future*', the authors identify three operational imperatives, each of which involves counter-offensive operations against, in turn, the enemy plan, his attempt to reconcentrate his efforts, and finally against his reserve forces as they are committed.

However, it does seem incongruous in the year following Colonel General Gareev's historic speech to the RUSI in October 1988, when he espoused the new Soviet doctrine of defensive defence, to be restudying offensive operations. Surely NATO is a purely defensive alliance, and is not the removal of an offensive capability precisely the sort of arms reduction currently being sought from the Warsaw Pact? This chapter will re-examine the counter-offensive as a technique of warfare and assess its relevance to operations in the Central Region during the final decade of the 20th century, taking into account not just the important political, economic, and technological factors, but also applying some classical military theory in support of the debate.

Given the inability of modern science to foretell the weather accurately more than a few hours ahead, it would seem foolhardy to attempt to predict the military balance in Europe in the mid 1990s.

161

However, several general assumptions may fairly safely be made which will give an indication of the way Europe might look from a military perspective as we head towards the next century.

From Mikhail Gorbachev's speeches, and particularly from his book *Perestroika*,[3] it is clear that he sees the continuing economic decline of the Soviet Union as a threat to the very existence of the Soviet Empire itself. His fears seem well founded; in *The Rise and Fall of the Great Powers*,[4] Paul Kennedy charts the inevitable disintegration of a great power whose economic strength, relative to that of its competitors, declines to the shambolic state of the current Soviet economy. Gorbachev has clearly identified the problem as a political rather than an economic one, and has directed his restructuring accordingly. At the same time he sees no immediate prospect of a military invasion of Soviet territory by the West, and believes none to be likely for the next 20 Years or so. However, such an invasion remains a real concern for the Soviet leadership, and a concern with plenty of historical precedents. Consequently Gorbachev has identified a period of about 20 years during which time he must turn the Soviet economy around if it is to be in a position to meet the potential military challenges of the 21st century. To achieve this economic revolution, he must restructure the Soviet political system and, critically, reduce the current crippling allocation of national resources to the military, while still maintaining an internally, as well as an externally credible defence posture.

As with all other Soviet military thinking, an historical model is being used to validate the changes. Current Soviet studies are centred on Khalkin Gol as the basis of defensive operations and Kursk for the counter-offensive. The new doctrine will probably be based upon a deep security zone containing light covering forces and border guards forward of well-prepared static defensive 'fortresses', with dug-in communications and battle positions as well as extensive obstacles. Behind this defensive area will be all-arms corps and brigade-sized formations, with a well developed counter-offensive capability. This concept of operations has some significant advantages for the Soviets; apart from looking very defensive and thus seeming less provocative to the West with a consequent reduction in tension, it could be maintained with less than half the current complement of the Group of Soviet Forces in Germany (GSFG). Furthermore, being smaller the concept will be easier to modernise as new equipment becomes available. Probably most important is the apparent willingness of the Soviet General Staff to accept the military logic of the reforms and to co-operate in their execution.

The West's response to these initiatives is harder to guage. Despite President Bush's important arms-control initiative in Bonn in May 1989, there is still a considerable divergence of view between the 16 members of NATO. The situation is further complicated by the apparent shift to the left in political allegiance demonstrated at the recent elections to the European Parliament and perhaps soon to be repeated in national elections in the next three or four years. Despite many of the variables being unquantifiable, it seems likely that:

- NATO will remain broadly united politically;
- the United States will remain committed to Europe but with reduced forces;
- NATO's willingness to consider the first use of nuclear weapons will continue to erode;
- NATO defence expenditures will decline in real terms;
- arms-control agreements will reduce all types of military equipment held in the Central Region; and
- threat perceptions of member nations will continue to decline.

Taken together these factors indicate that a review of the NATO strategy of flexible response should take place, perhaps being replaced by the 'defence in depth' strategy proposed by the Soviets.[5]

Within the context of this changing political and military environment, it is necessary to examine the part played by the counter-offensive in current Central Region operations so as to identify the developments already taking place to accommodate, not just changes in force structure and threat perceptions, but in technology as well.

Despite Soviet restructuring to a more defensive posture, it is likely that the forces of the Western TVD will retain an offensive capability. A Soviet offensive operation may well take longer to mount than one with current dispositions; but with a significantly reduced American in-place force commitment and with the likely reluctance of Western European nations to mobilise until it is too late, the likelihood of an attack in the Central Region achieving at least a degree of operational surprise remains high. With the battle of Kursk as an historical precedent for a future concept of operations, the characteristics of a Soviet attack will remain:

- surprise;
- mass;
- high tempo of operations; and
- overwhelming concentration of force.

A Soviet offensive will no longer be an attack in strength on the broad front currently envisaged. However, at the selected breakthrough points the concentration of force is likely to be irresistible, especially with a NATO defence characterised by:

- linear deployment;
- little operational depth;
- few in-theatre operational reserves;
- insufficient preparation time; and
- reluctance to use nuclear weapons.

Furthermore, this type of deployment makes surprise by the defender very difficult to achieve and could render NATO commanders susceptible to enemy deception, as decisions on the lateral movement of forces to create a point of main effort have to be taken early in the conflict.

The key to success in the current concept of defensive operations is the creation and timely committal of sufficiently powerful reserves to prevent either a catastrophic penetration of the linear defence or a strategic turning manœuvre around one of the flanks of the Central Region. A failure to counter either enemy offensive move is likely to result in a loss of cohesion and total collapse of the defence of the Central Front.

However, even without the changes forecast to take place in the next few years, certain problems have already been identified in carrying out the counter-offensive part of the NATO concept.

Insufficient Reserves

The bulk of 3rd (US) Corps, the key Central Region reserve formation, is located in the United States and considerable logistic, not to mention political effort will be required to make it available for operations in time. Most of the remaining, so-called operational reserves held at army group level are divisions with other commitments to the FEBA corps. While the need for counter-action reserves at army group level is not disputed, the danger is that the FEBA corps will be so weakened by their removal that they will end up being committed early merely to bolster the self-induced weakness on the FEBA.

Interoperability

Despite the efforts in recent years to improve the ability of divisional-sized formations to operate across corps boundaries, there are still very real interoperability problems in the fields of doctrine (including the most basic of subjects, such as terminology and fire-support measures),[6] communications, and logistics. The result may well be the piecemeal committal of such reserves as the army group commanders can muster with consequent failure to produce a decisive result.

Disruption

Allied to all of the above points is the disruption that would be caused by the movement of a corps-sized formation in the rear of a Central Region army group. Moving on six major routes and with no enemy interference, a corps still takes more than 24 hours to drive past a point in columns nearly 400 km long. Consequently, because of the NATO linear system of logistic resupply by main supply routes, the committal of a reserve corps has the effect of shutting down the logistic resupply of those corps whose rear areas it crosses for anything up to 36 hours – probably long enough to seriously endanger the FEBA defence it was trying to support.

Warning Time

Because of the unwieldy nature of a corps-sized reserve formation, and despite the considerable efforts made in recent years to speed up the necessary battle procedure, it still takes some 96 hours to commit a reserve corps to battle. Consequently decisions on the time and place of decisive counter-action have to be taken extremely early in the conflict and with the barest of intelligence information. This makes commanders susceptible to enemy deception measures and encourages them to delay their critical reserve-committal decisions until dangerously late in an attempt to improve the intelligence picture. The automation of the Intelligence Preparation of the Battlefield (IPB) may assist, but the problems of data handling and data fusion and the vulnerability of computers to sophisticated deception should be the subject of another complete study.

Transparent Battlefield

Even if sufficient information on the enemy is gathered so that the timely committal of a sufficiently large reserve force can be made, there still remains the very considerable problem of getting it to its target undetected. Surveillance and target-acquisition equipments are now so sophisticated that it seems impossible for a counter-offensive force to operate anywhere on the battlefield without detection and interdiction. The Soviet recce/strike complex seems ideally suited to this type of operation and a whole range of new surveillance equipments are being developed which should further enhance this capability. An example of this exploitation of technology to react rapidly to intelligence inform-ation is the deployment of the new Soviet PASUV command and control computer system. This equipment is now fielded to most headquarters in GSFG and provides commanders with ADP assistance in the calculation of operational norms as an aid to decision making. It is believed to reduce the planning time required for the preparation and dissemination of orders by a factor of six, cutting the planning time for an army level attack from a position of close contact from four hours to 40 minutes. Additionally the Soviet ability to lay scatterable mines is already significant; the new, larger, multi-barrel rocket launchers with greatly increased range and payload will dramatically improve this capability and further reduce the effectiveness of counter-action forces.

Despite the significant problems faced by counter-offensive forces today and in the near future, they remain the key to success in battle. Unless a defending force can create and commit to battle a worthwhile counter-offensive force it is doomed to failure. The failure might be delayed and might only be expressed in political rather than military terms, but a failure it surely will be. Thus considerable thought has gone into improving the current capability of counter-offensive forces, not just in the procurement of equipment more appropriate to counter-offensive operations, but in a whole range of measures, including tactical doctrine and command and control philosophy. The new range of armoured fighting vehicles is far more agile than its predecessor. The Abrams/Bradley, Challenger/Warrior, Leopard 2/Marder families of vehicles are all fast, reliable and well-protected vehicles capable of covering great distances very quickly. This should allow greater dispersal and deployment from greater depth to aid survivability or to achieve a reduction in the necessary warning time to allow for the acquisition of more intelligence. However it is interesting to compare a recent Exercise REFORGER counter-offensive operation and one made by General Patton's Third Army on the move north towards Bastogne in December 1944. Despite all the new equipment, Patton's Army was the quicker, and with a real enemy. Further, his Army with its lighter equipments was less restrained by bridge and route restrictions than a NATO corps would be today. Interestingly, the weight of his main equipments equates closely to today's Warsaw Pact equipment, which is markedly lighter than NATO's.

Directive Control

One simple but significant means of speeding the committal of a counter-offensive reserve is the development of a command and control philosophy which does not require the passage of detailed orders and co-ordinating instructions and can cope with degraded communications in a fluid and highly confused battle situation. The recent adoption by the British Army of the concept of directive control, whereby commanders merely give their subordinates their overall intent and the tasks, resources, constraints, and any essential co-ordination and then allow them to get on and develop their own concept of operations, is a major departure for British commanders and one that is causing much discussion and interest at the Staff College at Camberley.[7]

Smart Munitions

If it proves difficult to get a sufficiently powerful counter-action force into battle in time, then the technology exists to supplement the fighting power of the direct-fire systems with precision-guided submunitions from indirect-fire weapons. Thus MLRS with Phase 3 munitions and similarly equipped ATACMS should be able to mass considerable destructive capability in support of a conventional counter-offensive. It might be tempting to believe that this type of weapon system could replace future direct-fire weapons as the main means of counter-action. It is perhaps worth including a brief review of Lanchester's attrition theories as an aside at this stage as they seem pertinent to this important debate.[8] The elegance and logical simplicity of Lanchester's equations, so popular in the first half of this century, seem to have lost favour with the scientific community and been replaced by much more complex Lanchester models and other totally different concepts, such as aggregate firepower indices and probability simulations of combat. However Lanchester's basic laws – the square law and the linear law – still provide a useful insight into the relative merits of direct-fire and indirect-fire weapon systems. In simple terms, direct-fire weapons can be concentrated against individual targets and fire can be switched from one target to another. Direct-fire weapons are thus subject to the square law, which gives the total effectiveness of a force as:

$$(\text{weapon effectiveness}) \times (\text{numerical size})^2$$

Hence the scientific basis for the Soviet dictum that quantity has a quality all of its own. Thus minor improvements in the effectiveness of individual weapon systems or in the level of training of crews have little effect on the overall effectiveness of a military force because of the disproportionate effect of the squaring of the numerical-size factor. However, indirect-fire systems do not have the same ability to switch their fire from one individual target to another, despite modern surveillance systems, and thus their effectiveness is governed by Lanchester's linear law. Overall effectiveness is now a simple function of:

$$(\text{weapon effectiveness}) \times (\text{numerical size})$$

Thus when considering the balance of investment in direct and indirect weapon systems, particularly in the counter-offensive role, the fact that the numbers of direct-fire weapon systems will be squared to produce their overall effectiveness should not be ignored.

Airpower

Another means of concentrating firepower to support a conventional counter-offensive force is the application of air power. Offensive air support is particularly effective in the preparation of a target for counter-action by disrupting the enemy force and isolating that part of the enemy about to be attacked. Air power is at its most effective when used to delay and disrupt forces out of the immediate contact battle, and should only be tasked with the destruction of enemy forces in close air support of friendly units *in extremis*. This use of air power in direct support of the ground operation is, of course, in addition to the much more important tasks of air interdiction and offensive counter air. The delay and disruption of deep follow-on forces and the creation of a favourable (or less unfavourable) air situation will remain key elements of counter-offensive operations.

Airmobile Forces

A crucial problem in current concepts for the employment of counter-offensive forces is the time taken for the committal of conventional armoured reserves. In an attempt to overcome this problem by exploiting modern technology, several NATO nations have produced air-mobile formations. These forces are generally based upon infantry brigades but with additional anti-armour weapons. Their primary task is to occupy counter-penetration positions in depth to delay and disrupt an enemy breakthrough to give armoured reserves time to deploy. If equipped with effective anti-armour weapons and deployed in suitable terrain, such as built-up areas and ground dominated by wooded features, they could be a potent force. The critical resource for the operational commander in this counter-penetration battle will be time and an air-mobile reserve with its unique speed of deployment can provide him with sufficient time to allow the deployment of more powerful reserve forces. However, forces of this nature do have some significant intrinsic problems. They will inevitably be short of combat support, particularly artillery ammunition, and will seldom have sufficient warning time to prepare a robust defensive position. While their deployment capitalises well on the mobility of the helicopter, once in position they lose all mobility and become extremely difficult to redeploy. Furthermore, their deployment requires excellent anticipation based on the sort of intelligence that is unlikely to be available.

These difficulties result in a defensive, reactive concept for the use of air-mobile forces which, whilst it certainly overcomes some of the problems inherent in the use of armoured reserves, creates some sizeable ones of its own.

Attack Helicopters

The attack helicopter appears to provide a unique means of overcoming many of the problems currently encountered by conventional armoured and air-mobile counter-offensive forces. They can be widely dispersed to avoid detection, can concentrate very rapidly over great distances to produce large quantities of accurate direct-fire, anti-armour weapons, as well as being able to adjust any indirect fire used in their support. An attack helicopter counter-offensive force does not cause the logistic chaos of its ground equivalent as it manœuvres in the rear areas and is not dependent on a long logistic tail to maintain it. Unlike a ground force, it can return with comparative ease to its logistic support. Indeed, the attack helicopter seems so suitable to the currently envisaged range of counter-offensive tasks that one wonders why, with the exception of the US Army, the West has been so slow to embrace it. Perhaps we should not be surprised for it was Captain A. T. Mahan who observed that,

> changes in tactics have not only taken place after changes in weapons, which reasonably is the case, but that the interval between such changes has been unduly long[9]

some years before Lord Haig was making his famous statement about there always being a place on the future battlefield for the well-bred horse! Perhaps he was right as the British Army still has more horses than it does helicopters (and the French Army more horses than tanks!).

However the significance of the attack helicopter does seem to have been appreciated at last, and the British Army in its concept paper on the employment of helicopters in the Central Region has moved away from the helicopter transportation of conventional infantry to a much more aggressive use of this exciting new weapon system.

There is a perfectly natural tendency to attempt to improve military effectiveness by exploiting new technology or new circumstances to enhance particular aspects of weapon- or system-performance. Thus main battle tanks have increased in size as their chassis have been required to carry larger calibre weapons with more powerful propellant charges in an attempt to achieve frontal arc penetration of projected enemy armour. This technological development spiral has created cross-country movement and logistic penalties which deny some modern tanks the range of operational mobility and agility that they need to provide the shock action they were originally designed to deliver. Similar developments can be observed in conceptual thinking: the French preoccupation with the strength of the offence before World War I was matched by the development of a largely static defensive concept behind the Maginot Line in the 1930s. While these conceptual developments might well have been made in response to military experience and technological development, they had no basis in sound military theory, which then, as sometimes now, did not appear to have been a major factor in the decision-making process.

Thus, while acknowledging the fact that the attack helicopter does seem to overcome many of the modern difficulties inherent in the practice of offensive counter-action, it is worth re-examining military theory to ensure that current operational concepts are soundly based and that the application of new and exciting technology is not taking conceptual thinking off at a tangent.

Attrition Theory

Although attrition warfare is often confused with a static or positional form of warfare, with close-packed bodies of armed men being committed to a series of bloody battles, it has been the accepted norm since its perfection under Napoleon at the start of the nineteenth century. The key to his success can be summarised in his four phases of attrition warfare:

- manœuvre and seize key terrain;
- weaken opposition by wearing down attacks while building own reserves;
- decisive attack using all resources against the vital enemy sector; and
- pursuit.

Clearly there is a great deal of opportunity for manœuvre during all phases of this battle, not just during the first and the last phase, but to concentrate force and counter-attack during the wearing down and decisive battles. This style of war is anything but a mindless committal of massed troops, but is simply a recognition of the fact that, all other things being equal, a large army will beat a small one. The theory received added authority when Clausewitz refined and developed it after his experiences in the Napoleonic Wars. He laid even greater emphasis on the need for overwhelming concentration of force and singleness of purpose to win the *Vernichtungschlacht* or decisive battle. This view is best summarised in his famous quotation:

> The best strategy is *to be very strong* [italics in original]; first in general and then at the decisive point.[10]

The key to success in an attrition battle is the creation and recognition of an enemy 'culminating point'. Clausewitz defined the attackers' culminating point as that point at which, encouraged by the enemy's exhaustion, the defender seizes the initiative and advances in a surge which is stronger than the original attack.[11] The US Army seized on this strategic concept and developed it at the tactical and the operational level. In the 1986 version of FM 100-5 the culminating point is defined as:

> a point where the strength of the attacker no longer significantly exceeds that of the defender, and beyond which continued offensive operations therefore risk over extension, counter-attack and defeat.[12]

Thus the defender will succeed in this battle if sufficient success can be achieved during the wearing-down battles to create an enemy culminating point, while the defender still has sufficient strength to launch the decisive attack and subsequent pursuit.

It will be immediately apparent that the current concept of operations in the Central Region is in accordance with this well-proven military theory. Napoleon, Clausewitz, and Jomini would all have instantly recognised the correctness of current plans and would have been satisfied that the plan contains the four crucial stages:

- The key terrain is already identified and is seized before hostilities begin.
- An extensive wearing-down battle is fought on the FEBA, with reserves committed to counter enemy penetrations of the linear defence.
- Armoured reserves are held at army group and regional level to deliver the decisive blow one the culminating point has been reached.
- Pursuit will be the natural successor to a successful decisive attack.

Despite the theoretical correctness and simplicity of the plan, many modifications have been made to cope with perceptions of Soviet strengths and to incorporate new weapon systems. The key problem is NATO's perceived inability to create the all-important culminating point, an inability caused by both the possession of insufficient forces and by lack of depth to allow the inevitable frictions of war to assist in the process. Unless sufficient attrition can be caused during the FEBA battle the preconditions for a decisive attack will never be created. Several methods of enhancing the performance of NATO corps in this critical phase of the battle have been employed:

Separation of Enemy Echelons

By use of concentrated air power the arrival of subsequent enemy echelons can be delayed, so that the FEBA corps have the opportunity to maintain favourable force ratios when in contact and time in which to reconstitute reserve forces before the subsequent echelons arrive. This is really the only influence that the regional commander can have on the conduct of the land battle once his reserve corps has been allocated to an army group.

Extension of the Contact Battle

With the limited range of current ground weapons most of the necessary attrition has to take place in a narrow sector within a kilometre or so of ground troops. This makes defending forces vulnerable to surprise attack and susceptible to early penetration. In turn this forces the premature committal of reserves which should really be husbanded for the decisive counter-attack. New weapons, like ATACMS and MLRS with Phase 3 munitions, now give ground tactical commanders the opportunity to start this attrition process much earlier, effectively extending the depth of the contact battle zone to nearly 100 km and giving the FEBA corps commanders a better chance of achieving sufficient attrition to create the culminating point.

Offensive Counter-Force Operations

Until recently, in the British corps at any rate, counter-offensive operations were ground-orientated and devoted to maintaining the cohesion of a positional defence by counter-attack and counter-penetration. However, since Field Marshal Bagnall's time as Commander of 1st British Corps and subsequently of NORTHAG, the emphasis has switched to more aggressive tasking of reserve formations charged with destroying the enemy by counter-stroke rather the seizure of some ground objective. This technique clearly has a far greater destructive potential and should further enhance the effectiveness of the FEBA corps in the attrition battle.

Shaping the Battlefield

The technique of shaping the battlefield is a sophistication of the wearing-down phase and an attempt to avoid the inevitably reactive nature of an attrition battle. Consequently the FEBA forces, in addition to their important role of defeating selected enemy echelons, also have the task of holding areas of key terrain to facilitate subsequent counter-offensive action. These counter-offensives could either be offensive counter-force operations, as previously described, as part of the wearing-down phase, or could be orchestrated at a higher level to facilitate the decisive attack once the culminating point has been reached.

However, for all these refinements of the classic military theory of attrition, NATO is left with the uncomfortable truth that this type of battle inevitably favours the larger force. It is not surprising that many Central Region exercises end with the premature committal of operational reserves in a counter-offensive operation against a particular Soviet echelon, but before the culminating point has been reached and with further Soviet echelons available to exploit a NATO defence stripped of any viable operational reserves.

Manœuvre Theory

So if the application of attrition theory seems inappropriate, even with new technology and more mobile, aggressive operations, it might be worth examining manœuvre theory as an alternative, especially as there are many historical examples of small, well-trained armies beating numerically superior forces by[13] the application of manœuvre theory. The first point to be clear about when discussing manœuvre theory is that there is a great difference between 'manœuvre' as a tactical technique and 'manœuvre theory' as the basis for a style of war. The manœuvre as a tactical technique is defined by NATO as:

> The employment of forces on the battlefield through movement in combination with fire, or fire potential, to achieve a position of advantage in respect to the enemy in order to accomplish the mission.

This is merely a means, a highly effective means, of applying military force. The employment of a reserve armoured division in a counter-stroke operation during a FEBA battle as previously described is a good example of manœuvre as a technique applied to a battle based on attrition theory.

Manœuvre warfare, or the application of manœuvre theory, is rather more complex and its significance lies, not in *what* activity takes place, but in *why*. Indeed many of the particular elements of the battle may be precisely the same as the elements of an attrition battle – the difference lies in the purpose behind the activities. Most authors on the subject find it difficult to provide a clear, succinct definition, but J. F. C. Fuller[14] provided a clear description of manœuvre theory in four phases:

- *to distract* – that is, to bewilder the enemy;
- *to fix* – that is, to deprive him of the power of movement;
- *to manœuvre* – that is, to make the utmost use of our own power of movement; and
- *to hit* him unexpectedly or in superior force at the point selected.

Throughout this process the aim must be clear – it is not primarily to destroy the enemy, but to unhinge him, to render him inoperative and to destroy his will to proceed. There are many historical examples of this unhinging process: the surrender of General Mack at the Battle of Ulm in 1805 with hardly a shot fired, and the collapse of the French defence of the Western Front in 1940 while still possessing a considerable overall superiority are but two.[15]

This unhinging effect will not necessarily be brought about simply by causing attrition, particularly if fighting an opponent like the Soviets who are prepared to accept substantial losses in the achievement of their goals.[16] Neither will the effect necessarily be created by holding or seizing a particular piece of ground. However, every military force has some particular feature or characteristic that is at the heart of its strength. FM 100-5 describes this as:

> that capability, characteristic or locality from which an armed force derives its freedom of action, physical strength or will to fight.[17]

This is an adaptation of what Clausewitz would have described as the enemy's 'centre of gravity'; he wrote:

> One must keep the dominant characteristics of both belligerents in mind. Out of these characteristics a certain centre of gravity develops, the hub of all power and movement, on which everything depends. That is the point against which all our energies should be directed.[18]

Thus to succeed in a battle of manœuvre the first imperative is to identify the enemy's centre of gravity and then to devise a concept of operations to attack it successfully.

Enemy Centre of Gravity

An analysis of Soviet operational doctrine reveals the key feature as the ability to commit successive echelons to battle in a *timely* fashion.[19] Throughout Soviet military writing the importance of time is a recurring topic. An example of this occurs in the Soviet *Dictionary of Operational, Tactical and General Military Terms*, where combat mission is defined as the:

> Most compressed and clearly formulated definition of the goal to be achieved in a given type of combat operations by a *definite deadline* or during *some period of time*. In the offensive, the combat mission consists of the destruction of the most important groupings of the enemy and the winning, by the *set deadline*, of a definite line or area.

Time is important to the Soviets because it is a key element in the concept of tempo as a battle-winning factor. The whole concept of tempo and the conduct of operations in the medium of time rather than of force or ground can be explained by the use of physical formulae.[20] In simple terms kinetic energy is the product of mass and velocity in the equation:

$$\text{Kinetic energy} = \tfrac{1}{2} M \times V^2$$

Thus increased speed has a dramatic effect on the subsequent energy produced, as it is squared. However, this simple equation, although widely used by some commentators, is not particularly relevant to military analysis. First, mass is not just a function of the numerical size of a force. It involves all the many ingredients of fighting power as described in the new British military doctrine[21] including weapon effectiveness, morale and so on. Furthermore, it should be looked on as usable mass rather than total mass, for, in close country or when advancing forces are strung out during a route march, only a small proportion of the total force may be available for combat at a given point in time and space.[22]

Similarly velocity is too simplistic a factor. In military terms speed is not the critical ingredient but it is the ability to maintain speed against a resisting enemy. This is the true significance of tempo which could be defined as:[23]

the rate at which an attacking force moves against a resisting enemy force over the medium of terrain.

Thus a modified equation could be:

$$\text{mass} \times \text{tempo} = \text{momentum}$$

The creation of this momentum or impetus by the achievement of a large concentration of usable fighting power together with a high tempo of operations is not seen by the Soviets as an end in itself, but as the means of dictating the overall tempo of the battle. It is this ability to dictate the tempo that is the real meaning of initiative, and it is initiative that allows one side in a conflict to decide the time and place for the committal of forces. Similarly if the enemy's tempo[24] can be disrupted then his mass may become a liability rather than an asset as he struggles to reimpose his will on the conduct of battle. Further disruption may force him to change his plan, which can cause him to:

- replan;
- refocus concentrations;
- organise lateral movement;
- expose command and control assets;
- commit forces piecemeal; and
- lie to his superior.

This activity is well described by the US Army as cascading disruption and illustrates graphically the effect on the advancing enemy of a successful attack on the Soviet tempo.[25] The critical fact is that this disruption can be exploited by further attacks, which in turn create more disruption and still further opportunities for deeper and more powerful manœuvre, leading eventually to the unhinging effect that manœuvre warfare was designed to create. Thus a significant difference between the application of attrition and manœuvre theories is that the former produces a style of warfare that tries to *dissipate* the energy created by a large enemy mass and associated high tempo of operations, while the manœuvre theorist attempts to *prevent* the energy being created in the first place, by attacking the key component of momentum – the enemy tempo.

With the aim of attacking the enemy's operational tempo in mind, it is now necessary to reassess Fuller's phases of manœuvre warfare to identify where counter-offensive action should play a part.

To Distract

It would be inappropriate to dwell in this chapter on plans for operational deception, but few plans are ever successful without some element of surprise, and deception must be one of the key means of achieving surprise on the future battlefield.

To Fix

This is the key phase in the manœuvre battle. If the enemy can be deprived of this ability to manœuvre throughout his depth, then opportunities for deep manœuvre by NATO reserve forces will be created, and the unhinging of the enemy will become a possibility. However, this fixing must be thoroughly effective or the whole concept will break down. Fixing of the enemy does not just mean fighting a robust battle on the FEBA, but must include depriving the immediate follow-on forces of the lead divisions of their ability to manœuvre as well. This attack against enemy forces in the area 15–30 km from the FEBA, sometimes called 'shallow FOFA', denies them the ability to exploit tactical successes achieved by their leading regiments, but it is a critical deficiency in current NATO capabilities. However, a solution to this capability gap has already been identified by General Sir Peter Inge,[26] the previously Commander of 1st British Corps, when he proposed a concept of counter-offensive operations involving a combination of attack helicopters and MLRS, used aggressively in a tactical counter-offensive to exploit a fleeting opportunity, and thereby disrupting the enemy's ability to achieve a high tempo of operations.[27] If followed up by further counter-action, the preconditions may be created for the subsequent phases of the manœuvre battle.[28]

To Manœuvre and To Hit

These two phases are classical tasks for a counter-action force. There will clearly be a role for the continued use of the attack helicopter in these phases, but to create the sort of shock action necessary to bring about the unhinging of the enemy a robust and powerful armoured formation is likely to be required.

Thus in a concept of operations based upon manœuvre theory the counter-offensive has a far more significant part to play than in a classical attritional battle. Although it will be the repeated and relentless manœuvres and strikes by tactical counter-offensive forces in concert with concentrated air power that will fix and disrupt the enemy advance, it will be the rapid exploitation of these tactical successes by larger counter-offensive forces, synchronised and orchestrated at an operational level, that will bring about the unhinging of the enemy by a successful attack on the enemy centre of gravity. This is certainly not a new idea, although it does not seem to have been applied to our current concepts of operations in the Central Region. General Donn Starry identified three tasks for the operational commander in the Central Region:

- deny the enemy access to the objectives he seeks;
- prevent enemy forces from loading-up the assault force with reinforcing echelons and thus achieving by continuous combat what might be denied by a stiff forward defence against reasonable odds.

These first two are pretty standard attrition-based missions, but the third reveals a deep understanding of the purpose of manœuvre warfare:

- find the opportunity, seize the initiative – by manœuvre to attack and destroy the integrity of the enemy operational scheme, forcing him to break off the attack or risk resounding defeat.[29]

If manœuvre theory is adopted as the basis of a style of warfare in the Central Region, then counter-offensive forces will clearly have a greater part to play than ever before. At the tactical level, these forces will be required to carry out the pretty conventional, but nonetheless important, task of maintaining the cohesion of the defence by counter-penetration and counter-attack. However their primary tasks now must be:

- the fixing of the enemy throughout his tactical depth; and
- the relentless exploitation of tactical success to disrupt the enemy tempo and create the opportunities for operational counter-offensives.

There will be the temptation to concentrate all the highly effective assets, like attack helicopters, at the higher levels to support the operational plan; but it should be clear that tactical commanders at corps and division will also need the full range of counter-offensive equipments; not just fast moving, robust, armoured forces, but also attack helicopters and MLRS Phase 3 to ensure that the fixing of the enemy takes place throughout his tactical depth. Sufficient forces must also be held at a low enough level to ensure that the successes achieved really can be exploited, and that the enemy does not have the opportunity to reimpose his own tempo on the conduct of the battle and wrest back the initiative from the defending forces.

However the real changes in counter-offensive forces will be seen at the operational level. There will still be a requirement to provide reserve forces with the conventional defensive tasks of:

- destroying catastrophic enemy penetrations of the FEBA; and
- preventing a strategic turning manœuvre around one of the flanks.

But these tasks must not be allowed to interfere with the primary mission of an operational counter-offensive force:

- the rapid exploitation of tactical success achieved by a FEBA corps as it fixes the enemy advance and disrupts his tempo.

To be effective, reserve forces at the operational level must contain substantial combat power; however they must also be:

- swift into action (fleeting opportunities will not be seized by forces taking 96 hours to deploy);
- survivable (dispersed in hides and during deployment)
- capable of operating without causing logistic chaos in the rear areas.

These characteristics would seem to be mutually exclusive. It would take a corps-sized formation to provide the necessary combat power, and yet such a formation fails to meet the other criteria. What is required is a formation with the relative agility of an armoured division but the combat power of a full corps. In NORTHAG the Army Group commander already has a number of reserve divisions earmarked for action in support of his operational plan. In a future conflict, with the likely inability of the Soviets to attack simultaneously in strength across the whole front, all commanders must be alert to the possibility of removing forces from 'economy of force' sectors either to support a defensive point of main effort or to create additional counter-offensive reserves. Thus all armoured formations of every FEBA corps must have the option of becoming involved in counter-offensive operations as a part of their mission, and these must be properly balanced all-arms forces. The temptation to tailor a division for a specific piece of ground in a specific defence plan must be avoided. However, the earmarked army group reserve divisions are likely to be in the forefront of operational counter-action, but to be effective they must be supplemented by substantial quantities of additional combat power. Modern technology now provides the means of achieving this with long-range artillery (particularly rocket artillery such as MLRS Phase 3 and ATACMS), concentrated air power (particularly in depth to isolate the intended target), and, probably most significant of all, the attack helicopter, with its unique ability to concentrate large quantities of accurate, discerning direct fire very rapidly and over great distances. However, this type of operation will be successful only if the speed of reaction of a small force like an armoured division can be exploited to produce surprise attacks against enemy weaknesses from unexpected directions. This activity will inevitably require extensive co-ordination, not just in wartime to produce the necessary concentrations of combat power, but in peacetime as well to produce the necessary joint doctrine, training, and command and control arrangements. An unwieldy international 'reserve corps' headquarters is not the answer, but a co-ordinating headquarters centred on the infrastructure of a rear area security division could achieve the task and would certainly have considerable political advantage in addition to the military benefits of such an arrangement.

At the regional level, the problems for the employment of the reserve corps are just as acute. If the key to the battle is the rapid and relentless exploitation of successes created by the army group reserves, then a lead-time of 96 hours and the associated problems of enemy interdiction and logistic disruption to the FEBA corps probably make the current concepts of employment inappropriate to a battle of manœuvre. Circumstances would seem to dictate that the largest force that can be committed in a single section of time and space is an armoured division, albeit heavily reinforced with additional combat power. Historical precedent would also suggest that the timely committal of a small but powerful force, particularly if an element of surprise can be achieved, is far more effective than a much larger force that arrives too late, having been detected and interdicted *en route*. There is a natural reaction within the Central Region against any attempt to penny-packet decisive reserves into a piecemeal plan of committal. However, that is not what is being proposed – merely that the employment of the armoured divisions of the reserve corps be synchronised in time and space and not looked upon as a single entity capable of delivering a single massive blow. Rather it should be seen as a series of much more mobile armoured divisions capable of delivering a rapid and relentless series of synchronised counter-punches. Each of these attacks could then be supported by *all* the available indirect-fire, air and attack helicopter support available to the operational commander. This is not a plan that proposes the piecemeal committal of reserves but a concept that allows the operational commander to carry out his own task – the synchronisation of tactical activity to achieve operational goals.

The case for the adoption of manœuvre theory as the basis of a concept of operations in the Central Region seems overpowering. Although much of the modern equipment currently being procured is in support of an attrition-based concept, it is nonetheless highly suitable for a true battle of manœuvre. What is required is an acceptance of the importance of the underlying theoretical base of operational concepts and a willingness to embrace manœuvre theory as the basis of a whole style of warfare and not just manœuvre as a tactical technique. The significance of this decision should not be underestimated and will have far-reaching implications in equipment procurement, the structure of forces, and the organisation of training; indeed in every facet of military life. However, it will provide the forces of the Central Region with a soundly-based concept of operations which has a real chance of success in the changing years of the next decade and beyond.

CHAPTER 12

Command and Control of the Joint Army Group/Tactical Air Force Battle at the Operational Level

GENERAL SIR MARTIN FARNDALE

COMMAND in battle is a very personal matter. Any two commanders faced with the same situation will produce two different solutions, based on each's personality, character, judgement, and knowledge. Thus the training, selection, and appointment of commanders in the first place is of the greatest importance and will have a major effect on the outcome of battle. Nevertheless there are rules of the game which cannot be ignored. These concern the ability of a commander to assess his enemy correctly, impose his will over him and over his own command, to position himself correctly on the battlefield, and to make the correct decisions in time for them to be carried out by his subordinates. As the size of the battlefield, the pace of battle and the flow of information continue to increase, this all becomes more and more difficult to get right.

Because the art of command is so personal I have to address it so, using my own interpretation and experience, although I want to avoid this as much as possible and try to describe the daunting task that faces army and corps commanders in battle today. Inevitably what I have to say refers mainly to the Central Region. I want to look at the broad rules of the game and then to produce a set of principles or guidelines which could refer to operations at this level anywhere. Nothing I say can be precise or firm and no commander should attempt to adopt the command system I propose verbatim; rather he must adapt the principles to his own situation and personality. Although the principles should not change, the method of executing them will be continually changing with technological developments.

First, I want to look at the role of the commander at the operational level, as distinct from the commander at the strategic and the tactical levels. Then I will try to establish the principles. Next I will describe, in very general terms, a concept of operations at the operational level to see what it is that the operational commander is trying to do. Finally, I will suggest a system of command and control for the joint land/air battle at this level.

Role of the Commander

The art of war is divided broadly into the three areas of strategy, operations and tactics. The former is conducted at the politico-military level and is all about the allocation of priorities and resources to different theatres of war. Today it is also about the control of nuclear weapons. The second, or operational level, is concerned with the business of fighting the campaign within a theatre by commanding the formations and resources allotted to it. And the third, or tactical level, is concerned with fighting the enemy in the battles of the campaign in any one theatre. The essential difference between the operational and the tactical level of command is that the planning horizon, in terms of time, area and force capabilities, of the former considerably exceeds that of the latter.

Commanders at the strategic level are concerned with the overall management of the war. This is normally conducted from the seat of government, or as in NATO, from the Alliance Military Committee. Even so the direction of the war at this level does require command techniques to ensure that orders are timely and unambiguous, that objectives are crystal clear and that confidence is passed down the chain of command. History is littered with examples of failure: the strategic direction given to Hamilton at Gallipoli, Milne in Macedonia in World War I, Gort in France in World War II, or Stockwell at Suez in 1956. On the other hand the clarity of that direction at Alamein and on D-Day in World War II and in the Falklands campaign in 1982 ensured a confidence and will to win right down the chain of command which is so vital to success. Strategic commanders must give clear, long-term objectives to operational commanders, then allot them the priority their campaign has in the war and the resources with which to conduct it.

At the operational level the commander's role is to so employ his resources so that he achieves his strategic objectives. To do this he must first have so trained his command that they accept and fully understand his concept of operations and can carry it out. Then he must have an efficient system of finding out about his enemy and of quickly sorting out and assessing all the data collected. Then he must plan to seize the initiative, get on to the offensive and go all out to win. This means constantly planning ahead for the next battle. He must issue orders in good time for his subordinate tactical commanders to act. His main battle responsibilities are therefore:

- to monitor the contact battle in order to create the opportunity to commit powerful reserves;
- to command and control the deep battle against enemy follow-on forces (FOFA);
- to co-ordinate any rear area battle that develops;
- to prepare for nuclear operations.

To some extent he is involved in battle management at this level but he must also command otherwise he will never dominate his campaign. In addition, there will be times when he must also show personal leadership qualities.

At the tactical level, commanders are first and foremost leaders, because their ability to command in the true sense is limited by the orders of operational commanders above them. Nevertheless, within limits, there is certainly a requirement to demonstrate the ability to command as well. The blend between leadership and command will vary with level. For example, at battlegroup level commanders must be prepared to lead from the front as Colonel Jones did in the Falklands. At brigade level in an emergency, and probably in commanding counter-action the same applies, but at this level a commander must allocate some of his time to forward planning. Divisional commanders, in effect, have a foot in both the operational and the tactical camp, but normally they are tactical commanders because with modern communications it is possible to fight a division as a formation and to move it around rapidly. But, for example, an airmobile division operating at army group level, will be committed by the army group commander, but will operate under the operational control of a selected corps commander. These broad rules also apply to the conduct of air operations, except that most are conducted at the operational level (for example, the counter-air campaign and air interdiction) on a much tighter rein by the tactical air force commander. Combat at the tactical level in the air force refers to the much more personal business of fighting individual aircraft. The principle that airpower is best used concentrated at key times and on key targets ties up very well with the broad sequence of the land battle: first the contact battle to restore force ratios and to create the opportunity to seize the initiative, and later the commitment of powerful reserves at the operational level by the army commander in order to destroy the enemy's point of main effort.

The Principles

We will now leave the strategic and the tactical level of command and concentrate on the principles of command at the operational level. These principles refer to the maintenance of continuous command whatever the casualties and pressures of war. Again I must stress the personal nature of command and the need to adopt the principles to situations and personalities.

Operational commanders must:

- have studied the art of war at the operational level and have experience of command at subordinate levels. Experience is vital because judgement is of the essence when weighing the balance between a set of similar options. This does not imply having elderly commanders, far from it;
- be able to inspire confidence in their subordinates. This means that they must be known in their commands and this is especially so in allied formations. Confidence is essential here when a commander of one nation has to order men of another into situations where many will die;
- be fit and robust and possess courage, single-mindedness and optimism, otherwise they will not be able to survive the pressures involved. Once committed to a plan it is more than anything the commander's drive, energy and determination which will achieve success;
- study their opponent and aim to move with such accuracy and speed that they get inside their opponent's decision-making cycle and thus remain one jump ahead throughout;
- place themselves at the right place on the battlefield at the right time;
- having given orders, monitor progress and all battle functions without interference, but be ready to step if in things start to go wrong.
- be available and approachable to their subordinates and to their staffs;
- allot plenty of time to think well ahead and to consider all possible options. In this way they will be prepared for bad news and ready to act;
- visit subordinates when such visits have a purpose.

In short, a commander must dominate his command, set an impeccable example at all times, remain a shade aloof but also approachable, not allow himself to get involved in detail and concentrate his whole effort on his long-term objectives. By doing this he can constantly steer the efforts of his staff in the right direction, yet remain flexible to adjust to what they discover and recommend. For example, a commander will know how long his resources will last; he therefore knows that he must seize the initiative quickly and destroy his enemy by getting on to the offensive as soon as possible. This gives him a broad sequence of events that he wants to achieve. Once the enemy has committed himself, he must then decide as quickly as he can where his point of decision is to be, that is, the place where he wants to fight his key battle, so he can gear all his energies to achieve it.

There are two broad types of command at any level which are complementary to each other. The first is command before combat has started or when a commander's command is not in contact. This is the time for a commander to leave things to his staff. But there is much for him to do at this stage. First he can visit his units, talk to his men, visit battle positions, gun areas, logistic installations and reserves, doing his best to inspire them with the task ahead and giving them confidence. Whilst doing this he can also assess their morale and will to fight and he can check that his orders are, in fact, getting right down to the fighting men; he can also note their needs and the problems for staff action on his return. Today with helicopters he can cover much ground in a day. He can also visit subordinate commanders to ensure that they understand his concept (especially in a multinational force); but he must not interfere with local tactical plans unless they are clearly very wrong. It is at this time that the commander is acting much more in his capacity as a leader. Second, he can think. Time spent quietly assessing the situation developing in front of him will be well spent. Third, he can rest. He must not allow himself to get over-extended and tired at this stage.

The second type of command occurs when a commander's force is in combat. Here nothing must distract him from the business of winning the battles of the campaign. He must spend as much time as necessary at central communications and intelligence with his command group, monitoring and studying events in order to select the moment to give the orders that will enable him to seize the initiative, get on to the offensive and go all out to win while his resources last. He and he alone can authorise major action; the plan will be his and he must take full responsibility for it. What is more, the time-window for action will be short and he must be present when it occurs. He can delegate much of the execution of his plan once he has given his orders. Much of his time must therefore be spent at his headquarters, but, once he has approved the plan and given his orders, provided he has good communications, he can and should move around; indeed on occasions he must. Whatever he does, however, he must never allow himself to be away from his headquarters without communications.

Operational Concepts

Before deciding how these principles might work in practice it is necessary to examine a possible sequence of battle. A joint land/air battle ranging over many thousands of square miles relies on a very large team of commanders, probably of several nations, of both services and of all arms and services in the army, at all levels, all pulling in the same direction within a concept that they all understand and believe in. This is what training in peacetime must have achieved before the war starts. No commander can be everywhere, and he must rely on his subordinates doing the right thing at the right time. They can only do this if they thoroughly understand the concept of operations which will spell out the army commander's method of defeating the enemy. Every subordinate commander must be crystal clear as to his task and the part he has to play in that concept. Whether he is a forward corps, division or brigade, whether a reserve formation, an artillery, engineer or logistic commander he must understand how to conduct his battle to conform with the concept and so place his command correctly within it. For this he needs clear objectives, a clear definition of his resources, and then outline orders and considerable freedom of action.

For example, a corps commander may be told that his task is the defeat of the lead echelon attacks without calling on army group reserves. A reserve divisional commander might be given a series of possible options and the sort of situation that might cause him to be committed. Air and artillery commanders can be given a series of priorities and zones and told to achieve maximum attrition of the enemy before he reaches a given area. Thus a broad sequence of battle emerges but still with plenty of flexibility in it. Orders will be sufficient to enable commanders to predict what their superiors are trying to do, so that they can position their own commands in context and be poised and ready in the right place for the next phase. They can also allocate their resources so that they have enough remaining for the critical moment when it comes. Intelligence staffs can direct their energies in the right direction without too much supervision, and logistic staffs can build up the right stocks at the right place at the right time. Thus even if there is massive electronic interference or combat destruction, paralysis will not set in.

Care must be taken not to make a concept into a plan nor to spell it out in too much detail because no one can foresee how the battle will go and flexibility is essential until the moment of decision arrives. A commander at the operational level must be constantly testing his thinking against the principles of war. After all, he is looking for the moment when he can commit his reserves with maximum surprise and effect, to achieve a concentration of force at the right place and the right time but with sufficient forces remaining to maintain momentum, once he makes his move. Therefore it is the concept of operations at army group/tactical air force level that is all important. For only at this level can the best possible allocation of force be made as the enemy commits himself. From this concept the corps commanders can make their plans and give orders to tactical commanders.

A possible sequence might be as follows. Once deployment, reinforcement, and preparation are complete and the initial hostile act has occurred, the priority will be on intelligence and on the outcome of the initial tactical battles to find out where the enemy's main point of effort is. At the same time, and of equal priority, will be the conduct of the first part of the air and long-range artillery battles, which will include air-defence and air-interdiction attacks on enemy air assets and counter-battery attacks. Throughout this battle of attrition at long range it is essential to try to reduce the adverse ratio which will inevitably be present in the early stages. Then, as the enemy commits his first echelon reserves, corps commanders must understand that they must have their own reserves poised and ready to strike. By this time the true enemy plan should be emerging and the army commander can begin the battle drill necessary to commit his own reserves. At this stage he will also be supervising the build-up of more reserves in order to maintain the momentum of his attack once it is launched. He must also realise that his resources are finite, and that once these reserves are all committed he will have to call for nuclear weapons. Planning for this must be occurring all the time; this too will need his broad direction and priorities.

A System of Command

It is now possible to examine a system of joint command to fight this battle at the operational level: a system which covers the conduct of battle at army group/tactical air force and corps/ASOC levels. Such a system must be robust enough to survive modern war, including nuclear operations; it must have considerable redundancy and it must also be responsive enough to cope with the ever increasing speed of modern combat. Assuming, therefore, that the commander has prepared himself and trained his command, what structure does he need and how best to use it? Since all battles will consist of some combination of fire and manœuvre integrated together, he must ensure that above all these two functions are properly catered for.

At corps level the commander needs an artillery, an air and an engineer commander alongside him at all times. He also needs an air-defence, a heavy artillery and an aviation commander at his headquarters, who are commanding their aspects of the battle under his priorities but under the direction of the chief of staff. It is at this level too that all agencies connected with the collection of information report, and there must be a rapid system for converting this into intelligence, presenting it to the commander and passing it upwards and downwards.

At army group level the commander works closely with the commander of the tactical air force. Their staffs work under the direction of their chiefs of staff and it is imperative that they can work well together. More could be done at this level to integrate staffs, particularly in the fields of intelligence and target assessment. At this level too there could soon be a need for an artillery commander to co-ordinate the long-range rocket capability that shortly comes into service in large numbers. This must attack targets across corps boundaries and be well tied in with the air-interdiction battle. He could also co-ordinate the ground-to-air defence battle with air operations, which, with the new command and control systems coming into service, he will be able to do. These are two functions that need firm and clear direction if the best is to be got out of them, especially since both link closely to air operations at this level. The operations staff have neither the knowledge, time nor capacity to do this on a permanent basis. Such a commander can also relieve the commanding general of the detail of nuclear planning. Unless this is done much of the effect of these powerful weapons will not be exploited to the full. However, much can be done by developing a joint, integrated army/air force air-interdiction cell at the joint headquarters to fight the FOFA battle.

During the battle there will be times when the commander is drawn forward to cope with unexpected and critical situations. It will seldom be wise for the army and the air commander to leave the headquarters together on the same mission. However if the army commander does go to visit one of his corps, it will be essential that an air force one- or two-star general goes with him, with power to act on behalf of the tactical air force commander.

The commander's relationship with his chief of staff is critical. The two must respect and understand each other fully. They must also have full confidence in each other and know instinctively and accurately how to act in the absence of the other. The chief of staff must know how far to go in the absence of the commander and feel confident in doing so. The commander must feel that, once he has given his orders, they will be carried out within acceptable parameters and that the chief of staff will conduct the battle in accordance with them. The chief of staff must, however, be quick to appreciate new situations developing and modify his plans accordingly or, if necessary, approach his commander with recommendations. Montgomery and de Guingand and Balck and von Mellenthin in World War II are examples of the system working well. Moreover, in these days such a relationship will often have to be conducted across national boundaries and this calls for a very special ability to understand and to get on with people on the part of both.

As war clouds gather, the commander must assert his influence, he must anticipate events and ensure that his staff have clear direction and priorities. He must then contact his subordinates to ensure that they too are clear as to the developing situation. He may be able to summon them to his own location to brief them and to have informal discussions about their problems. Again, this is the more important when commanders of several nations are involved. This could well be the last time they are all together, so it is an important meeting to enable the commander to stress key issues, go over salient points of the concept and bind his team together.

As the enemy attacks, the requirement is for a first rate flow of information being addressed by joint land/air intelligence staffs to produce a single, agreed, and, as far as possible, verified, situation for both land and air commanders to assess and use for planning. Ideally this should be an extension of normal peacetime practice, and the staffs concerned should not have to be moved as hostilities begin. This means a location with sufficient protection to survive early air attacks. By this time commanders will have completed their initial visits, watched the process of deployment, outloading and preparation in progress and have made such adjustments to their plans as may be necessary in order to cope with the evolving situation. They will have talked to a selection of their subordinate commanders and men and have a feel for their mood, morale, and capability.

By now the army and air force headquarters will be deploying to their 'main' war locations. Here the first problems begin. There is a theory that such headquarters should be in a permanent hole in the ground with full conventional and nuclear protection and with permanently fixed communications. There is merit in this solution and it is much favoured by air force commanders, as it fits their operational requirements very well. However, because such a headquarters can never move, it must be well to the rear so that it has a chance of continuing to function no matter what happens in battle. This is fine for airmen who are issuing their orders to static airfields and installations, themselves located well to the rear. But it has problems for the soldier. First, no matter how carefully sited, such a headquarters could well turn out to be in the wrong place for the land battle. Second, its location is bound to become known to the enemy who will certainly try to destroy it or at least to neutralise it. The human brain is very effective at making plans to achieve this as history shows. The immune fortress at Eben Emael on the Maas was penetrated and captured by the Germans in just 20 minutes in 1940. But more than that, the land battle is bound to evolve in an unpredictable way and this will inevitably draw the army commander forward at least from time to time. Where then should the commander be in battle?

There is, of course, no precise answer but there are some principles. With modern communications the land commander at both army and corps level should be as far forward as he can be for most of the time. He must have with him his command group and sufficient staff to handle the end product of the work of the chief of staff and the main staff who remain at main headquarters, which is the centre of the communications and intelligence web. But what is 'forward'? It means the army commander being located at a forward headquarters not more than 30 minutes' flying time in a helicopter from each corps main headquarters

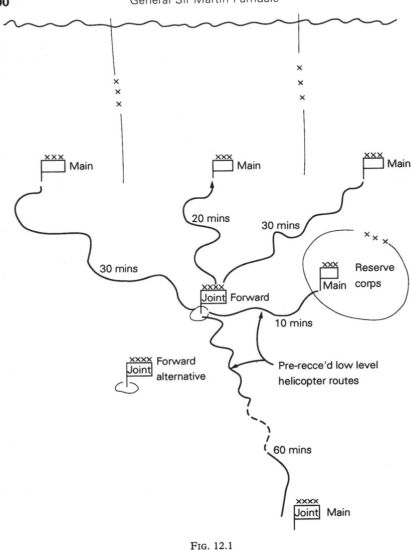

FIG. 12.1

Command and Control at the Army Group/Tactical Air Force Level.

and one hour's from his own main headquarters. For a corps commander the times are 20 minutes' flying time from each divisional main headquarters and 45 minutes' from his own main HQ. These forward headquarters must have enough capability to exist on a 24-hour basis and to handle all aspects of the battle in an emergency. Ideally there should be a duplicate HQ or 'step up' so that the actual point of command can change frequently. An army commander visiting a corps headquarters must not necessarily expect to see the corps commander himself, as he may well be forward. However, there is an option to meet, discuss the battle with the corps chief of staff and even to go further forward himself.

With such a command layout deployed, the command group can place itself on the battlefield at one of several places, giving it a good chance of being at the right place at the right time. They can move by helicopter on pre-reconnoitred routes flying ultra low, our own air defence having been warned in advance. At army group level at least two helicopters are needed, spreading the command group between them.

A word here about deputy commanders: many armies have them and there is some merit in them in a high pressure, fast moving and relentless campaign, but their job is always difficult to define. There is no real job for them while the commander and the chief of staff are up and about, although there is some merit in their being available when the commander is resting. They could sit in a resting step-up headquarters following the battle and ready to take over should disaster occur. But such a commander would be hard to justify in peacetime and yet, if he did not exist in peacetime, he would not be of much use in wartime. On balance, therefore, it is better not to have a special deputy commander. The right man to take command immediately the commander becomes a casualty is the artillery commander who, by the nature of his job, has been living the battle alongside the commander and is best placed to do so until either he is formally appointed or another is found.

The Command Cycle

Commanders are responsible for conducting operations in their areas of responsibility and these areas must reflect their ability to conduct operations in them. There is a tendency to make them too big, especially at corps level. Currently a corps commander has integral weapons to deal with an enemy out to only about 30 km. He can only do more if given the resources to do so (normally air power). This can extend his area out to some 80 km leaving the area beyond as the direct responsibility of the army commander.

If the concept demands that the corps commander must destroy the leading attacks himself, he must be left to get on with it. Nevertheless the army commander must monitor progress and provide such additional resources as he can, normally air power and/or airmobile forces. Meanwhile the army commander is preparing to use his own reserves to destroy the next wave of attacks in whatever format they arrive. Such operations will involve a concentration of firepower of all types and the committal of two or more armoured divisions. The battle drill to conduct such operations must begin about 48–60 hours for operational reserve divisions before the attacking force is required on its objectives and rather longer for corps-sized reserves. However, no enemy will be so obliging as to perform so predictably that this is made possible in precise terms. Thus the command system for the committal of reserves at the operational level must be flexible and simple. Inevitably reserves of this scale will have to be committed through more than one forward corps, and inevitably the artillery of more than one corps will have to be integrated together with that of the attacking formations. The sheer size of the problems of co-ordination of movement and passage of lines will require rapid and accurate staff work according to firm priorities.

In addition, the command relationships have to be laid down with great clarity. Are reserve forces being put under command of forward corps for them to mount offensive operations, or are the attacking formations passing through the forward corps and reporting direct to the army commander? What are the priorities for guns, engineers, aircraft, helicopters, routes and logistics? To do this successfully it is best, in the case when operational reserve divisions (usually two to achieve the required combat power) are being committed, to put them under the operational control of the in-place corps responsible for the attack. For corps-sized reserves it is preferable that the attacking corps commander 'grow up' with the situation so that he can see the problems emerging and start his staff working. He can do this best by being located close to the army group headquarters. It then soon becomes clear which is the most likely option and which in-place corps must become the master corps for the operation. Once this has occurred the plan is confirmed and the orders given so the army commander can order his rover group to move to the in-place corps headquarters which is most concerned with the operation, usually the corps responsible for securing the line of departure. The rover group is led by a deputy chief of staff. It should consist of an officer from each staff function fully briefed on the details of the plan. Also to that rover group should go representatives from the attacking formation(s), tactical air force headquarters, and from any other corps involved. Invariably the army commander should go himself to launch the operation and to stress personally the key features of the plan. Unless he does this the staffs of several nations meet about a plan which could be relatively new to them and much time could be lost in debate and discussion when the time for that had long since passed. On Exercise REFORGER 87 with all five corps headquarters of Northern Army Group in the field and 3rd US Corps doing the attacking, this system was used many times and in the end orders using the cover group method were taking only some two hours to complete.

Once per day it is essential for key members of the staff to come together to update the commander and, where necessary, present him with his future options. This procedure can also be quite quick. It serves to ensure that all staff branches are drawn together on to the same data baseline for the next 24 hours. But more important, it enables the commander to assess the situation, approve options and state his priorities for both the short and the long term; where necessary he can give orders. These should be joint army/air briefings, although both services need their own detailed meetings as well.

It is here that liaison officers can be of great value. There are two ways of using them. Either they can be based at army group headquarters and 'slipped' on missions from time to time, or they can remain located at corps headquarters and be called in once every 24 hours to attend the commander's briefing. At the end of the briefing they can be called together for a few minutes to be given any special and personal messages for the commanders and then return to brief the latter, having heard the full situation as seen at army group headquarters.

The main disadvantage of this system is that liaison officers have to be continually on the move, often over long distances. It could be better to exchange liaison officers between army group and corps headquarters on a more permanent basis; whatever way it is done they are of the greatest value.

After the commander's daily briefing it helps if a personal statement of his assessment and outline plan is sent to corps commanders giving them early warning of his intentions and an opportunity to ask questions before the chief of staff issues the battle directive. By sending these messages by computer, with corps commanders standing by their terminals, a quick and effective exchange of views can be achieved and, what is more, it helps to overcome any language problems and misunderstandings.

Usually by this time it is clear that one corps may be under much more pressure than the rest, and it is therefore appropriate for the commander to visit it by helicopter. He can be there in 30 minutes and spend an hour being briefed on the situation and listening to their concerns. Providing he has a senior airman with him, authorised to act for his commander, and providing he checks with his chief of staff that nothing else has changed, he can issue more orders whilst there. This would normally be a reallocation of resources, air power, artillery or logistics, permitting a very rapid reaction to a fast moving battle. Such visits can only be of the greatest value to clear up any misunderstandings which can so easily occur even with the best staff work.

The Future

The system I have described does work, but only just. It still requires much better communications at the higher levels and much improved information technology (IT) to make it function properly. I believe that, as we move into the next century, the pace of battle will increase further, the long-range, indirect, fire battle will increase in importance, and the need to commit even more powerful airmobile and armoured reserves even more quickly will occur. This system will cope provided nations really do agree to concepts of operations and structure and train themselves in accordance with single directives. Any nation which tries to go it alone, produce its own concepts, equipment and training doctrine will have a counter-productive effect on the whole.

I do not believe there is a case for removing a level of command. This will work on exercises, but in reality it will overload any one level, and then when this sustains casualties it will collapse in a fast moving battle. The increased accuracy of modern weapons will mean far greater destruction and casualties, and the effect of destroying a headquarters will be the greater. Far better to have more smaller, harder hitting formations so that if one is destroyed there are others available. But this means very slick and reliable communications and battle procedures.

Conclusion

My aim has been to give some idea of the practical problems facing corps and army group commanders and one possible way of solving them. This concept of command was created to meet the very special situation facing Northern Army Group in the mid 1980s. However, the system was created with the next generation of equipment in mind, Ptarmigan-type communications, Wavell-type IT systems, airmobile formations, powerful attack helicopters, MLRS and other long-range rocket systems, and more powerful and faster moving tanks, guns and APCs. Nevertheless it must evolve with modern technology and change. But I doubt if the principles will change. In the horror and chaos of modern conflict on a large scale, when the destruction is very great and casualties are very high, the need for commanders who survive to be able to impose their will over the enemy and their own forces, to be able to assess rapidly what is happening, to be at the right place at the right time and to get inside their opponent's decision-making cycle, will be greater than ever.

CHAPTER 13

Command and Control: A Falklands Analogy

MAJOR-GENERAL JULIAN THOMPSON

THE AUTHOR'S qualifications for writing this chapter are twofold. He has had much experience on the Northern Flank of the Alliance over a period of 10 years, both on the staff and in command, at various levels up to and including brigade commander and has spent much time walking the ground for operational planning purposes. The clue to his second, and more important qualification is contained in the title, *Command and Control*, having commanded a brigade of approximately 5,500 men in war.

Brigade commanders, even in war, are not usually concerned with planning and command and control at the strategic or operational level. But in a miniature war, the Falklands campaign of 1982, the author certainly got involved at the operational level, in that he was faced with the problem of translating political intent into military action, and was therefore forced to think at the operational level in order to identify the operational objective, the seizure of which would result in achievement of the strategic aim. And, although he might not have planned the strategy, his actions had a considerable bearing on it. In that campaign, for the planning phase and the first 10 days of the land battle, he was the operational level land commander. Although his command was small compared to a central European scenario in terms of numbers and destructive power, the implications of success, or otherwise, were politically devastating. This was clear to him at every stage in the operation. The translation of political intent into military action at this level was an area of great difficulty; and would have been helped by a clear directive received at an early stage, a subject to which we shall return.

It might be useful at this point to show what the command arrangements were, because there have been some misconceptions about them in the past, usually on the line of command and who exactly was the Task Force commander. The organisation was as shown in Figure 13.1.

195

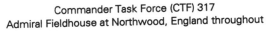

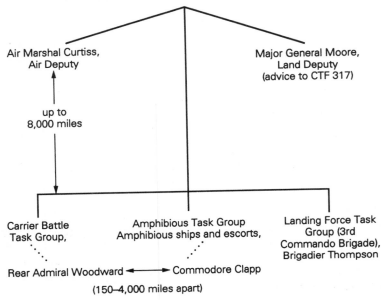

FIG. 13.1

Original Command Chain in the Falklands Campaign.

All Task Group commanders reported direct to Admiral Fieldhouse at Northwood. Commodore Clapp and Brigadier Thompson travelled south in the HQ ship, the LPD, HMS *Fearless*.

We shall address the amphibious phase of the campaign first, because this involved planning and command decisions at one-star level (Commanders Amphibious and Land Force Task Groups), that would have an effect on the whole outcome of the war, and ultimately on British standing in the eyes of the world. It was only in the joint headquarters aboard the command ship that the necessary information required to knit together that complex military operation, an amphibious landing, was held in sufficient detail. This is not to say that the proposed plans were not approved in outline by the Task Force Commander at Northwood and his superiors. But from the outset, the concept, including the shedding of options that were not feasible for a variety of reasons, and the detailed plans themselves, were the outcome of much thought, discussion, and hard work by Michael Clapp, Commodore Amphibious Warfare, the author, and their staffs. It is important to realise that they were planning operations in an area of the world of which few in the task force had personal knowledge. There were no plans in existence to cater for any landings to recapture the Falkland islands, nor any other reaction to an enemy invasion for that matter. Although no plan survives contact with the enemy, to misquote Moltke, having a plan at the conceptual stage of planning an operation, even if most of it is ultimately rejected or it is torn up and pasted together in a different form, can often be better than starting with a blank sheet of paper. Information on all the matters that concern a commander about to carry out an operation of this kind: beach gradients, surf conditions, beach exits, and enemy locations, was sparse or non-existent. There had been no planning exercises nor any study of the ground in the years leading up to this operation; rather different to the situation in the Central Region or anywhere else in the NATO area. It is also important to remember that, for good political reasons, the task groups had sailed from the United Kingdom in a considerable hurry, and without direction. This state of affairs lasted for some time. Indeed at a 'council of war' called by the Task Force Commander at Ascension Island on 17 April, 12 days after the task groups had left Britain, there was still discussion on fundamentals such as whether to land on East or West Falkland: an operational-level decision, because the outcome would affect the whole conduct of the war.

In contrast to most operations at the brigade level of command, where the commander is given his objective, phase lines, beaches, and so forth, and told to work out the details, all these, and much more, were selected by Clapp and the author, after studying what intelligence there was, and after taking advice from one officer with extensive local knowledge. Before arriving at the final, detailed plan, it and two other options had been passed in outline to Task Force Headquarters at Northwood. These other options were designed to take advantage of the situation, should the enemy decide to throw in the sponge at the approach of the landing force; in the author's opinion this was never very likely. Eventually the preferred option was approved. On the same day a directive was received. As time was by then running short, the orders for the amphibious landing had already been prepared by the Brigade staff in the headquarters ship some days before, based on the preferred option. These orders were given to all concerned on the day after the receipt of approval and the directive. At no stage during this time was the seizure of Port Stanley given as the operational objective. The Landing Force Commander and his staff arrived at this conclusion themselves, and tailored the plan accordingly.

The directive read as follows:

You are to secure a bridgehead on East Falkland, into which reinforcements can be landed, in which an airstrip can be established and from which operations to repossess the Falkland Islands can be achieved.

You are to push forward from the bridgehead area so far as the maintenance of its security allows, to gain information, to establish moral and physical domination over the enemy, and to forward the ultimate objective of repossession. You will retain operational control of all forces landed in the Falklands until I establish my Headquarters in the area. It is my intention to do this, aboard *Fearless*, as early as possible after the landing. I expect this to be approximately on $D + 7$. It is then my intention to land 5 Infantry Brigade into the beachhead and to develop operations for the complete repossession of the Falkland Islands.

Although it had been clear for some days that another brigade would be coming out, and that General Moore would be taking up the reins as land force commander, this was the first order to emanate from divisional headquarters. It was also the last until $D + 9$. General Moore joined the ship carrying Headquarters 5th Infantry Brigade at Ascension Island on 20 May, $D - 1$, and steamed south. The radio fit on board his ship was unsatisfactory, and he could not communicate at all with headquarters forward, until he stepped ashore on 30 May. So although the command chain changed on 20 May, to that shown in Figure 13.2, *de facto* it remained as in Figure 13.1 until 30 May. All signals from the Task Force Commander at Northwood were sent to General Moore, and fortunately were copied to Commander 3rd Commando Brigade, who took the appropriate action on the assumption that approval would be forthcoming.

It was important that Clapp and the author consulted each other at all stages in planning the amphibious operation, and took account of each other's requirements, which sometimes conflicted. Again, this is not often found at one-star level. Decisions affecting the degree of inter-service co-operation, and compromises on the push-pull of the differing imperatives of each service at operational level, are usually made at least corps – in the Central Region, between the Army and the Air Force and on the flanks of NATO between the Army/Marines, the Navy, and the Air Force. But there was no room for a unilateral approach to planning or the execution of the plan in the Falklands operation, whatever the command level. Both Clapp and I had experience of exercising in north Norway, therefore the use of the sea flank, in the development of their plans was almost second nature. The option they favoured, and which was approved by their superiors, was to land at San Carlos Water. The selection of this beachhead was in itself an example of compromise, and the need to satisfy the demands of more than one service. No other beachhead in East Falkland came anywhere near combining all the necessary specifications. It had one drawback from the landing forces point of view: the distance to Port Stanley, 50 miles as the crow flies. But this disadvantage was outweighed by a host of more pressing needs.

Even when the plan was agreed, there were a number of matters that had to be resolved by compromise, or by conceding that one's opposite number had an overriding case for 'doing it his way'. One example will suffice. From a landing force point of view, an H-hour as soon as possible after last light was preferable. This would give the maximum hours of darkness to land most of the infantry, the air defence, and the artillery,

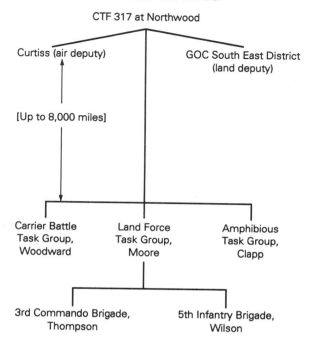

FIG. 13.2

Command Chain from 20 May, 1982.
All task group commanders reported direct to CTF 317.

and make a start on the logistic off-load, particularly of gun ammunition. This was important in the light of the shortage of helicopters and the slow turn-round times of the limited numbers of landing craft; three waves of landing craft were needed to land the infantry alone. None of this would have mattered had the air battle been won. But the prospect of carrying out the landing in daylight, in the face of air attack was not attractive. Seen from a naval point of view, the threat, and hence the preferred H-hour was different. Again because the air battle had not been won, Commodore Clapp wanted to transit the last 250 miles in darkness, with an H-hour at first light. His main worry was the air-launched Exocet. Once in the beachhead area of San Carlos Water, an air-launched Exocet attack could be discounted. A compromise was agreed on, by which the first half of the run-in towards the entrance to Falkland Sound was done in daylight, still within range of enemy air, but at the outer edge of his radius of action. The final, and potentially most dangerous part was done in darkness, with an H-hour of 2.30 a.m.

Because of delays, only the first wave landed in darkness, and the off-load was thereafter conducted while the amphibious ships and their escorts were under air attack, which resulted in considerable delays. However, this was preferable to running the gauntlet of the Argentine air force, with vulnerable troopships and transports, in daylight and well out to sea.

There was also at least one example of a lack of appreciation of another service's problems, a lesson for future operations world-wide. The headquarters at Northwood decided that the time zone for the operational area would be Zulu time (GMT), four hours behind local time. To the crew of a nuclear ballistic missile submarine, which never surfaces, and who are therefore oblivious of sunrise and sunset, carrying on as if they had not crossed four time zones matters little. For psychological reasons, soldiers find it better to link timings to night and day. Operating in the appropriate local time is also more satisfactory when talking to the local population, or arranging host-nation support.

The landing at San Carlos was planned to be in three phases, infantry in the first two of them, landing on four beaches, to secure the vital ground surrounding the beachhead. The third phase consisted of landing guns, air defence, and ammunition. One commando was kept afloat as reserve. Once the landing started the author was faced by the usual question, where to position himself to exercise command and control?

His command method on amphibious exercises was to stay in the command ship until the leading commando or battalion was ashore, and then fly ashore by helicopter. Concurrently his tactical headquarters vehicles and staff were landed nearby. This provided a 'foot on the ground' for command, while he roved by helicopter, vehicle, or on foot. This left him free to command and control the brigade as it came ashore on the same or adjacent beaches or landing zones and moved off to its objectives. His main headquarters, including his chief of staff, would remain on board until ordered ashore, usually within 24 hours. Their task was to monitor progress overall. As the tactical situation ashore unfolded, he ordered the necessary changes to the plan, often as a result of visits forward to commanding officers. The chief of staff who was totally 'in his commander's mind', modified the landing plan to comply with his orders. During this critical phase the chief of staff was co-located with the Commodore's staff, and able to consult them. This was most important, because the Commodore controlled all the means of ship–shore movement. On this operation the wide dispersal of the beaches, chosen for good tactical reasons, meant that, if the Brigade Commander positioned himself on one of them too soon, he might be in the wrong place when a crisis occurred elsewhere. However, he had every intention of starting to rove by helicopter as soon as possible, while the tactical headquarters was landed at the best place from a command

and control point of view, in the centre of what would be the beach-defence layout. Main headquarters would follow that night, stepping up to tactical headquarters.

In the event, communications did not work well to begin with; this is always a possibility because of the need to maintain radio silence before landing and exacerbated by the inadequate radio fit in the command ship; this has been recognised and reported after every exercise for years, but not rectified on the grounds of cost. Bad communications, the air attacks on the ships (which, while they were in progress, closed decks and sent helicopters to take cover in folds in the ground), and the shooting down of two brigade light helicopters by the small enemy ground force all led to an increasing sense of frustration at the lack of information. Two things were clear: first, the air situation was even less promising than had been forecast, and, second, now that the intelligence that there were few enemy in the beachhead area had proved correct, there was little point in keeping the reserve afloat, where they risked being sunk at any minute. They were ordered to land forthwith, and the necessary craft were extracted from the landing craft stream to collect them from their ship.

Eventually the author got away by helicopter. As always, there was no substitute for going forward, and I was able to come back at last light with a much clearer picture of the situation. This is no reflection on the highly efficient brigade staff, but merely proof that there is no substitute for talking face-to-face, particularly when communications are less than perfect. In this campaign they never were particularly good, and communications are likely to be considerably worse in a future war, whether in the Central Region or elsewhere, simply because of the massive effort that the enemy will put into disrupting them. Only if commanders at all levels are operating within the intent of their higher level commanders will they be able to continue to fight effectively when communications have been lost. This will be even more important on the Central Region where movement and battle will be at a much faster pace than in an out-of-area operation.

By the end of the first day it became clear that logistics would dictate the pace and texture of the battle; and they did so to the end. A few examples will suffice. Because of the adverse air situation, plans to keep most supplies afloat until they were needed had to be changed; and for the next few days all helicopters and landing craft were engaged in moving stocks ashore. The stores and plant to construct the air strip at San Carlos were lost in *Atlantic Conveyer*, so the strip was built mainly by hand using repair panels intended for the runway at Stanley. Air support for the land forces was never satisfactory until GR3 Harriers could be based forward; and impossible until the strip was built and sufficient fuel was available. Because of the precipitate departure of some of the stores ships from the beachhead, on the orders of the headquarters at Northwood, much of the equipment for the fuel installation was sailed before it could be unloaded, and was subsequently split up and distributed among several ships. In some cases, when the whereabouts of the equipment could be established, the ships were recalled for unloading. Where the correct item could not be found, the engineers had to make do and redesign the layout of that part of the installation. The speed at which this fuel installation was built was the critical path in the logistics build-up. Until it was dispensing fuel, not only for Harriers, but for helicopters, refuelling the latter was a matter of queuing up for a refill from one-spot decks from ships in the beachhead, in the pauses between air attacks. More helicopters would have resulted in longer queues. And helicopters were in desperately short supply. The most pressing customers for their services were the artillery for ammunition. The movement of guns and ammunition took precedence over all other loads, including rations. In the final battle, one battalion in 3rd Commando Brigade was without rations for 72 hours.

The author's orders to his Brigade before landing reflected what he understood the directive to require. In particular he stipulated that any major moves 'for the complete repossession of the Falkland Islands' (which could only be to close up on Port Stanley) were to wait until the second brigade arrived; but that forces would be pushed forward to gain information and to establish physical and moral domination over the enemy and to forward the ultimate objective of repossession. With all the helicopters and landing craft fully engaged in off-loading and the dominance of the enemy air force in daylight, particularly outside the air-defence umbrella of San Carlos, to push forward substantial forces from the beachhead immediately would have been tactically unsound. Even if the troops advanced on foot, their resupply would be tenuous, dependent as it was on helicopters in an adverse air situation. Without the advantage of foresight, it was not possible to forecast how supine the enemy land forces would be, and it was right to assume that any advance would be resisted, or at least harassed. To counter this would involve ammunition expenditure, the movement of guns, and logistic resupply outside the beachhead; for which, until more helicopters arrived, there was insufficient lift. Finally, even if the brigade breasted up to the enemy around Port Stanley without undue interference, since it lacked adequate means to move ammunition and other supplies forward there was little that could be done on arrival, particularly after the contents of each man's pack and ammunition pouches had been expended.

However, well before landing, the author had made his tactical plan in pursuit of what he assumed to be the operational level objective. He had selected the route to Port Stanley to approach the high ground overlooking the town from the west and north-west. This was chosen to take account of two factors, one tactical, the other logistical. Intelligence assessments at brigade level indicated that the enemy would expect an assault from the south or the north-east. This view was not fed from higher headquarters, but followed from an examination of what was known about his troop deployment and on trying to get into the mind of the enemy. The line of reasoning was based on the knowledge that a number of Argentine officers had trained in American military establishments and would be likely to espouse American methods, particularly their amphibious tactics: usually frontal assaults supported by massive firepower. As allies of the Americans, the British would be likely to employ the same tactics, so it was assessed that the enemy would expect a head-on assault, landing as near Port Stanley as possible. Consequently there was every likelihood that initially he would treat the landings at San Carlos as a feint or subsidiary landing, and not alter his dispositions. Subsequent events confirmed this assessment, as did radio intercepts and enemy after-action reports.

The boggy and rocky terrain was totally unsuitable for wheeled vehicles, and the landing force had only a limited number of oversnow tracked vehicles which could cope with the going, albeit at a very slow pace. To save valuable helicopter lift, it was necessary to use the sea flank to take the heavier loads, such as artillery ammunition, at least part of the way. The deep inlet of Port Salvador which would take ships up to LSL size was ideal, reducing the length of the helicopter line of communication by two-thirds. It could not, however, be used until the high ground overlooking the inlet had been secured. Failure to do so could have resulted in an earlier version of the bombing of ships at Bluff Cove, or, more correctly, Fitzroy.

To further this plan, starting on the night of *D*-day and for several nights thereafter, Special Forces and other patrols were lifted forward to key ground along the route and on to Mount Kent. The latter being the highest feature on the vital ground overlooking both the approaches to Port Stanley from the west and Port Salvador. Special Forces' task was to reconnoitre and prepare to receive the brigade when it moved forward by helicopter.

The nearest enemy forces over which it was possible to establish physical and moral dominance, as required by the directive, were at Darwin and Goose Green, some 23 to 25 km away. A battalion raid on these two settlements was therefore planned. It was subsequently cancelled when it became apparent that the diversion of effort in terms of helicopter lift for artillery to support the raid would severely hamper the move forward of the SAS to seize landing zones for the eventual move forward of the brigade. At this stage the author was being summoned to the satellite communication system at least twice daily, to be asked about the plan for the move out of the beachhead, and it was clear that political pressure was being applied to get moving out of the beachhead and 'invest' Stanley, before the arrival of 5th Infantry Brigade, despite the wording of the directive. For the reasons given above, he was unable to refer to General Moore for confirmation that this early move suited his plans. He therefore brought forward the plan for the move forward of the brigade. This relied on the use of the four Chinook heavy-lift helicopters and 12 medium-lift helicopters being brought south in the ship *Atlantic Conveyer*, in addition to the helicopters already in the beachhead, to lift the brigade forward in a series of night moves. The ship was sunk the day before she was due to arrive, taking all but one Chinook and all the Wessex helicopters to the bottom. However, the pressure to move was maintained and, in addition, there was a clear order to take Darwin and Goose Green. Some rapid planning took place, which resulted in one battalion assaulting Darwin and Goose Green, while a battalion and a commando marched via Douglas Settlement and Teal Inlet to join up with a commando lifted forward over two nights to Mount Kent.

Possibly because the Goose Green operation was, in the author's mind, an operational diversion from the aim of getting on to the high ground overlooking Stanley (and his opinion has not changed), he did not pay enough attention to its planning and execution. It might have helped if the requirement to capture Goose Green and Darwin could have been articulated as a change in intent for perfectly understandable political reasons. In particular, he blames himself for not taking his tactical headquarters and another battalion or commando down to fight a co-ordinated battle. These were considerable errors on his part. This is not to imply any criticism of the battalion, which won a 'soldier's battle' with little assistance from anybody. In this battle he used the liaison officer system to good effect, sending with the battalion a battle-experienced officer who had fought in the Dhofar. He had a radio on a one-to-one direct link to the brigade commander. The liaison officer's experience enabled him to read the battle and to keep the brigade commander in the picture as it unfolded. This reduced the number of times the busy commanding officer had to be summoned to the radio or give a situation report. The liaison officer was particularly useful when the commanding officer was killed and the second-in-command took over. The second-in-command could do without a brigade commander breathing down his neck while he was trying to pick up the pieces, find out what was going on, and assume command. The liaison officer was able to report on progress, and pass back the new commanding officer's intentions. In this role an officer accustomed to the sights and sounds of combat is invaluable; he can read the battle, and is not unduly distracted by noise and confusion. An inexperienced officer might be unduly affected by his first battle experience to the detriment of his judgement. The use of a liaison officer is not a substitute for face-to-face command or direct radio conversations between commanders, but is a very useful command tool. He is in van Creveld's words, a 'directed telescope'.

Darwin and Goose Green had been in British hands for two days and the moves described above were well under way when General Moore arrived at the beachhead. He immediately endorsed the existing plans, and the author handed over the land force command, reverting to the command of his brigade alone. Space does not permit any description of the two night battles in which his brigade subsequently took part and the follow-up of the defeated enemy, all of which were considerably more satisfying professionally, and less frustrating, than what had gone before. But by this time the author was merely a brigade commander, not a land force commander, and brigade-level decisions are outside the scope of this chapter.

A number of lessons were learned, or rather relearned. A study of military history shows that the lessons learned each time are rarely, if ever, new. At first glance, not all of them appeared to concern command and control, but they were matters that impinged on planning and had to be born in mind throughout.

First, and without apology for putting it first, there was the overriding importance of logistics. General Sir David Fraser has written: 'In any battle the size, composition and tactical handling of the effective force at the critical point may determine the outcome; but in any campaign the ability to produce this force depends not only upon the overall strength of the army, but upon the lines of communication and supply.'[1]

The second lesson, and linked to the first, in the huge expenditure of ammunition in war, and the need to plan for it. There is a correlation between Alanbrooke's statement in 1923, as a member of the Directing Staff at the Staff College, 'in our pre-war concepts we had failed to appreciate the true influence of fire-power in modern battle', and the false lessons learned in peacetime training about ammunition expenditure. This is because on peacetime exercises, to paraphrase Alanbrooke, the devastating effect of artillery and other fire cannot be realistically simulated, and troops behave as if that effect did not exist. Moves take place without the expenditure of ammunition, and the logistic imperatives are never allowed to assert themselves.

The third is the need to command from the right location; this must be a place where the commander can carry out three command and control functions:

- keeping himself informed, by seeing for himself, or by speaking, face-to-face, or on the radio;
- be able to consult those who will assist him in sorting out any problems and making his plan, for example, his gunner, or his helicopter commander; and

- having made his plan, or modifications to an existing plan, be able to pass his orders to those who have to carry it out.

If the commander is in a position where he is not able to do any one of these three except for brief periods, when, for example, he is moving by helicopter, he is in the wrong place. Depending on the nature of the battle, the 'right' place will vary; it could be a vantage point, a command vehicle, or a command post; there are a number of options. And the 'right' place may change as the battle develops.

Fourth is the value of the 'directed telescope'.

Fifth is the need for a worked-up staff, who understand how the commander operates, and who are trusted by the subordinate units. This calls for stability in our peacetime organisations, so that staffs are not hurriedly thrown together at the last moment.

Sixth is the need for subordinates to be given clear direction, and then be left to carry out the task, with as much moral and practical support as possible. Modern communications give those in the rear the ability to over-command their subordinates, over unlimited distances. Van Creveld has described an Austrian officer in 1859 writing of 'the fear which seized him' on hearing that an Austrian general commanding in Italy was in direct communication with Vienna by telegraph. 'This fear proved to be well-founded. A commander who is tied down this way is really to be pitied; he has two enemies to defeat, one in front and another in the rear . . . everything combines to rob the commander of his force and independence, partly by accident, partly by design.'[2]

Finally, without well-trained, well-led, and determined troops, the most brilliant commander, the best plan, and the slickest command and control system, are all to no avail.

CHAPTER 14

Interdiction and Follow-on Forces Attack

AIR CHIEF MARSHAL SIR ANTHONY SKINGSLEY

THE TITLE of this chapter might seem to imply that two separate entities are being discussed. However, the chapter is intended first to show that the topics are very closely related, and thereafter to explain from a Central Region perspective the concept of Follow-On Forces Attack (FOFA), the capabilities needed in order to meet the mission, how its prosecution is envisaged and how it applies to the future. There are those who are under the misapprehension that FOFA is a concept for the future. However, FOFA is not new; it is planned and can be executed with today's systems, equipment, and staffs. Certainly improvements are necessary to enhance our capability to accomplish FOFA and thereby to deter aggression and, should deterrence fail, to defend Central Europe.

A definition of interdiction is 'operations conducted to destroy, neutralise or delay the enemy's military potential before it can be brought to bear effectively against friendly forces'. With this in mind, it is possible to trace a basic evolution of interdiction, the origins of which are difficult to ascertain. However, the concept became evident when commanders started looking beyond tactical engagements. For example, a case can be made that interdiction was the intent when, in 1704, the Duke of Marlborough and Prince Eugene intercepted the forces of Marshal Tallard in Bavaria at Blenheim, thereby both preventing them from joining the armies threatening Vienna and preserving the integrity of the Grand Alliance.

The first documented, effective use of interdiction was the sea-borne blockade waged by the British Navy against colonial ports in the American War of Independence. This was so effective that a special fast frigate and tactics were developed to counter the greater sea power and the larger vessels of the blockading fleet. Perhaps from this experience the Americans were convinced of the utility of a blockade to prevent war materials from reaching an adversary dependent on imports for the sustenance of their warfighting capability. In the American Civil War the application of the Union's superior naval forces in such a manner sealed the Confederate States' fate early.

The first effective use of submarines in maritime interdiction was during the First World War. Used primarily against commercial vessels instead of warships, in an attempt to blockade Britain, the unannounced attack on unarmed shipping was considered heinous and eventually brought the United States into the war. The success of this sea interdiction, however, provided the basis for its extension into World War II.

As with the submarine, the aircraft brought a new dimension to war, and while the use of air power did not decisively affect the conduct of World War I, events in the war had a profound effect on the use of air power. Marshal of the RAF Sir Hugh Trenchard, regarded as the father of the RAF and the leading proponent and pioneer of strategic aviation in World War I, was impressed with the fact that aircraft could be used to attack the enemy at places other than the front lines, where the German Army's means of supply, subsistence and replacement could be destroyed. This mission for the new air arm had to wait for the future, however, because the air resources were too scarce for such a project. Trenchard did, nevertheless, direct the attack on German airfields, which dramatically reduced the German capability both to attack Allied rear areas and to support ground forces in the field. This type of air interdiction is considered so important and specific in intent that today it is classified as a separate mission called *offensive counter air*.

World War I revealed the extent to which military capacity depends on industrial capacity to manufacture the tanks, submarines, lorries, aircraft, artillery and ammunition necessary to wage war. This increased mechanisation of war incorporated another product necessary to utilise this military potential: oil. Manufacturing capability and the system for its delivery to combat units were obvious targets for the new concept of air interdiction.

The extent to which British, and later American, forces depended on the sea lanes of the North Atlantic for the build up of supplies and equipment was exploited by the German use of submarines, as sea-lane interdiction became an objective of the Axis in World War II. With a more extensive fleet organised into groups for attack, German U-boats targeted specific convoys from just off the American coast all the way to Britain. While the life line was never severed, the loss of much of these supplies and equipment had a debilitating effect on the Allied prosecution of the war. But this was a protracted campaign for which counter-measures were developed and in which Allied industrial capacity was able to compensate.

The air interdiction of Germany's war manufacturing capability was also protracted. Portions of this strategic bombing campaign which were directed against specific interdiction targets were quite effective; for example, the delay in aircraft production resulting from bombardment of aircraft and engine factories permitted, in large part, the attainment of allied air superiority. But even the ravaged economy of Nazi Germany was able to overcome this and in the end it was the interdiction of the fuel supply which kept the available aircraft on the ground.

A more dramatic effect occurred when air interdiction was co-ordinated with the land commander's operational requirements in specific campaigns. The three examples which follows illustrate the importance of this synchronisation, known today as 'jointness'.

In the Italian campaign in early 1944, Allied forces languished in virtual stalemate. Despite Allied air superiority, the Germans faced only minor problems owing to the inconsistency and the lack of focus of the air interdiction effort. Operation DIADEM, beginning in May, co-ordinated the operational ground campaign with the air interdiction effort, which focused on the reserves and the resupply network of the engaged German forces. The Germans were forced to abandon rail traffic south of Florence, as air interdiction was initially concentrated on this network. This forced them to transport supplies by road, tieing up scarce vehicles, wasting fuel and degrading the tactical mobility of their combat units. Massive and continuous diversions of tactical vehicles proved necessary, resulting in severely reduced combat capability. The Germans were unable to respond rapidly, and those units which attemped to move on the road during the day incurred heavy losses from tactical air interdiction. The stalemate was over.

At the same time, Allied air interdiction was preparing the way for the invasion of Normandy. Normandy was chosen as the invasion because, *inter alia*, it was within range of fighter aircraft operating from southern Britain, and it could be effectively isolated from the rest of France. The bridges across the Seine and Loire rivers west of Paris were destroyed in the weeks and days before the landings. The specific intent was to keep the force ratios at the beachhead at a manageable level. As the British and Canadian forces landed at *Gold*, *Juno* and *Sword* beaches, the movement of Panzer reserves was disrupted and delayed until the Allies obtained a foothold. By the time the Panzers were able to engage, they had been weakened by continuous air attack. Once the beachheads were estab-lished, it became a race to build up forces. This race would normally have been won by the German land transportation, but, because of the delays caused by the destruction of the rail system and the many diversions caused by fighter-bomber attacks on road traffic, it was won instead by the Allied amphibious supply. During the breakout Operation COBRA, the ground scheme of manœuvre was again co-ordinated with air interdiction of the German forces. Constrained to movement at night and with battle plans disrupted by the delay of critical divisions, the Germans were unable to match the operational mobility and pace of the Allied attacks.

Application of this principle of synchronisation in a defensive situation, such as in the Ardennes counter-offensive, is directly applicable to the central European situation today. A rapid breakthrough and a high rate of advance to Antwerp by 6th SS Panzer Army would have isolated 1st US Army and 2nd British Army from their supplies. This breakthrough attempt was foiled by a combined operation of ground and air forces. The terrain was not conducive to the movement of armour. However, the air interdiction which could fly in the prevailing poor weather was able to produce delays in the advancing armour until ground forces could reach better defensive positions. When the weather finally cleared, air interdiction closed many routes and stopped the fuel and ammunition critical to the German advance. The offensive was over, and, as the German forces withdrew, Allied fighter-bombers interdicted a bridge over the Our river at Dasburg. As the forces bunched up behind this obstacle, other fighters systematically destroyed 3,000 vehicles.

Moving forward to the confrontation which existed in Europe over recent years, a wide range of scenarios could be envisaged. However, the most probable includes a period of mobilisation which results in massed forces facing each other along the inner German border. The area is limited and too small for the Soviet Union forces to crowd into near the front. Moreover, such a deployment would provide all too easy targets for NATO air attacks and would restrict the movement of Soviet manœuvre groups. Thus the Soviet doctrine of echeloning their forces has been developed, not only as a counter to the nuclear threat, but also to 'meter' their forces to the front. This would allow exploitation of breakthrough opportunities developed by the initial echelons and provide fresh combat forces, while keeping the pressure on beleagured and tired NATO forces.

Although well-equipped and well-trained, NATO ground forces are vastly outnumbered with both less sustainability than the Soviet forces and only limited interoperability. This level of conventional inferiority can be traced to the unwillingness of NATO nations to make available the personnel, money and resources established as necessary at the Lisbon Conference in 1952. Instead of matching the Soviet conventional power maintained in Eastern Europe, the NATO nations decided in 1954 to allow their security to rest on the nuclear capability of the United States, with any attack inviting massive retaliation. The evolution of NATO strategy through 'trip-wire' to 'flexible response' is well known and documented. Conventional capability has been markedly improved over the years in support of flexible response, but a severe imbalance remains, made more serious by the steadily improving quality of Soviet equipment. Thus, even today, a political decision to escalate to the use of theatre nuclear weapons remains an element of Alliance strategy. The remorseless growth of the Soviet Union's own nuclear capability, however, plus a changed political climate, led by the end of the 1970s to increasing pressure for the nuclear threshold to be raised. This demanded improved covential capabilities and a prolonged conventional phase to any hostilities before the resort to nuclear weapons became unavoidable. One of the best ways to achieve this was thought to be to interdict the successive echelons of Soviet forces before they could engage NATO forward defenders and thus provide an opportunity for Allied ground commanders to seize the initiative. The aim would be to relieve the weight of the attack both in magnitude and in time, in order that our tactical commanders could manage the tactical battles at the FEBA. Time would also be needed both to commit reserves where they would be of most benefit to the operational commander's scheme of manœuvre and to regroup and reconstitute tired defenders. In short, the Soviet follow-on forces must be made to fight their way to the front, expending time, energy, munitions, capability, and morale in the process.

Considerable work had been carried out on this concept over a number of years by 2 ATAF and Northern Army Group, but it was not accepted as an ACE-wide philosophy until the early 1980s, when the US Army adopted it as a result of studies into the Air/Land Battle. The then SACEUR, General Bernard Rogers, received a briefing under the title *Attack of the Follow-on Forces*. Although the briefing did not get an easy reception, the merits of the concept were apparent, and it was relatively quickly adopted as ACE policy, under the slightly amended title of Follow-on Forces Attack – 'FOFA' was a more appealing acronym than 'AFOF'! SACEUR's endorsement gave a very important focus to the interdiction philosophy and considerable impetus to the acquisition of the necessary, improved systems.

FOFA is defined as: 'Military actions to delay, disrupt and destroy the enemy's follow-on forces and to neutralise other military resources in depth before they can be brought to bear effectively against NATO forces'. There is a clear resemblance in this definition to that of air interdiction: 'Air operations conducted to destroy, neutralise or delay the enemy's military potential before it can be brought to bear effectively against friendly forces at such distance from friendly forces that detailed integration of each air mission with the fire and movement of friendly forces is not required'. It should by now be apparent that this similarity is no accident, since the concept evolved from the work previously carried out in the Central

Region and, therefore, already reflected in the definitions in NATO tactical manuals.

The NATO Military Committee and SACEUR subsequently identified those key missions which are vital both to deterrence and, should the Soviet Union launch an attack, to the restoration of NATO's territorial integrity. It is not surprising that FOFA is one of these. It is foreseen as being prosecuted in an integrated campaign along with forward defence, designated 'defeat of the lead echelon', the gaining and maintaining of a favourable air situation, and rear area operations, which maintain our own forces' freedom of movement. Each of these elements is essential to an integrated conventional defence campaign in the Central Region. For example, it clearly makes little sense to expend valuable assets on follow-on forces if forward defence cannot be maintained.

It is important to highlight that we do not expect to stop follow-on forces completely. This would be an impossible task which would be sure to dilute the power we do possess. The objectives of FOFA, derived from the military requirements and strategy, are to:

- delay forward movement and deployment of Soviet forces which are not engaged at the front lines;
- disrupt command and control, and movement and engagement plans;
- cause attrition to the forces, particularly armour, as they deploy forward into intermediate and final assemblies; and to shape the battlefield by having control over the movement options which are available to the Soviet commander.

In today's rapidly developing battlefield, target studies have shown that it will be more important to focus on the combat forces themselves than on their logistic supplies. Very often what would appear to be lucrative targets may have to be rejected because more critical elements need attention. FOFA has to be a sustained effort conducted from just behind the forces in contact, to as far into the depth of the enemy as our means of attack can reach. Continued attacks on his forces, both day and night, will not allow the enemy sanctuary, will cause him to divert resources to their protection and will keep the pressure on them as they fight their way to the front.

Planners will identify targets for engagement within a wide range of target sets. These targets must be selected to accomplish specific objectives related to specified units moving forward. The phrase 'target sets' is used because attacks on all types of target are necessary to produce the desired cumulative effects of delay, disruption and destruction. Hard, fixed targets, such as brigades and areas where roads and railroads congest, called 'choke points', cause considerable delay if they must be by-passed or repaired. Destruction of command and control centres, both hardened and soft, mobile varieties, if identified, can cause disruption of routes of advance and timing, especially when combined with the bridge and choke-point attacks. Destruction of soft, mobile targets, such as support vehicles and equipment, which are deploying with the follow-on forces will disrupt engagement plans, since self-evidently this equipment and support are needed or they would not be there. However, the primary targets, and the principal objects of concern for our land commanders, are the main battle tanks and armoured fighting vehicles which will eventually engage NATO forward positions.

But, FOFA is not new. The targets are still the combat forces which are assessed to pose the greatest threat to the battle at the FEBA and thereby to a cohesive forward defence. Thus FOFA is simply an evolution of interdiction which focuses more clearly on the critical elements of the enemy's attack plans. It is thus very much part of a defensive campaign, although it involves operations deep into enemy territory. The massive superiority in numbers of the Soviet armour and artillery has compelled us to focus on these forces and their support. The pace of modern warfare also forces us to apply interdiction in the operational context instead of in the strategic. There is no time to wait for effects to be evident. Therefore FOFA must be conducted in a co-ordinated manner in accordance with the ground force commander's scheme of manœuvre.

Since we must focus our limited resources on specific units and types of target during the FOFA campaign, there are three critical elements which must be improved to enhance our capability to attack follow-on forces. First our surveillance forces must have the means to locate and identify moving units. This will require constant surveillance with the capability of indicating moving targets. Stand-off airborne radar systems which operate over our territory and look deep into the Soviet rear areas will down-link data to command centres for immediate use. Thereafter closer looks may be required from battlefield overhead and penetration systems, with a variety of sensors, to provide a robust and survivable suite of systems. To give us the data that are needed in near real-time, these systems will need to feed into and ideally be controlled by NATO C^2 headquarters. Since they are acquired by nations, however, the essential is that they must be interoperable, both with one another and NATO command and control systems. This must be a designed requirement.

Our second requirement for FOFA is an ability rapidly to collate data input from many different systems, assess what has been collated and manage the output in order to ensure that the appropriate commanders have the information before making engagement decisions. Such a responsive command and control system must be assisted by computers which can match indications received from various sources to provide an analysis of all information gathered on the critical units being observed. An analysis of this kind is greater than the sum of its individual parts, because future movements and plans can be predicted which will open up many attack opportunities and options. It is obvious that the inputs to be processed (and the outputs to operational commanders) must have standard formats and all these systems must be interoperable. With this rapid reporting of intelligence gleaned from the collected data, existing engagement plans can be integrated and executed at the approximate time. Although computer-assisted, this process requires trained staffs knowledgeable in the collection systems being analysed, both in Soviet movement doctrine and tactics, and in our own attack capabilities.

This brings us to the last of our three requirements for effective FOFA: adequate weapons systems and weapons. From the outset, timeliness must be stressed, for it does little good to have near real-time information on enemy dispositions and movement if one cannot do anything about them. The intent of the use of modern technology in our surveillance, target acquisition and reconnaissance, and automatic, data-processing-assisted analysis and distribtion is to reduce the time from observation until engagement. This detection–decision–attack cycle must be completed and initiated again and again while enemy forces are concentrated for movement. Our procedures for the employment of air power must recognise this requirement. The destruction or mining of choke points will cause traffic to stop and bunch up, as is seen in a motorway traffic jam. Similar attacks on the rear of the backed-up traffic will trap many targets and continued attacks on the queued-up vehicles should achieve significant attrition and disrupt engagement plans.

We need effective munitions to achieve these tasks. PGMs and air-delivered mines are available, but we need better anti-armour weapons with improved kill ratios, such as air-delivered dispensers with multiple terminally-guided submunitions. Moreover, the systems should be able to accomplish their missions in all types of weather, despite Soviet countermeasures, both day and night. Therefore, some sensors and weapons systems must be optimised for night or bad weather operations to ensure that follow-on forces will not have a sanctuary during these periods, when they are most likely to be moving forward. Maximum disruption to Soviet movement plans will require accurate timing, using the information discussed earlier. Additional delay can be created by attacking bridging and mine clearing equipment, which must work its way through stalled vehicles. Moreover, as the enemy forces deploy further forward, attack management may be employed to channel their movement, thereby enabling prediction of the best time and place for additional attacks and preparation by NATO ground forces for engagement at the FEBA.

If we are to meet our objectives, the attack on the follow-on forces cannot be piecemeal. It must be planned as a campaign, and it must be a joint land and air, co-ordinated and concentrated effort, which is followed up until the objectives are met or until the objective priorities change. To have the desired effect it must be prioritised, according to the land force commander's operational plan and scheme of manœuvre. He will set the objectives. Therefore, it is important that FOFA is directed from the joint operational level of command. In the European Central Region, this exists at the joint AFCENT/AAFCE war headquarters and the two joint Army Group (AG)/Allied Tactical Air Force (ATAF) headquarters, NORTHAG/2 ATAF and CENTAG/4 ATAF. At each of the AG/ATAG HQs, joint interdiction planning cells are established, which allocate not only air force aircraft to FOFA targets, but also, where available, army air and missile systems which can reach targets.

Mission assignments are further planned and tasked at Allied Tactical Operations Centres (ATOCs) and, in some cases, Air Support Operations Centres (ASOCs). Support for each mission, such as electronic warfare, suppression of enemy air defences, air-to-air refuelling, air-defence escort and surveillance system target updating, is allocated at the AG/ATAF and co-ordinated by the ATOCs in the same fashion. This process ensures centralised control and decentralised execution. When timing is the most critical element, which in FOFA is often the case, this arrangement is essential.

The requirements for surveillance, command, control, communication and intelligence (C^3I), the weapon systems, and the weapons needed to fulfil the FOFA mission will be expensive. However, the value of these systems is immeasurable. Simply providing NATO with a capability to extend conventional defence, while our political leaders convince the Soviet Union to halt its aggression is a sound return on investment. Moreover, these individual systems provide much more valuable support across the spectrum from training, through crisis management and transition to war, to war itself. The surveillance systems, particularly the stand-off collectors, are probably the most costly, but also provide the most collateral support. Indications of forward movement, concentration of forces and intentions can be determined from combinations of radar surveillance, with all-source intelligence. Thus early warning of impending crisis can be provided. This same non-obtrusive observation can support treaty verification by monitoring movements, communications, procedures and electronic emissions, which in turn may trigger on-site inspection or political enquiries. If these situations lead to a political crisis, the variety of stand-off and space detectors will provide our political leaders with a timely and accurate picture of Soviet civil and military preparations. This will ensure that decisions, such as the reinforcement decision, are based on definite signals and force movements, which provide clear intent to escalate the crisis. The deployment of their forces will be closely observed, which will provide our ground force commanders with the necessary intelligence to achieve the optimum deployment of covering forces in all types of warning scenario. The command, control, communication and intelligence systems, which fuse all of the data provided by NATO and national intelligence gathering systems, will be invaluable in providing rapid and accurate information for the support of political and military decisions throughout the crisis period. The development of trends, which can be compared to the original or subsequent databases, can show clear intent of either increasing or decreasing tension. The electronic, air and ground orders of battle will be continuously updated and provided to planning staffs to enable them to co-ordinate as much as possible before the outbreak of hostilities.

Should the Soviet Union decide to initiate hostilities, FOFA weapons systems could engage enemy forces throughout the depth of the Soviet Union operational area. Mechanisms that kill armour for FOFA will also kill armour in the FEBA area and have application for counter-battery fire. Mines that block river crossings in the Soviet rear will also delay or cause unacceptable losses upon initial echelon forces or others attempting breakthroughs. Area denial mines for crossroads and choke points will also deny areas near the FEBA, stop or hinder manœuvre groups and deny airfield operations. When mixed with timed anti-personnel, anti-armour and anti-material sub-munitions, extensive delays may be introduced, as well as harassment of the limited operations that are possible. Finally, night and all-weather penetration capability, as well as applying 24-hour a day pressure, will allow operations to proceed with reduced vulnerability of our attack aircraft.

Looking to the future against the backdrop of arms-control negotiations, possibilities now exist for dramatic force level and force structure changes. We look forward to substantial indications of a true change in the Soviet force structure from an offensive orientation to a defensive one. This will entail substantial unilateral Soviet cuts, a levelling of opposing forces and a disengagement along the central European borders.

Arms reduction should decrease the likelihood of military adventurism and thus enhance stability in central Europe. The final force levels are yet to be agreed, indeed are difficult to foresee precisely, but at any level we must be able to detect, locate, identify and, if necessary, stop follow-on forces from breaking through our remaining defences.

Whatever changes in Soviet concepts develop in the new circumstances of reduced and balanced force levels, it seems that the need for them to move fresh forces to the *Schwerpunkt* of the contact battle will remain and may, indeed, become even more critical as they may have much more difficulty achieving the force ratios necessary for effective attack. A more fluid and mobile battle area might well result, in which the ability to move forces quickly (or to prevent such movement) could assume critical importance. Certainly it would be true that if each side were led to reinforce through a breakdown in the hoped for stability, the Soviets could do so much more rapidly than the United States; FOFA in such circumstances would be a key capability for NATO, and there is no need for current work to be invalidated by arms control processes. On the contrary, we must take care that the agreements reached do not weaken our FOFA capabilities, a particular danger since FOFA, while in fact an integral part of a defensive capability and posture, can so easily be portrayed to the general public as offensive in nature. The deterrent value of the capabilities we have discussed in arguably more than ever valid and valuable in the probable circumstances of the next century.

In conclusion, as we look forward to our longer-term military requirements, we need to take full account of the possibility of significant force reductions which could have a major impact on the military concepts of both sides. While it may seem self-evident, we must be firm that any reductions take account of our need to retain the capability to defend ourselves if attacked. The arms control process is currently proceeding at a pace at which it could acquire a self-sustaining momentum, where such primary objectives could be easily forgotten amid other pressures.

We need to keep constantly in mind that our objective in arms control, which all right-thinking men and women must welcome and wholeheartedly pursue, is *enhanced security* at lower levels of armaments. The FOFA capability will have an important part to play in that enhanced security. We have a capability today, which has evolved from a more specific focusing and highlighting of the work Central Region planners have long carried out on interdiction – the antecedents of which go back many decades in military history. Emerging technologies will improve that capability, and at the same time enhance other conventional missions, provide indications and warning, allow better forward defence preparation and give political leaders assistance in making crisis management decisions. The improved capability that we are planning will be every bit as important in surveillance, in crisis management, in deterrence and (if necessary) in combat, in the greatly changed circumstances that seem to be in prospect in the 1990s. Through today's understandable euphoria, adequate provision for our security will continue to be a requirement.

(This essay represents the personal thoughts of the author and is not necessarily endorsed NATO policy.)

CHAPTER 15

Logistics Since 1945: From Complexity to Paralysis?

MARTIN VAN CREVELD

THE PURPOSE of this chapter is to present a brief outline of the development of logistics since the end of the Second World War. The discussion will be divided into two parts. First, I shall analyse the most important problems confronting modern military logistics and the attempts, successful or otherwise, to deal with them. Secondly, an attempt will be made to assess the interaction of logistics with warfare under present-day technological conditions.

To start, however, with a definition of the subject. In my book, *Supplying War*, I based myself on Jomini and defined logstics as 'the practical art of moving armies and keeping them supplied'.[1] Looking back from the vantage point of 12 years on, this definition is probably too narrow. I should now like to include under the rubric of logistics all the manifold functions that are required to keep an armed force provided with the necessities of life and combat, from the moment that its supplies leave the factory gates to the time they are consumed or expended in the field. Obviously this definition includes such standard quartermaster functions as the procurement, storage, transportation, and distribution of supplies. Less obviously, it also includes the manifold control, requisitioning, and record-keeping services that are needed to co-ordinate those functions. I do not, however, propose to discuss the processes whereby military suppliers are produced, this being a subject which is better classified under economics or mobilisation.[2] Nor does the present chapter have much to say concerning fields such as technical maintenance and repair services, even though their relevance to the problem of logistics is obvious.

Looking back, the most obvious change that has taken place since the end of the Second World War is that warfare has become much more capital-intensive. Calculating on a per-man basis, the amount of equipment in an American infantry regiment – lavishly equipped to

219

begin with – has risen as follows between 1943 and 1971: machine guns 74 per cent, vehicles 102 per cent, anti-tank weapons 159 per cent, radio sets 565 per cent.[3] Even greater was the change undergone by a Soviet rifle division between 1939 and 1973: while the number of personnel declined by a quarter, the number of radio sets in the unit increased five-fold, that of tanks 16-fold, that of armoured personnel carriers 37-fold, and the amount of horsepower per man 10-fold from three to 30.[4] Between 1967 and 1976 alone Soviet rifle divisions, undergoing modernisation, increased the number of artillery tubes in their tables of organisation by 60 per cent and that of multiple rocket launchers by almost 400 per cent.[5] Even so, these figures and many similar ones that could be adduced probably underestimate the true extent to which modern warfare has been penetrated by technology. Any discussion of artillery, for example, should mention the switch from towed to self-propelled weapons. Also, diachronic statistical comparisons leave out numerous kinds of equipment, ranging from helicopters through missiles and RPVs (remotely piloted vehicles) to every kind of electronic device, which did not even exist when World War II came to an end.

Logistically speaking, the two most important consequences of the introduction of more and more machines were growing complexity on the one hand and a much increased volume of supplies on the other. Concerning the first problem little need be said; by way of illustration, let the reader realise that the fuel-control system of a modern jet engine alone can consist of over 4,000 separate parts.[6] A logistic system intended to support even a single operational air base, for example, must have at hand tens if not hundreds of thousands of different items, ranging from the tiniest electronic components to the largest types of ammunition, which may weigh several tons. Probably the majority of these can be stored under ordinary conditions, but some will require special facilities designed to prevent deterioration. Some items can remain on the shelf and do not need to be inspected, but others – sophisticated modern munitions in particular – require periodic check-ups and maintenance. Some last almost indefinitely, but others have a specified lifetime and must be used, reconditioned, or discarded. Some are consumed on a day-to-day basis, but others are required only periodically or else on an irregular basis that is difficult if not impossible to forecast. It will be evident that co-ordinating all these different items, let alone the personnel and facilities needed for their use (both of which also form part of the logistic system) represents a formidable task indeed. As warfare becomes more capital-intensive, the dimensions of that task tend to expand not arithmetically but geometrically, since everything must be co-ordinated with everything else.

The second major consequence of the use of more and more hardware in war is, of course, the enormously increased volume of supplies needed to keep forces operational. Whereas the requirements of military men stay constant, more or less (the 'luxury' items so often inveighed against constitute a small and diminishing fraction of all supplies), those of machines tend to grow and grow. The result is that, unit for unit and operation for operation, the amount of supplies required-ammunition, fuel, and spare parts – has gone nowhere but up. Again, a few figures will illustrate the trend. In 1941–42, a well-equipped German Panzer division and its support required perhaps 350 tons a day when engaged on active operations.[7] The considerably more lavishly equipped Allied forces operating in France in 1944–45 required much more, perhaps as much as 650–700 tons per divisional slice.[8] By the time of the Korean War, the figure was in excess of a thousand tons.[9] What it would take to sustain a full-scale, prolonged, conventional war on NATO's Central Front nobody knows, but figures as high as 1,500 tons a day have been mentioned in the literature. This is the result, among other things, of having tanks and aircraft with bigger and more powerful engines, artillery pieces firing heavier shells more rapidly, and a much larger number of automatic weapons – the result, in short, of technological progress in every field.[10]

To deal with complexity, the sheer task of managing the flow of supplies required, modern armed forces around the world have resorted to automatic data processing. The computers routinely used for administration, command, control, and communications are equally evident in the field of logistics. Probably their most important jobs consist of helping to plan the statistical consumption models on which the system is built, record-keeping, calculation, requisitioning, and inventory control. It is indeed difficult to imagine how modern armed forces could keep themselves supplied – how they could even keep track of all the different kinds of item they need or have in stock – without the aid of computers. On the other hand, nothing is easier than to spell out the shortcomings of automated systems and the ways in which they can break down. As compared with humans, computers are short on both flexibility and resourcefulness. Unable to improvise, they must have every instruction exactly spelt out, a demand that may be easier to meet during the calm of peace than in the confusion and stress of a real-life campaign. Computers are also quite vulnerable, both physically and to all kinds of electronic interference, ranging from EMP (electro-magnetic pulse) to sabotage.

The first theatre of war which saw a logistic system that was even halfway automated put to the test was Vietnam. Seen from the global (macro) level, the American achievement in moving two million men across the Pacific and keeping them supplied on a scale which has never been exceeded before or seen was remarkable; however, on the micro level many of the field units which depended on the system regarded it as a disaster.[11] By contrast, the British success in fighting so far from home during the 1982 Falklands War was extraordinary, and the Israeli logistic system in Lebanon in the same year (owing in part to lessons drawn from the 1973 War) also did very well. Still, in both cases, the fighting was of only limited scale and duration. Moreover, the bases from which the forces drew their supplies were never subjected to attack. Hence, and with all due respect, neither case can be considered a real test from which lessons applicable to any central European battlefield may be drawn. I may be wrong, but I have the uneasy feeling that, if hard ever hits hard, a fully automated logistic system may be worse than none at all.

Since the advent of large scale motorisation in the Second World War, the most important categories into which the supplies of modern armed forces are divided comprise: (1) ammunition; (2) POL (petrol, oil, lubricants); and (3) everything else. As circumstances differ, it is difficult to say anything conclusive about the relative quantities involved: obviously a force engaged on an unopposed pursuit will require more POL than one that is fighting a pithead battle or defending itself against attack, whereas in the case of ammunition, the situation will be the opposite. As a rule of thumb, however, the proportions are perhaps ammunition: 30 per cent, POL: 40 per cent; everything else: 30 per cent. The miscellaneous 30 per cent includes less than 10 per cent pertaining to the needs of soldiers (food, drink, clothing, market-tender wares, and medical supplies), as opposed to those of machines. I have already said that, whereas the requirements of personnel remain fixed over time, those of machines grow and grow. In so far as present-day warfare is not radically different from that of 40 years ago – in both cases it is a question of moving about by means of internal combustion (or jet) engines and of firing metal into the air – there appears to be little prospect of reducing the quantities required and thus easing the logistic burden.

At this point, mention must be made of precision-guided munitions, or PGMs, which 10 or 15 years ago were expected to solve, or at least ease, the logistic problem by providing a one-shot-kill capability. Much has been written concerning the cost effectiveness of such weapons, particularly as fired by men against tanks or by aircraft against targets on the ground; notwithstanding, their undoubted effectiveness, however, the hoped-for savings have failed to materialise. One reason for this is that many guided weapons (medium- and long-range anti-aircraft missiles, for example) require complex ancilliary equipment to operate, equipment that itself tends to turn into a logistic burden. Another is the fact that the standard response of ground forces attacked by such weapons is to smother them with vast quantities of more or less unaimed suppressive fire from artillery, machine guns, and anything else that can consume ammunition fast. Finally, in the cases of many – perhaps most – guided weapons the hoped for one-shot-one-kill capability was simply not achieved (on the Golan Heights in 1973, the Syrians fired 50 missiles to down a single Israeli aircraft). Thus modern warfare has failed to meet expectations. The electronics experts' promises notwithstanding, instead of substituting few expensive for many cheap weapons it has turned out to be both very lavish *and* incredibly expensive. Whether such expenditure can be sustained for long even by the greatest military powers may be and has been doubted, but this is a question that lies outside the scope of the present chapter.

Passing now from the demand for supplies to the means by which it can be satisfied, again there is no escape from the conclusion that developments have been much less rapid than has been expected. Twenty five or 30 years ago, serious strategists from Henry Kissinger down earnestly demanded that a replacement be found for the internal combustion engine.[12] There was much loose talk about substituting flying jeeps and hovercraft for land-bound transport. 'Artists' conceptions' in professional periodicals showed armed forces being supplied by guided missiles which, having been fired into the stratosphere and descending by parachute, would stick their sharp noses into the ground like burrowing anteaters. There were also visions of giant, land-walking machines. Resembling nothing so much as the fighting engines depicted in H. G. Wells's *The War of the Worlds* (1898), they would stride over field, marsh and forest carying their logistic burdens. Needless to say, not one of these esoteric devices has materialised. Recently some experimental walking machines, delicate and extremely complicated contraptions, have been constructed, only to be put into museums. Missile transport has never even been tried, and had it been tried it would have foundered on the expense, small payloads, and inaccuracies involved. Flying jeeps have just not taken off. Consequently, ground-bound transport apart, the most important means that logistics may employ are conventional aircraft, helicopters, and the occasional hovercraft.

During the Second World War conventional aircraft were extensively used for logistic purposes, and such use remains possible today. Technological advances have replaced the old DC-3 by the C-5B, thus increasing the range of transport planes, their burden carrying capacity, and their cost-effectiveness (so long as none of the monsters is lost) out of all recognition. There has, however, been a price to pay. By and large it consists of an even greater dependence on extensive and vulnerable facilities for take-off and landing. Since such facilities cannot be located close to the front, they required transfer from one mode of transport to another which is time-consuming, complicated, and very expensive. Nor are such facilities capable of being moved quickly to follow the forces' advances or retreats.[13]

Various techniques exist (and have long existed) for dropping supplies from aircraft. However, they often involve severe limitations as to accuracy, the kind of material that can be dropped, and the extensive nature of the preparations required. Though helicopters do not suffer from these limitations, class-for-class they cannot compare with fixed-wing aircraft in point of range, speed or burden-carrying capacity, whereas ton-for-ton they are much more expensive to operate. Existing hovercraft suffer from much the same shortcomings as do helicopters. They are even more noisy and vulnerable than the latter, nor are they suited to every kind of terrain. This discussion of airborne transport could be brought to a close by noting that hovercraft, helicopters and aircraft often have important advantages when it comes to rushing comparatively small amounts of critical supplies to locations that would otherwise be difficult to reach. Now, as four decades ago, however, they on their own do not even come close to providing the logistic capability need to support large-scale military operations on land.

When the Second World War came to end only the British and the American Armies were completely motorised. Two other large armies, the German and the Soviet ones, were still to a large extent dependent on horse-drawn transport. The growth of the motor-car industry during the postwar decades has long caused the horse to disappear. However, it has not changed the situation whereby the motor truck, moving on wheels and hence requiring roads, is the fundamental means by which field armies are supplied. Mechanised supply vehicles have been developed and are in routine use by every modern army. Yet it has proved impossible to put even a considerable fraction – not to say all – of the supplies needed for large-scale conventional operations on tracks. Paradoxically, the most important reason for this itself lies in the domain of logistics, given the penalities that tracked vehicles impose in terms of spare parts, maintenance, and the consumption of POL.

Motor trucks themselves have developed, but not very greatly so; some models dating from 1944–45 are actually still in service, kept there by their ruggedness, simplicity, and ability to run on low octane fuel. In any case, any commuter knows that whether or not he reaches his destination on time depends less on the quality of his vehicle than on that of the road network. Of even greater importance is effective traffic control, which, however, is almost immune to technological change. There have been some advances, it is true, in ancillary equipment designed to expedite the loading and unloading of motor transport, leading to the elimination of bottlenecks and a faster turnover; I am thinking of movable conveyor belts suited for field work, forklifts, containers, pallets prepacked with supplies and ammunition, and the like. The effect of such developments is likely to make itself felt more in the field of tactics than in that of strategy. Given the vastly increased volume of logistic support required, they are like drops in the ocean.

To conclude, during the decades since 1945 several trends have interacted and, between them, shaped the field of logistics. While conventional warfare as such underwent comparatively little change, it became much more capital-intensive. The growing number and variety of machines in use brought a remarkable increase in the complexity of the logistic system, which could not be entirely offset even by far-reaching automation; with the result (although this is but one of several factors) that readiness can be a problem even in peacetime.[14] The second most important development, stemming from the same cause, has been the increase in the volume of supplies required. While considerable progress has also been made in the field of transportation, particularly air transportation, it has not been anywhere sufficient to offset that increase. This probably means that talk about the fast pace of modern warfare is largely illusory; in fact, there is reason to think that neither the forces' maximum speed (the 'tempo' at which they operate, to use Soviet terminology), nor their radius of action from base has grown by very much.

From the point of view of NATO, this is probably good news. If, as I suspect, Second World War calculations remain fundamentally valid, then Warsaw Pact armoured forces pouring across the East German and Czechoslovak borders would not be able to sustain anything like the 50 miles a day operational norms set out for them in Soviet military publications.[15] Nor, most likely, will they be able to proceed much further than 200 miles from base before they are brought to a halt by their own logistic requirements and compelled to reorganise. They may thus be able to reach the Rhine in a single drive, but it is very doubtful whether, faced with any kind of opposition, their reach can extend nearly as far as the Channel coast. Moreover, if logic and history provide any guide, declining logistic freedom should help the strategic defence. This is what took place in the First World War and, though hard data are scarce, may have taken place again during the recent Iran–Iraq War.

On the reverse side of the coin, one sometimes wonders whether any kind of economic infrastructure in the world can still suffice to sustain the mushrooming demands of large-scale, conventional warfare. Such warfare is also being undermined by other factors, including the spread of nuclear weapons and the ever-present fear of escalation on the one hand and of terrorism on the other; hence it may well be on its way out. This makes it all the more important that armed forces should be able to operate in marginal, underdeveloped parts of the world.

Given that modern armed forces are dependent on motor transport they find it harder and harder to operate in places where the road network is underdeveloped. Given their dependence on supplies that cannot be procured locally but must be brought up from base – another factor that is the outcome of mechanisation – a situation may be created where the bulk of the forces are occupied in developing and protecting bases and lines of communication instead of fighting. Where conventional army meets conventional army this will probably lead to the triumph of the defence and a battle of attrition. In the case of anti-guerrilla operations the consequences may be more serious still. In Vietnam the American Forces plus those of the Republic of South Vietnam consistently outnumbered the Viet Cong/North Vietnamese Army. Yet so preoccupied were the former with the need to meet the logistic demands created by their own technology that this superiority was not reflected on the battlefield, where the number of manœuvre battalions on both sides actually available for fighting was approximately equal.

Thus this chapter must end with a warning. The capital-intensiveness of war, and with it the logistic demands that it generates, are reaching the point of diminishing returns if indeed that point has not been passed already. If modern armed forces are to remain viable instruments of making war, then some radically new methods for dealing with these problems will have to be found. Otherwise they will probably go the way of the dinosaurs, nor are signs lacking that this development is already taking place.

CHAPTER 16

Sustainability: a Concept Which May Come of Age

MAJOR-GENERAL I. S. BAXTER

A Britain prepared to defend itself – and thereby incidentally to defend peace and the balance of power in Europe – is a Britain whose armed forces in peace are designed to enable us if necessary to decide the issue of a long struggle.
Enoch Powell in an address to the Oxford University Conservative Association, 12 June, 1989.

Sustainability: the Concept Defined

The world is now seeing one of the most significant changes in superpower postures in the last 45 years and its full impact on East–West relations has yet to be fully assessed. Arms-control negotiations and political initiatives are all aimed at maintaining security in Europe, with lower standing force levels and smaller nuclear arsenals. The Soviet Union wishes to be seen to be moving from an offensive to a defensive posture. The reality, however, is that the Soviet Union owes its superpower status largely to military strength. Despite pressures to implement far-reaching economic and social reforms, Soviet military power is likely to remain predominant. Whatever the political intent, it is the military capability which must be recognised and focused upon. The NATO Alliance therefore faces the major task of seeking means to maintain deterrence in the new political and military environment.

In the revised scenario it is a matter of balance, and nowhere is this more important than in the area of sustainability, which has been highlighted as the most critical, long-term shortfall for NATO as a whole. SACEUR wrote recently that 'more than any other field, sustainability requires a consistent level of new investment'.[1] Sustainability, however, is a most complex issue; it is certainly more than just logistics. It is a combination of interlocking factors that provides a qualitative and quantitative assessment of a force's ability to complete its mission. The recently agreed NATO definition of sustainability is:

The ability of a force to maintain the necessary level of combat power for the duration required to achieve its objectives.

By contrast Martin Van Creveld describes sustainability in a wider context as 'The sum of national character, organisation, combat efficiency, leadership and good administration.'[2]

It is of interest to note that the Russian term (and Soviet military concept) that most closely equates to NATO's sustainability is *zhivuchest* or 'viability', defined in the *Military Encyclopaedic Dictionary* as:

The capability of troops (forces), weapons, military equipment, rear installations, or command and control systems to preserve or quickly restore their combat supply (the capability to fulfil their appropriate military task).

At first sight not so unlike the NATO view perhaps, but this Soviet concept of sustainability or viability differs fundamentally from NATO's in that it is assessed quantitatively. It is calculated in great detail. The commander does not have to guess whether he can 'sustain' his battle; he will know on a scientific basis whether he can or not. The Soviets use military history to enhance their understanding of procedures, to help solve military problems, to establish a statistical base for future planning,[3] and for mounting the various phases of battle.

My purpose in this chapter is to examine further the concept of sustainability in the context of the Central Region land/air battle in the early twenty-first century, compared with the present day, and the implications for resource allocation. I intend to pursue my study from the viewpoint of the practical soldier. Sustainability is vital to the defence of the Alliance, yet it is arguably the most neglected and misunderstood area of military study at the present time.

NATO 40 Years on

The Political Dimension

Quite dramatically, NATO, on its fortieth anniversary finds itself at one of the most difficult crossroads in its short but undeniably successful history. From its origins in the depths of the Cold War, the Alliance has grown to a total of 16 nations, united by the common aim of deterring Soviet aggression by the threat of a common and unified response. In the 1950s the deterrent posture of the Alliance was based on the nuclear umbrella provided by the United States. Since then the advent of medium- and short-range nuclear weapons has allowed the member nations to adopt a strategy of 'flexible response'. In 1989 the INF Treaty has been ratified, conventional-force reductions are on the superpower political agenda, and there is the real prospect that further nuclear reductions will find political acceptance. Faced with these developments, how well is NATO sustainability suited to the present-day threat?

The Battlefield Today

Since the Second World War there have been many advances in technology which have had an impact on strategy, tactics, and the equipment found on today's battlefield. However, much of the posture on the battlefield has been determined by the reliance on a strategy of flexible response, a conventional performance, and sustainability underpinned by a nuclear capability. The result is a military philosophy which concentrates on forward lines and the teeth of the organisation. Sustainability has therefore not received the due and balanced consideration required to establish a viable defence capability, as opposed to posture.

In the Central Region the NATO forces are aligned in a 'layer cake' of national corps. Yet few of these forces are able to operate effectively together, as there are few NATO standard equipments. Lack of effective standardisation and interoperability, *inter alia*, dictate that logistic support remains a national responsibility with little potential for rationalisation and improvements in efficiency. Yet standardisation, interoperability, and collaboration remain NATO goals. NATO defines interoperability as 'The ability of systems, units of forces to provide services to and accept services from other systems, units of forces and to use the services so exchanged to enable them to operate effectively together.' However, after 40 years of the Alliance, progress on interoperability has been minimal. In NORTHAG, for example, each of its four corps has its own tactical communication system (ZODIAC, AUTOCO, PTARMIGAN, RITA), none of which is interoperable with each other nor indeed with NATO communications, without expensive, vulnerable and unreliable interfaces. Within NATO there are five different tanks with four guns of different calibres and four anti-tank helicopters with different anti-tank missiles. The brief success in common small arms ammunition ended when 7.62 mm ceased to be the NATO standard calibre. In comparison with standardised Soviet and NSWP equipment, NATO's low level of interoperable equipment puts the Alliance at a considerable disadvantage.

The same lack of rationalisation and co-operation in NATO extends to the national defence industrial bases. There is much duplication. It cannot be sound to have 11 firms in Alliance countries building anti-tank weapons; 18 firms in seven countries designing and producing ground-to-air weapons; and 16 companies in seven countries working on air-to-ground weapons.[4] These weaknesses are acknowledged and the recent NATO Conventional Defence Improvements exercise has established a plan of action to encourage member nations to give a greater priority to more effective procurement co-operation. Commercial pressure has also enhanced multinational development in the European defence industries with the development and production of MLRS, Tornado, Milan and latterly EFA, but there is scope for further progress.

The Soviet Union possesses the capacity for industrial surge production to follow on its initial reserve stockpiles. In marked contrast, the United Kingdom, in common with virtually all other members of the Alliance except the United States, has no industrial strategic stockpile of critical items. Historically resupply planning has concentrated on what is the worst-case scenario, involving minimum warning time and large-scale attack. Such an attack allows little room for surge production from industry prior to the conflict; consequently, there is a gap between preferred strategy and realistic capability. Few resources are committed to improving responsiveness and therefore little reliance is placed on industrial resupply. This theme is developed later.

One of the more visible and obvious measures of sustainability is, the provision of stockpiles of combat supplies and *matériel* that are essential for the armed forces to operate. Soviet stockpile policy allows for 60 to 90 days of resupply. Despite NATO guidance requiring national stockpiles of 30 days of supply and a percentage of reserve equipments, collectively Alliance stockholdings are dangerously short of these levels and only one nation has made provision against the commitment agreed by NATO Ministers to consider providing for sustaining stocks beyond the 30 days goal.

Sustainability: the Current Perspective

Whilst some efforts are now being made to redress progressively the balance, particularly in the area of logistic sustainability, 'the harsh realities of politics and economies in the defence arrangements of NATO dictate that a 'shop window' array of expensive military weapons and equipment is held to add more to deterrence than equally expensive stockpiles of combat supplies and war maintenance reserves of equipment'.[5] Although more attention is now being directed at the impact that sustainability has on overall capability and deterrent posture, by 1989 sustainability had certainly not come of age.

The Progress towards Sustainability in the Future: NATO 65 Years on

The Battlefield of the Future

Before the prospects for sustainability in the early twenty-first century are considered, what of the battlefield of the future? The pace of technological advance, together with social and demographic changes dictate that the battlefield in 2015 will be significantly different from that of today. Although nuclear weapons are likely to be retained by the superpowers, their shadow over the battlefield could be much reduced and political developments may lead to a parity of *in situ* ground forces.

In the land/air battle of 2015, both the increased 'transparency' brought about by improvements in surveillance technologies, data manipulation, the development of effective homing munitions, together with the much greater emphasis of mobility, will demand that operations be conducted around the clock, in a similar pattern to the way maritime warfare has developed since electronic detection became the norm. There will be no respite at night and darkness will no longer provide a cover for rest or resupply. It will be a battlefield characterised by devastating firepower delivered from every dimension, a battlefield which will be frightening, confusing and exhausting, more extensive in time and space than ever before and one in which the opportunities for sleep, replenishment, evacuation, servicing, and repair will be rare, and one which will put a premium on human endurance as well as on the reliability and the easy maintenance of weapon systems.

The ability of the NATO forces to sustain the required level of combat power to achieve their objectives will be severely tested in this environment. Radical ideas and initiatives will be required to ensure an adequate level of sustainability in terms of manpower and equipment, as well as of the organisation and systems that support the deployed forces.

Manpower

The effects of the 'demographic trough' will dominate considerations for the future manning of the forces, and the problem will by no means be confined to the United Kingdom. By 1998 the pool of potential recruits in United Kingdom will have fallen by 28 per cent from a 1985 peak; the equivalent reductions in the Federal Republic and the United States are 40 per cent and 15 per cent respectively. From 2000 recruiting will not only face stiff competition from industry and commerce in this country, but also from abroad, especially with the free movement of labour within the EEC European Community after 1992. Demography and economic pressure will, therefore, almost certainly reduce the size of the United Kingdom's armed forces significantly by the year 2015. The shortage of males in the conscript groups in the Federal Republic have prompted the development of a new army structure (*Heeresstruktur 2000*) which will rely more heavily for key logistic services on civilians in peacetime, who will then be co-opted as reservists in war. By contrast, this is a problem the Soviet Union will not experience so drastically, although the proportion of ethnic Russian and other Slavs will drop as the number of Central Asians increases.

These manpower constraints will force research into new technology in order to save on manpower. Robotics, the use of labour-saving devices, such as automated mechanical-handling equipment and reduced crew sizes, will need to be pursued vigorously, if force levels are to be maintained. Technology, however, will not be a panacea, as it will breed a complexity that is expensive to produce and maintain.

Manpower constraints will force a rationalisation of functions both nationally and within the Alliance. Vital functions such as casualty evacuation (CASEVAC) will need to be extensively restructured. Presently such evacuation is a national responsibility; as an example four CASEVAC chains exist in the rear NORTHAG area. Future systems will need to be internationally integrated with all elements working to standard procedures. Host nation assistance will be required to shorten CASEVAC lines and save resources otherwise required to assist with the evacuation.

The extensive use of reservists to supplement the fighting order of battle will be required, as happens at present. The availability of specialist skills, however, will be more important than numbers. To maintain adequate skill levels within the forces it will be necessary to target areas of expertise (IT specialists, communications experts, and mechanical/ electrical engineers) and then effectively requisition these skills for the war effort. Legal powers to ensure this co-opted manpower performs the tasks will be needed. Reservists for the teeth arms will also be needed, but could be mobilised much as today. Timely reinforcement however will require regular practice and a streamlining of procedures to get reservists to their equipment and deployment areas as quickly as possible.

The whole question of reinforcement, including both standing forces and reservists, will be crucial to force sustainability. Within Europe the rationalisation of transport links will aid rapid intra-continental movement. One foresees several channel fixed links with a nexus of high-speed rail and road links. These links would need to be exploited to facilitate reinforcement plans. The Atlantic link would probably remain much as today, and much of the credibility of the Alliance will continue to depend on SACEUR's rapid reinforcement plan, which is not amendable to any high-speed transport solution.

Equipment Sustainability

On the battlefield of the twenty-first century, equipment costs will continue to represent a large proportion of the Defence Vote. Rising equipment costs will heighten the impetus to achieve greater standardisation, as will the greater European commercial standardisation brought about by the advent of the Single European Act. Certainly the high investment costs of the defence industries will highlight the potential for co-operation. Continued commitment to the Independent European Programme Group (IEPG), established in 1976 to foster co-operation and competitiveness, will promote collaborative ventures. 'Reciprocal purchasing', favoured by many in British procurement circles, would be only a temporary palliative before economic realities make collaboration a necessity.

However, perhaps more fundamental is the fact that currently national concepts staff, for all practical purposes, work independently of each other, although some co-operation exists under the auspices of the EUROLONGTERM Working Group, a EUROGROUP committee. Consensus in this area would break new ground and provide a much needed early thrust towards consensus procurement policies. Another force for equipment (and procedural) standardisation would be the establishment of joint doctrine. The problems of operational integration in the Central Region are well illustrated by the current position in the development of close air support (CAS). For the United States, CAS is provided in direct support of the American corps, in Britain it is provided by 2 ATAF and in Germany it is integrated into the German corps. Such diversity of approach is likely to result in diversity of doctrine and consequently of equipment requirements.

A further area where substantial improvement is feasible is in the development of a defence-industrial database to increase the potential surge production. Dr Ewan Anderson, from the University of Durham (and currently a commander in the RNR), is conducting this research for the MOD. From British defence-industrial base dealing with in excess of three million items, his research shows that for most equipments the strategic components comprise between 5 per cent and 10 per cent of the materials bill, identified on the basis of lead time or restricted sourcing. Hence by pre-positioning a relatively small number of strategic components, surge production can be brought within the broad range of present planning. Research continues to establish how these findings relate to other families of weapons, but general deductions which can already be drawn are:

- The identification of surge-production potential for key equipments would eliminate a considerable weak spot in our crisis resupply situation.
- The availability of strategic components would enable crisis resupply considerations to be built into operational planning. Factors governing the availability of key equipment would be known in advance, to meet a range of crisis scenarios, including out-of-area operations.

Increasingly all aspects of reliability and maintainability (R&M) will become vital elements of sustainability. The importance of reliability was stressed in a recent National Audit Office report which estimated that unreliability increases MOD support costs by over £1 billion a year at current prices, and stresses that reliability must be given equal priority with performance and in-service dates. To improve equipment sustainability, all future equipment must be designed and produced with due regard being given to through-life costs, especially logistic support costs. The introduction of integrated logistic support (ILS) procedures developed by the Americans and perhaps to be adopted for use in certain NATO multinational projects, embraces many of these aspects in a formalised package. Increased reliability will in turn give rise to increased operational availability at reduced cost, both financially and in manpower.

Reduced manpower will force the pace on availability and repair; equipment will be designed to limit repair requirements and improve the supply of *matériel*. Modular construction using standard, interchangeable components should allow reduced spares holdings and increase the availability of common spare parts. There is scope for common tools and test equipment and the modular replacement of critical sub-systems. Common fuel types, pressurised refuelling (to reduce the time spent out of action), decreased vehicle fuel and water consumption, survivable tyres, rapid tyre repair, and common tracks would all increase availability. The use of widely available commercial spares and equipment would show significant cost benefits, both in terms of inventory holdings, and in the ability to requisition in wartime.

Repair techniques will be further enhanced by the use of artificial intelligence to estimate the probabilities of failure, interpret built-in-test-equipment (BITE) output and provide on-site advice on repair. Advances in metallurgy and the commercial development of new materials will assist with the development of speedy and efficient battle damage assessment and repairs. Much of the repair task, essentially black-box exchange, will be carried out by the operator on site, for which he will require some training.

Organisational Sustainability

With increased standardisation and the concomitant interoperability there will be a parallel pressure for co-operative logistic support. National logistic support has obvious peacetime advantages, especially in budgeting and provision. On the future battlefield the scope for cross-boundary operations and the possible development of multinational formations (a NATO multinational division?) make some interoperable logistic support essential.

Logistic support is an ideal area for applying collective solutions to common problems. Standardised procedures and definitions, agreement on stockpile-planning methodology (level of effort or threat related), meeting stockpile targets and common support philosophies would all enhance sustainability. Agreed stocks of combat supplies and warlike stores must be procured and positioned in sufficient quantities to provide for the first days of battle. However, there is a danger in placing too much emphasis on the NATO infrastructure forward storage-sites and locating a great deal of initial replenishment stocks in permanent bunkers well forward in the Central Region; committing logistic support to ground-dumped stocks to meet a fixed deployment plan may not necessarily be the best way to support a future war of manœuvre. Similar wariness will be extended to other logistic infra-structure facilities, such as existing pipelines and depots, to ensure that the umbilical cords of supply have sufficient flexibility to cope with the fluid battlefield in 2015.

Improved logistic sustainability could be achieved by integrating logistic support more fully with the operational levels of command. For example, logistic support in the British Army is based on the divisional level of command. A reorganisation of logistic support, which would give each brigade a measure of logistic independence, would add to operational flexibility on the highly mobile battlefield of the next century.

Finally, a mention should be made of some air force developments which will contribute substantially to Alliance effectiveness in any future land/air battle. In an era of ever-improving area-denial capabilities and precision-guided munitions survival to operate (STO) techniques will, given the necessary resources, enhance sustainability markedly. The plans initiated in the 1970s for the physical protection of airfields and which concentrated primarily on the hardening of facilities – the airfield survival measures (ASM) programme – will need to be updated and augmented. Survival techniques will have to be refined to incorporate increased SAM and SHORAD capabilities, better camouflage, concealment and deception measures (including greater emphasis on the use of modern technology and aircraft dispersal), and improved resilience embracing airfield damage repair (ADR), the recovery of facilities, and the restoration of essential services. Without doubt, however, the greatest challenge is that posed by dispersal – ranging from the relatively simple concept of dispersed to survive through that of dispersed to operate, with its dispersed operating locations (DOL) capable of accepting combat-ready aircraft for a single mission and/or sophisticated dispersal operating bases (DOB) with that full supply of logistics support needed to permit sustained day/night all-weather operations.

It is perhaps worth remembering here the size, cost, and complexity of current Harrier force operations, with their flying sites and logistic parts. The bill for this concept involving the Harrier GR3, a relatively unsophisticated weapons platform, is very expensive. Clearly the dispersal of non-VSTOL aircraft types will similarly impose high logistic costs, and efforts must be made to reduce these by considering the requirements for dispersed storage for all future aircraft at the design stage. Future aircraft will need to be designed to operate from operating strips and should incorporate, for example, measures to prevent FOD ingress, ruggedized undercarriages, low-pressure tyres, and STOL performance.

Future Sustainability and Resource Allocation

Priorities

Sustainability has lost its 'edge' in the post-1945 nuclear world. Emphasis placed on the short conventional war has allowed financial and manpower decisions to be made that have dramatically affected sustainability; but the penalty in a 'flexible response' world has been difficult to demonstrate effectively. In the future, with less emphasis on the nuclear threat and more likelihood of a longer conventional phase in war, sustainability (and its visibility and measurement) will have a far more direct effect on capability. It must, therefore, be accorded a higher priority in terms of resource allocation. Consequently, public and military opinion must be convinced of the necessity and requirement for visible sustainability in order to have a sound defence posture. Deterrence is not founded on the number of tanks in the barracks, but on the effectiveness of our weapons systems, the men and women operating them, and the reserves of men and *matériel* to support them in the completion of their task; 'capability' will become much more important than 'display'. *Blitzkrieg* on its own may well win a battle; it will not win the war.

Attitude to Costing and Funding

If sustainability is to be afforded its correct place in the spectrum of deterrence then resource and programme staff must acknowledge both its true cost and how it may be minimised. A concentration on front-end resourcing distorts the true financial picture. The lack of a whole-life approach detracts from efforts to achieve standardisation as the true cost effectiveness of these measures is felt at the rear-end of the operation and not simply in reduced cost per unit item. These rear-end costs can reduce to insignificance the unit procurement-costs not simply financially but also in manpower and systems. Currently approximately 30 per cent of Army manpower strength is absorbed in the support area; a recent MOD study, suggested that British spending on defence materials was in the region of £3 billion in 1986/87.

However the calculation of the whole-life cost of a weapon system is difficult. Recently the MOD's Balance of Investment Working Group, sponsored a study into costs of ownership to examine whether changes in resource considerations could achieve a more effective balance between programme and development acquisition and whole-life costs. Only when faced with hard facts can resource staffs make decisions (one would hope!). But the potential for benefit is enormous. Using ILS techniques the F18 aircraft requires 15 hours of maintenance per flying hour compared with Tornado which requires 30 hours. The effect is increased availability with fewer aircraft and reduced support costs and manpower.

Funding once allocated must then be guaranteed, otherwise financial wisdom is sacrificed for short-term solutions to resource problems. It took three years to get Tornado to the NATO Staff Target Specification at a cost of £250 million following the dropping of a £37 million R&M programme.

Allied to a whole-life approach for equipment is the need for a 'total force' approach within the military system. Our concentration on the importance of 'front-window' deterrence has led to an unco-ordinated approach to policy and doctrine. The full effects of changes in tactics and new equipment, for example, are addressed in isolation. Sustainability penalties caused by these changes are expected to be solved by self-help measures, often to make the above the line costs smaller in programme terms. Again this is a form of false economy which needs addressing now, to ensure a properly orchestrated approach to sustainability over the next 25 years.

Burden Sharing: Division of Labour and Role Specialisation

Burden-sharing was seen, at least initially, as reducing pressure on those elements of the American defence budget dedicated to NATO commitments. However, it does provide a useful medium through which to achieve efficiencies. Much suspicion surrounds burden-sharing, as it can potentially be interpreted as an excuse for burden-shedding. Applied properly it could be regarded as the fairest way of ensuring that, not only the burdens of defence are shared equitably, but that the operational benefits are equally distributed. The NATO Airborne Early Warning Force was established in this manner, and in the longer term NATO plans to investigate the potential of extending this concept to other areas, including mine warfare, amphibious shipping lift, air defence, and FOFA.

Burden-sharing will not solve all the potential difficulties of fielding increasingly costly weapon systems. Some division of labour or 'role-sharing' may prove inevitable, although this does conjure up images for some of constrained national sovereignty and of providing excuses for others to shed unpopular or expensive tasks. Specialisation will, however, allow the Alliance to use scarce resources and skills in a cost-effective and efficient manner.

The Prospects for Success

This chapter has attempted to illustrate that the potential exists to achieve the required levels of sustainability on the future battlefield by early in next century. The reader, however, should not be left with the feeling that this potential will necessarily be achieved, or achieved easily. Sustainability is a complex subject and it has been neglected. Because of its complexity, it has been equated in many minds with logistic sustainability, which is but one part of the whole.

If sustainability is to achieve its rightful priority for resources allocation in the 2015 scenario, it will need a significant shift in attitude by both the political and the military hierarchies. It requires a shift away from 'shop-window' deterrence to one of measuring and calculating capability. Measurement is itself a complex area. What has to be calculated is the readiness, capability, and endurance of opposing forces. There is also the fundamental question of what is absolutely necessary to achieve the right level of sustainability for NATO forces. Unless progress can be made in measuring sustainability in an accepted way the shop-window approach will continue to be adopted, as this will offer the only reliable method of verification. And the operational commander, at all levels, will lack the real freedom of action to achieve his task that genuine sustainability would give him. Sustainability is a concept which must come of age on the future battlefield if NATO is to continue to deter aggression successfully, a theme also strongly advocated by SACEUR.

CHAPTER 17

The Central Region: a Strategic Overview

FIELD MARSHAL SIR NIGEL BAGNALL

THIS VOLUME is published at a time when we stand at a political and strategic crossroads. It covers a wide field, and it would overtax my ingenuity and your patience were I to try and cover every aspect of our studies. I will therefore confine myself to what I regard as being the salient issues. Let me then begin by summarising the principal points made by three of our contributors, which largely established the framework for subsequent chapters.

Lawrence Freedman in his opening chapter pointed out that the need for the Western Alliance was as great as ever during a period of experimentation in the East. Although it would be only sensible to expect a reversal, if the fragmentation of the Eastern bloc continues, it would be unrealistic to imagine that the current rate of defence expenditure would continue. Michael Carver related the birth pangs suffered by British politicians and policy-makers in deciding to make a land commitment to the defence of Europe. Since then it has been the aggressive and repressive attitude of the Soviet Union which has held the Alliance together, and any relaxation of this bellicosity will inevitably put at risk, not only our own contribution, but that of our Allies. Michael Howard and others have stressed the need for stability in the West, and the vital importance of the United Kingdom's contribution in maintaining this stability. Abrupt adjustments to our defences should then be avoided as the Eastern bloc resolves its future.

Although it has been generally agreed that we must keep our guard up and avoid disarming prematurely, it has also been accepted that political, economic, arms-control, and demographic pressures are going to reduce force levels. But as differences over modes of defence reveal, when it comes to the nature of future allied force requirements, and the United Kingdom's contribution in particular, there is not the same degree of unanimity. Though German arguments underlined the continuing need

239

to maintain the twin strategies of forward defence and flexible response, how this is to be achieved convincingly at a lower level of capability, remains undefined. While Christopher Donnelly made the point that, since only nuclear weapons were regarded by the Soviets as posing a threat to their existence, we should not be led astray by feigned anxieties over the level of Western conventional capability.

Several other contributors have argued for the removal of offensive and threatening weapons from the armouries of both East and West. But except for those who may have silently discounted the requirement, nobody has satisfactorily resolved the dilemma, that while any effective conventional defence has to have a counter-offensive capability, this capability could be used offensively in the first place. The balance between offensive and defensive weapons can be adjusted, but not tipped solely in one direction. Simon Lunn suggested that operational concepts, doctrine and the supervised storage of offensive weapons might be possible ways of raising confidence. But he then realistically went on to remind us that arms control can only contribute to achieving greater stability, not provide a solution in itself. David Greenwood proposed that individual nations should provide across the board capabilities, such as all-tank formations, with a view to achieving considerable economies. But the military remained sceptical about such fundamental restructuring, not least because of the problem of close tactical integration at the lower level. Abandoning a major military role in this manner also has considerable industrial, economic, and social implications, not all of which would necessarily receive standing Parliamentary ovations.

After considering strategy and force structures, the volume turns to war-fighting. Christopher Donnelly analysed the still latent Soviet threat, and emphasised the importance the Soviet Union attaches to gaining surprise, winning the air battle, and reducing force-to-ground ratios so as to enable a rapid breakthrough. Though there is little disagreement about the need for forward defence and flexible response, implementation of the former with smaller forces is militarily questionable, while to maintain public acceptance of flexible response in a situation of nuclear parity would require considerable political dexterity.

What we are really suggesting is that we need to do a number of things, which unfortunately do not sit very comfortably together. On the one hand, we want to be realistic and accept that there are likely to be substantial reductions in force levels and capabilities, yet, on the other, we resolutely declare that this must be done without undermining the Alliance's existing strategies of forward defence and flexible response. In other words, we are seeking to do more with less conventionally, while finding a way of maintaining nuclear deterrence without risking a decoupling from the United States, or turning Germany into a nuclear battlefield. Moreover, we need to remember that the time-scale for change is very limited and the restructuring of forces in anticipation of technological developments is hazardous.

As I have been invited to do so, and confident in the knowledge that nobody can be given the opportunity to challenge me, at this stage I would like to make some personal observations. The first point to make is that throughout there is little disagreement about the need for a British continental commiment, only its size and nature is debatable. So there is no requirement for me to rehearse any of the arguments for its continuation.

My second point concerns nuclear weapons, and here I confess to being something of a heretic, so few are likely to agree with me. I do not understand why so much has been made about the military utility of battlefield nuclear weapons. In my opinion their military, as opposed to any deterrent value, is just about nil. No sane politician is going to authorise their use until he or she is convinced that conventional defence has failed, and by then the situation on the battlefield will be far from clear. Command and surveillance facilities will have been so degraded, that precise targeting of enemy formations will be virtually impossible, and the dispositions of our own troops uncertain. Obtaining nuclear release is also a prolix business, further complicating the selection of targets in a kaleidoscopic situation. The only weapons that have a military utility are those longer-range ones which can be targeted by a variety of agencies, and reach out beyond the confusion of the immediate battle area. In other words, what is required is Lance's replacement, you can then scrap all the rest as being militarily valueless, and devote the resources saved to bolstering our conventional artillery, where we are woefully lacking. However, Lance is unlikely to be replaced and ground forces will have to rely on air launched tactical nuclear weapons (TASM).

The problem of having to do more with less is nothing new. Shortly after the First World War divisional frontages were some 6,000 yards in length and depth never got a mention. Without going through all the intermediary stages, today frontages are 20,000 yards long and 25,000 yards deep, while actual frontline manpower has been halved. This has only been achieved by three enhancements: greater mobility, greater weapon ranges and effectiveness, and vastly improved communications. These trends must now be intensified and hastened. Plenty has been said about mobility at the operational and the tactical level, so I will confine myself to making a few general points. First, winning the air battle is essential if enemy movement is to be restricted and our own made possible. Until this is achieved, except in the case of an overriding emergency, to divert air resources on to other tasks is to invite defeat through failing to identify clear priorities.

Secondly, mobility is not just physical but mental, it calls for quick reaction. If early decisions are to be reached, responsibilities at the various levels of command need to be defined. This is a battle I have fought and now that I am retired, which a considerable number of people were waiting for, I have probably lost. At the moment everybody wants to know everything, but if the conditions of war were imposed, they would end up by knowing very little; the signals collect like rolls of loo paper, the communications become choked, and the staffs swamped. Information priorities need to be imposed at every level, so that what is essential gets through, the remainder can follow on in slower time. But determining priorities is always uncomfortable, and it is easier to behave like ostriches.

Thirdly, by achieving greater weapons effectiveness, we should be able to reduce the quantities of the munitions required. Saturating targets by fire may become an outdated concept, and the present highly vulnerable tail of resupply accordingly reduced.

Fourthly, I repeat the age-long cry that weapons systems must be made compatible and logistics internationalised before operational and tactical flexibility can be fully realised.

To summarise the overall situation; given the requirement to meet various political and military considerations, there is nothing inherently wrong with having all the corps in line, so long as the need for operational-level reserves can be met. This can be achieved only if we do not attempt to hold everything, and national boundaries between corps are not regarded as physical ones. When allocating troops to tasks, the priorities must be to create mobile reserves, then to secure key terrain in the forward area; those troops that are left, and they will not be many, can be deployed to cover the gaps as best they can. To try and implement forward defence by holding everywhere is just about as effective as putting up a sheet of plate glass. The fewer your resources, the more necessary it becomes to adhere to priorities.

Finally, one thing I have learned over the years, is that new concepts must be introduced before the necessary changes can be made. To start the other way round only results in stonewall resistance and nothing changing. As Michael Carver has related, the proponents of mechanisation between the two World Wars, were continually confronted with the argument that it was all too expensive. If, when I was commanding 1st (Br) Corps, I had done more than to ask for air-mobility trials, or following these trials, had presented anything other than the minimum requirement when CGS, I would have met with concerted opposition on the same grounds. Such measures have to be introduced step by step and, as they gain respectability and support, funding slowly becomes available. So those of you now facing changes must be very clear about where you are going, then introduce your measures pragmatically as the opportunity presents itself.

Conclusion

MICHAEL DEWAR

MOMENTOUS EVENTS have taken place in Europe since late 1989. The chapters in this volume address these issues and map the way ahead. Clearly at a time of such significant change in Europe it is appropriate to review the likely evolution of NATO dispositions, force levels and intentions in the Central Region. The British Government for one has denied the need for and intention to undertake a defence review. Neverthless – whatever name it is given – there is going to have to be a process of re-examination of the West's defence needs. It would appear that in the early 1990s very few of the old assumptions of Western military policy will still apply. That reappraisal of force levels and structures is already under way in the United States, in Europe and in the Soviet Union. Certainly the old fear of a co-ordinated Warsaw Pact invasion of Western Europe quickly overwhelming NATO forces is now obsolescent. But what exactly will the threat be?

The likelihood is that, as part of the continuing revolution in Eastern Europe, the Warsaw Pact will simply disintegrate. But although it will be in the interests of all Eastern European countries to reduce the importance of military factors in their own countries, it will also be in their interests to be seen to continue to contribute towards a balanced, managed and responsible level of forces in Europe, particularly in the context of a reunified Germany. This could best be done within the context of a continuing Warsaw Pact. Moreover most East European leaders would prefer not to offend Moscow and make Gorbachev's already precarious situation even more so. That would be in nobody's interests. So a truncated Warsaw Pact is likely to remain in place – albeit as a more politicised organisation along NATO lines – certainly in the short term.

However, in the event of the Warsaw Pact's failing to maintain its integrity, it would not fundamentally affect the threat assessment to NATO. The Soviet Union accounts for by far the largest proportion of

Warsaw Pact forces and that country alone would continue to pose a threat to NATO of approximately the same size and nature as at present, discounting for the moment any arms reductions which will result from the CFE negotiations. Moreover the Soviet Union maintains a series of bilateral agreements with all Warsaw Pact members which, so long as those agreements are still in force, would ensure support and access for Soviet forces.

But whatever the future of the Warsaw Pact, German reunification is a fait accompli. Although in the long term it is possible that a reunified Germany will adopt a neutral stance in Central Europe, it is far more likely that she will remain economically and militarily part of Western Europe. As a balance to this, a truncated Warsaw Pact led by the Soviet Union might emerge, the main purpose of which would be to guarantee the existing eastern borders of a reunified Germany.

Additional to and separate from these possible scenarios, Gorbachev's promised force reductions on the Central Front, reinforced by the effects of the treaty on conventional forces in Europe, will further reduce the threat to Western Europe as perceived by NATO. In the light of all these emerging new factors how should NATO be shaped for the nineties?

First, public opinion in both East and West will demand substantial cuts in defence expenditure. The CFE process will encourage and aid this tendency. NATO forces are undoubtedly going to be smaller and will probably rely to a far greater extent on the use of reserves. American forces will remain – with the blessing of Moscow – in Europe but at much reduced levels. A half, perhaps three quarters of the American ground troops are likely to be withdrawn. The CFE ceiling of 195,000 US troops plus 30,000 elsewhere in Europe could be reduced by the turn of the century to a total of 75,000. Secondly, NATO will be able to assume a much longer warning of attack than is presently the case. Predictions until recently were for 10–14 days warning though this could be reduced in some circumstances to 48 hours. This demanded not only a high state of readiness by NATO but also assumed a very high level of in-place manpower and equipment. Whilst a surprise attack by a relatively small force for a limited objective might still be possible, the new set of constraints in a post-CFE Europe would make a concerted full-scale attack on Western Europe difficult to mount even in a period measured in months rather than weeks. This, of course, has all sorts of consequences for force structures and operational planning. Lastly, political rhetoric apart, neither Gorbachev nor Bush is at all likely to be prepared to dispense with the nuclear option. Indeed, the closer NATO and the Warsaw Pact move towards parity in conventional weapons, arguably they are even less likely to want to tamper with their nuclear capability. It may suit everybody's purposes for theatre nuclear weapons to be air-launched rather than ground-launched, but one thing is certain, these systems will remain in significant numbers.

Christopher Donnelly's chapter on the Central Front in Soviet strategy sounds a warning note that the reorganisation of the Soviet armed forces to accommodate the new defensive strategy will neither be straightforward nor without pain. That NATO is also thinking deeply as to how it will reshape its forces in the emerging scenario is evidenced by the chapters in this volume. That its six strands – modes of defence, the counter-offensive, FOFA, nuclear weapons, command and control, and logistics – are inextricably intertwined is, it is hoped, by now clear. A purely defensive defence system is unworkable, hence its connection with the counter-offensive. A defence that is able to reach out and cause unaccetable damage to enemy forces on enemy territory is more effective – and arguably a better deterrent – than systems which would confine the battle to German soil. Herein lies the connection between FOFA and both the defence and the counter-offensive. And, of course, the ramifications of the chapters on command and control, nuclear weapons and logistics pervade all other considerations. Each chapter concludes that in the greatly changed circumstances that seem to be in prospect for the 1990s, and despite the understandable euphoria resulting from the momentous year of change that was 1989, adequate provision for our security will continue to be a requirement. This volume goes beyond just stating the requirement. It puts some flesh on the bones and investigates ways forward at the operational level of war in the Central Region. What perhaps makes it particularly penetrating is that each strand – with the exception of nuclear weapons – is considered by both a military man and an academic. These two perspectives are seldom combined. Nor is the importance and relevance of history ignored by either the military or the academic contributors. This is not surprising at a time when the relevance of historical example in the study of contemporary conflict has recently been given a new impetus in the British Army. Brian Holden Reid's chapter giving a theoretical and historical perspective of the counter-offensive is a particularly good example of this technique.

This volume does not pretend to offer definitive solutions to NATO's future needs but it does point to and confirm certain trends.

There will be fewer men and less equipment in the Central Region in the 1990s. Manpower cuts arising from CFE 1 are likely to be minimal for NATO but, assuming that the process is going to continue, NATO could find itself with much reduced manpower densities on the Central Front by the mid-1990s. Traditional definitions of phases of war will therefore necessarily become increasingly diffuse. Although elements of the defence (the pivotal forces) may be static, much of the defence will be held in depth ready to react offensively once a main axis of penetration has been identified. All formations will have to be prepared to undertake both offensive and defensive roles, will be much more widely dispersed and will need the ability to project firepower over greater distances. The attack helicopter must be about to play a central role on the mechanised battlefield.

The more simplistic forms of 'defensive defence' have surely been overtaken by the pace of events in arms-control negotiations. The traditional notions of defensive defence explored ways of using *existing* force levels in a less provocative way. Hence the largely static nature of most defensive defence models. But much lower force densities mean that a credible defence must not only retain, but increase its mobility and flexibility to react to threats over long distances.

Lower force densities also imply an improved surveillance and target-acquisition capability. Clearly more warning time will be required in order to get mobile reserves to the 'right place at the right time' – a phrase much used by General Sir Martin Farndale in his chapter on command and control at the operational level. Peter Sharfman in his chapter on the future of FOFA also underlines the importance of procuring the right surveillance and target acquisition equipment, in this case Joint STARS. The information collected and collated by such a system must then be processed efficiently so that commanders have the relevant intelligence to issue the right directives. And directives they must be: on the more fluid and widespread battlefield of the 1990s it will be even more necessary to control large formations by directive rather than by over-specific orders.

In the longer warning scenarios that will inevitably result from lower force densities, NATO in particular is likely to rely more on reserves. Ways will have to be developed of ensuring rapid mobilisation of these reserves and their transportation – particularly from the United States – to the Central Region. This will entail a continuation, and perhaps even an expansion of the system by which large stockpiles of equipment and ammunition are maintained in constant readiness in Europe.

And finally, whatever the outcome of the SNF negotiations, there are clearly going to be changes in policy regarding in-theatre nuclear weapons. Whichever of the scenarios posed by Dr Phil Williams in his chapter on nuclear weapons in Europe in the 1990s emerges, there is likely to be both a reduction and a rationalisation of in-theatre nuclear delivery means. The most likely development is a move towards air-delivered stand-off weapons of either American or French design. Nuclear artillery and the Lance Follow-On are dispensable.

In the world of the 1990s there will still be a need for deterrence. Prudence dictates – as it always has done – that any state of affairs may not last forever. And whilst the possibility of a mad Soviet general or neo-stalinist successor to Gorbachev is so unlikely as to be virtually discounted, NATO must continue to demonstrate that is members are not enfeebled, whether the aggressor is the traditional enemy or a new one. The views expressed in this volume are likely to serve as a guide to our planning of the way forward for many years to come.

In early 1990 few would have envisaged that one NATO member – namely Turkey – would be closing her borders with Iraq and putting her armed forces on alert against the possibility of attack from that country. Nor are they likely to have imagined that virtually every member of NATO would be dispatching armed forces to the Gulf region and that, in the US case, they would number over 100,000 men. NATO therefore has to consider to what extent it is appropriate for its forces to be projected, if at all, outside the NATO area. Certainly NATO cannot be justified for 'out-of-area' contingencies alone. But assuming the Soviet Union continues to pose a residual threat and thereby remains the raison d'etre for the continued existence of NATO, it will become increasingly difficult *not* to use these in being forces for 'out-of-area' contingencies when and if they arrive.

Moreover, the United States is unlikely to be willing to remain the world's policeman for much longer. Burden sharing, not just in the European context, is fast becoming an increasingly important issue in the US. The European members of NATO may find that they are going to have to assume a higher proportion of this burden, certainly within the context of the defence of Europe and possibly in the wider context too. Budget constraints may force a degree of isolationism upon the US.

A reunited Germany's attitudes will also shape the future of NATO, perhaps more than any other factor. It is certainly possible that the new Germany will choose to exclude stationed forces from its territory; it is also possible that she may insist upon all nuclear weapons being removed from German soil. Clearly both decisions – if they were ever implemented – would be of immense significance to NATO. The first possibility might be circumvented by the creation of truly multinational NATO formations, possibly under overall German command; these would thus not be 'foreign' formations. The second possibility could mean that air launched tactical nuclear weapons (TASM) would have to be stationed elsewhere – in the UK, Italy and Turkey are possibilities. To what extent might this trigger the 'no nukes, no troops' clause which currently underpins the stationing of US ground troops in Europe?

These and many other issues face NATO in the 1990s and beyond. If anything the Revolution of 1989–90 has made the issues more complicated. The Cold War was dangerous but our reactions to it, and those of the Warsaw Pact, were well rehearsed, predictable and, above all, balanced. The balance has been upset; procedures are unrehearsed; few can predict with any certainty what next month will bring, let alone next year. It is in the Soviet Union's interests and in those of the United

States and of Europe to maintain balance and predictability through this period of change and 'build down'. That is why, despite unilateral initiatives, the Arms Control process must be kept in place.

An equally stable Central Region in Europe is likely to continue to be founded as it always has been – on a balance of power, the maintenance of adequate force levels, on a cohesive alliance and, finally, on the continued deployment of theatre nuclear weapons.

Notes

Introduction

1. Quoted in Brian Holden Reid, 'Is there a British military philosophy?', in J. J. G. Mackenzie & Brian Holden Reid, *Central Europe vs Out-of-Area*, (Tri-Service Press, 1990), p. 2.
2. Correlli Barnett, *The Collapse of British Power*, (Sutton, 1984 edn.), pp. 5, 10–12, 80–2, 132–4, 217–8.
3. Michael Howard, *The Continental Commitment*, (Penguin Books, 1974), pp. 43, 44–7; M. L. Dockrill, *The Formulation of a Continental Foreign Policy by Great Britain, 1908–12*, (Garland Press, 1986), pp. 115, 130–4; David French, *British Economic and Strategic Planning, 1906–15*, (Allen & Unwin, 1983), pp. 124–18, 132–3, 172.
4. J. J. Mearsheimer, *Liddell Hart and the Weight of History*, (Brassey's, 1988), pp. 93, 168–9.
5. Quoted in *The Origins of the Second World War Reconsidered*, ed. G. Martel, (Unwin Hyman, 1986), p. 153.
6. D. Cameron Watt, *How War Came: the Immediate Origins of the Second World War*, (Heinemann, 1989), pp. 284, 309.
7. M. L. Dockrill, *British Defence Since 1945*, (Blackwell, Oxford, 1988), p. 20.

Chapter 2

1. Nigel Hamilton, *Monty: the Field Marshal, 1944–1976*, (Hamish Hamilton, 1986), p. 699.
2. JP(48)16(Final) of 27 January 1948; Public Record Office DEFE4. 10.
3. Hamilton, op. cit., p. 702.
4. COS(48), 18th Meeting; PRO DEFE4. 10.

Chapter 6

1. The last few years have seen a proliferation of ever more detailed and sophisticated studies on the conventional balance by analysts, institutes, and study groups – some reinforcing the traditional perceptions, most challenging them and many taking fellow analysts to task for getting it wrong or missing the point. See for example the contributions in *International Security*, Spring 1989, vol. 13 no. 4.
2. This extrapolation essentially centres on taking a standard Soviet division as found in East Germany, where knowledge of the organisation, structure, and composition of Soviet forces is relatively high and then assessing the degree to which other WTO forces conform to this model. This leaves room for considerable agreement amongst the intelligence community as well as within the academic world.
3. Both NATO and the WTO have published data on their conventional forces relevant to the CFE negotiations. It was significant that even according to their own data and definitions the WTO conceded that it had substantial numerical superiority in the three categories of greatest concern to NATO: tanks, armoured troop carriers, and artillery, although at reduced ratios compared to those in the NATO force comparison.
4. General Rogers's 'widening gap' message touched two sensitive chords: the burden-

sharing debate in the United States and the nuclear debate in Europe. Concerned at this impact and at the validity of the message, NATO's political authorities undertook a major defence review in 1984 in order to identify major deficiencies in NATO's defence and the precise nature of the so-called 'gap'. It was found that the notion could not be substantiated in terms of numbers. Rather it was an overall military judgement that the WTO was improving its ability to implement its strategy faster than NATO was its ability to deny this strategy. As with all assessments of this type, it needed to be put in its proper context and appropriately qualified.

5. As the nuclear guarantor of NATO, the United States was never happy with the situation that suggested an early use of nuclear weapons. Hence American pressure for better conventional forces has been a persistent feature of Alliance life. The situation became particularly acute with the appearance of the Nunn amendments in the early 1980s. Much effort was expended by the Alliance in trying to persuade Congress that, in fact, the Allies were making the necessary improvements to their conventional forces by, for example, the adoption in 1984 of the Conventional Defence Initiative (CDI).

6. The exception to this was the work of the High Level Group in proposing the requirement of 572 INF warheads in 1979. However, it should be remembered that even here the initial number suggested ranged from 200 to 600: 200 was adjudged too low and 600 suggested a Euro-strategic balance; 572 was on the high side to allow for arms control, and the actual number was the result of operational rather than strategic criteria.

7. The CDI exercise represented an attempt to introduce priorities into NATO's Force Planning Process – to get the military authorities to say that some things were more important than others.

8. The negotiations in Vienna were known initially within the Alliance as the Conventional Stability Talks (CST). 'Stability' was dropped, however, at the insistence of the East.

9. For a detailed description of the evolution of the two sides' approaches in Vienna and the current status of negotiations, see the report of the North Atlantic Assembly's Special Committee on Alliance Strategy and Arms Control (Rapporteurs: Bereuter and Frinking), published in October 1989.

10. The WTO argument that manpower is as relevant as equipment and thus should be limited is not without substance. Alliance opposition to the formal inclusion of manpower derives from the frustrations of MBFR. Indeed, the same problem remains, the achieving of a satisfactory definition of when a soldier is a soldier and not a gendarme, land-based sailor, civilian reservist, nor construction worker, with all the accompanying problems for verification. Under the Alliance proposal, reductions of equipment would involve manpower. Information on resulting ceilings would be provided through the information exchange. This formula would avoid giving manpower the formal status of a Treaty Limited Item (TLI).

11. The percentage reductions on the Alliance side using Alliance data are between 4 and 13 per cent, depending on the category of equipment and the region of limitation. The corresponding WTO cuts, again using Alliance data, are between 40 and 60 per cent. Or to put it another way, the WTO will reduce approximately 100,000 Treaty Limited Items, and the Alliance approximately 8,000. However, it should be noted that for the Alliance the reductions are more severe in some sub-regions than in others.

12. A considerable amount of work has been carried out in both the East and the West on the issue of distinguishing between offensive and defensive systems and structures through schemes such as defensive defence, non-provocative defence, or structural incapacity to attack. Many of these schemes require a fundamental reorientation of military thinking that even in today's environment does not appear to be practicable or feasible. Others, despite accommodating the traditional military penchant for balanced forces, including fire and manoeuvre capabilities, have not yet persuaded military professionals of the credibility of their ideas. Nevertheless, there are a number of ideas from this alternative defence school which certainly merit serious attention, and it may well be that their time has yet to come.

Chapter 8

1. Challenger and Chieftain: current main battle tanks; TRIGAT: long-range, anti-tank,

guided missile system; Warrior: infantry armoured fighting vehicle; MLRS: multi-launch rocket system; AS 90: 155-mm self-propelled gun; Rapier and Javelin: anti-air missiles; HVM: high-velocity missile; STA: surveillance target acquisition; and Phoenix: surveillance and target acquisition system.

Chapter 9

1. C. von Clausewitz, *On War*, Bk. 6, Ch. 8.
2. Defensive defence, non-offensive defence, reactive defence, non-provocative defence, structural incapacity for attack, area defence, static defence, techno-defence, territorial defence, militia defence, non-nuclear defence, autonomous defence, and transarmament (in J. Dean, 'Alternative defence: answer to NATO's Central Front problems?', *International Affairs*, Winter 1987/88, pp. 61–82).
3. The notion of *Strukturelle Nichtangriffsfähigkeit* was apparently introduced by H.-P. Dürr and A. A. C. von Müller in 1983.
4. This notion was probably first used by von Müller in 1985/86.

Chapter 10

1. J. F. C. Fuller, *Lectures on FSR II* (Sifton Praed, 1931), p. 120.
2. Carl von Clausewitz, *On War* (Princeton U.P., 1976), ed. M. Howard & P. Paret, Bk. VI, 1, pp. 357–8.
3. Ibid., Bk. VI, 3, pp. 363–5; Bk. VI, 4, pp. 368–9.
4. Ibid., Bk. VI, 5, p. 370.
5. Ibid., Bk. VI, 5, pp. 370–71.
6. Ibid., Bk. VI, 9, pp. 390–1.
7. Ibid., Bk. VII, 5, p. 528.
8. Quoted in Michael Howard, *Clausewitz* (OUP, 1983), p. 39.
9. See J. Gooch, *Armies in Europe* (Routledge, 1980), pp. 33–4.
10. Quoted in J. F. C. Fuller, *The Conduct of War, 1789–1961* (Eyre & Spottiswoode, 1961), pp. 49–50; P. Paret, 'Napoleon and the Revolution in War', in Paret (ed.), *Makers of Modern Strategy* (Clarendon Press, Oxford, 1986) pp. 133–4.
11. Fuller, *Conduct of War*, pp. 93, 88.
12. B. Bond, *War and Society in Europe, 1870–1970* (Fontana, 1984), pp. 13–30.
13. Bond, op. cit., p. 19.
14. For a readable analysis of the opening battles of the Civil War, see W. C. Davis, *Battle at Bull Run* (Louisiana State U.P., 1977).
15. P. Griffith, *Rally Once Again: Battle Tactics of the American Civil War* (Crowood Press, 1987), pp. 49, 67.
16. E. Hagerman, *The American Civil War and the Origins of Modern Warfare* (Indiana U.P., 1988), p. 193. Griffith offers a different interpretation, see *Rally Once Again*, pp. 83, 90, 121–7, 132–33, 141.
17. Hagerman, op. cit., p. 269; on Sherman, see pp. 280, 284, 286–7.
18. Ibid., p. 274.
19. G. F. R. Henderson, *Stonewall Jackson* (Longmans, 1898), vol. II, p. 131.
20. Quoted in Bond, p. 47.
21. Quoted in M. Howard, 'Men against fire: the doctrine of the offensive', in Paret (ed.), *Makers of Modern Strategy*, p. 512.
22. H. Strachan, *European Armies and the Conduct of War* (Allen & Unwin, 1983), p. 128.
23. Quoted in Howard, 'Men against fire', p. 521.
24. Fuller, *Conduct of War*, pp. 126–7; D. Porch, *The March to the Rhine: The French Army, 1871–1914* (Cambridge U.P., 1981), p. 226; T. Travers, *The Killing Ground* (Unwin Hyman, 1987), pp. 53–4, 142–3.
25. J. F. C. Fuller, *On Future Warfare* (Sifton Praed, 1928), pp. 43–4.
26. G. C. Wynne, *If Germany Attacks* (Faber, 1940), pp. 150–7.
27. B. H. Liddell Hart, *Memoirs* (Cassell, 1965), vol. II, p. 26–7, 95.
28. B. H. Liddell Hart, *Foch: The Man of Orleans* (Eyre and Spottiswoode, 1931), pp. 343–4;

C. Barnett, 'A successful counter stroke, 18 July, 1918' in Barrett *et al.*, *Old Battles and New Defences: Can We Learn from Military History?* (Brassey's, 1986), pp. 40, 42, 44–5, 48–50.

29. T. Wilson, *The Myriad Faces of War* (Polity Press, 1986), pp. 583–7.
30. See, for example, J. Terraine, 'Military theory, military history', *RUSI Journal*, March 1978, pp. 73–4; J. J. Mearsheimer, *Liddell Hart and the Weight of History* (Brassey's, 1988), pp. 29–32.
31. B. Holden Reid, *J. F. C. Fuller: Military Thinker* (Macmillan, 1987), pp. 52.
32. On this point see, B. Holden Reid, 'J. F. C. Fuller and B. H. Liddell Hart: a comparison', *Military Review*, LXX, May 1990, pp. 69–70.
33. Fuller, *Lectures on FSR II*, pp. 59, 46, 36.
34. Liddell Hart, *Memoirs*, vol. II, p. 27.
35. Quoted in Barnett *et al.*, *Old Battles and New Defences*, p. 70; T. J. Granville-Chapman, 'The importance of surprise: a reappraisal', in Major-General J. J. G. Mackenzie & Brian Holden Reid (eds.), *The British Army and the Operational Level of War* (Tri-Service Press, 1989), p. 54.
36. B. Bond, 'Arras, 21 May, 1940: a case study in the counter-stroke', in Barnett *et al.*, op. cit., pp. 76–82.
37. J. Harding, 'The German operation in the Ardennes 1944', in Barnett *et al.*, op. cit., pp. 87–8, 95, 97, 103, 105–6, 112; J. F. C. Fuller, *The Second World War* (Eyre & Spottiswoode, 1948), pp 348–9.
38. E. von Manstein, *Lost Victories* (Methuen, 1958), p. 188.

Chapter 11

1. C. von Clausewitz, *On War*, (Princeton U.P., 1976), ed. M. Howard & P. Paret
2. Sun Tzu, *The Art of War*, (trans. S. B. Griffith, O.U.P., 1971), Ch. 4, para. 5.
3. M. Gorbachev, *Perestroika*, (Collins, 1987), pp. 83–98.
4. P. Kennedy, *The Rise and Fall of the Great Powers*, (Unwin Hyman, 1988), pp. 413–37.
5. B. H. Liddell Hart, 'The ratio of troops to space', *Military Review*, April 1960.
6. *STANAG 2099* lists current fire-support measures in force for each NATO nation and highlights the problems of interoperability.
7. S. S. Fitz-Gibbon, 'Colonel von Spohn's "Art of Command"', *British Army Review*, no. 91, April 1989, p. 7, provides a critique of current Army doctrine.
8. J. W. R. Lepingwell, 'The laws of combat', *International Security*, vol. 12, no. 1, Summer 1987, pp. 89–134.
9. A. T. Mahan, *The Influence of Sea Power Upon History*, 1660–1783, (1890), pp. 9–10.
10. Von Clausewitz, op. cit., p. 204.
11. See below, p. 147.
12. *FM 100–5*, Annex B, pp. 181–2.
13. W. S. Lind, *The Manœuvre Warfare Handbook*, (Westview, 1985), Ch. 1, pp. 4–8.
14. J. F. C. Fuller, *Lectures on FSR II*, (Sifton Praed, 1931), pp. 8–9.
15. A. Horne, *To Lose a Battle*, (Macmillan, 1969), pp. 325–60.
16. *Army Field Manual*, vol. 2, part 2, 'Soviet operations'; section 6 explains the Soviet view of acceptable losses and differentiates between the rate of attrition and total losses.
17. *FM 100–5*, pp. 2–3.
18. Von Clausewitz, op. cit., Bk. VIII, 4, pp. 595–6.
19. V. Ye Sarkin, *The Basic Principles of Operational Art and Tactics*, (Washington DC: GPO, n.d.), p. 168.
20. R. Simpkin, *Race to the Swift*, (Brassey's, 1985), pp. 81–115; this provides a detailed view of military action in terms of physics.
21. *Design for Military Operations: the British Military Doctrine*, (HMSO, 1989), pp. 4.2, 4.5.
22. T. B. Macaulay, 'Horatius' (in *Lays of Ancient Rome*, 1842) for a classical example.
23. A. M. Coroalles, *Fighting in the Medium of Time*, (unpublished SAMS monograph, 11 April, 1988).
24. R. Simpkin, op. cit., p. 106, provides a different definition of tempo as containing seven interacting elements: physical mobility, tactical rate of advance, quantity and reliability of information, C³ timings, times to complete moves, pattern of combat support, and pattern of service support.

25. US Army Operational Concept, *AirLand Battle Future – Heavy 2004*, October 1988 draft, pp. 1925; this defined NATO operational imperatives for the future; T. Donnolly, 'War of the future: fast paced, highly lethal', *US Army Times*, June 1989, provides an excellent summary.
26. General Sir Peter Inge, lecture to the RUSI, 15 June, 1989.
27. Lt General Sir John Learmont, 'Military theory and the helicopter', *AAC Journal*, July 1989; the author (Colonel Commandant of the Army Air Corps) provides a similar but more detailed analysis of the future role of the attack helicopter in the manœuvre battle.
28. J. F. C. Fuller, loc. cit.
29. R. Simpkin, op. cit.; foreward by Donn Starry, p. xi.

Chapter 13

1.. General Sir David Fraser, *And We Shall Shock Them*, (Hodder & Stoughton, 1983), p. 93.
2. M. van Creveld, *Command in War*, (Harvard U.P., 1985), p. 108.

Chapter 14

1. M. van Creveld, *Supplying War: Logistics from Wallenstein to Patton*, (Cambridge U.P., 1977), p. 1.
2. See G. H. McCormick & R. E. Bissell (eds.), *Strategic Dimensions of Economic Behavior* (Praeger, 1984), for the interaction between economics and strategy.
3. Z. B. Bradford and F. J. Brown, *The US Army in Transition* (Beverly Hills, California, 1973), p. 138.
4. Figures from N. A. Lomov (ed.), *The Revolution in Military Affairs* (US Air Force transaction, Washington D.C., 1975), p. 117.
5. Figures from J. Erickson, L. Hansen & W. Schneider, *Soviet Ground Forces: an Operational Assessment* (Greenwood Press, 1986), p. 33.
6. Figure from J. Fallows, *The National Defense* (New York, 1981), p. 39.
7. Van Creveld, op. cit., p. 185 quoting German Army High Command documents.
8. J. Huston, *The Sinews of War* (Washington D.C., 1966), p. 530, the planning figure for Overlord, incidentally, was as high as 800.
9. N. Brown, *Strategic Mobility* (Chatto and Windus, 1963), pp. 218–9.
10. Between 1939 and the early 1970s the salvo of a Soviet rifle division increased 31-fold; Lomov, op. cit., p. 31.
11. For a description of the way the system looked from the field see D. A. Starry, *Vietnam Studies: Mounted Combat in Vietnam* (Washington D.C., 1978), pp. 181–2.
12. H. Kissinger, *Nuclear Weapons and Foreign Policy: the need for Choice* (New York, 1957), pp. 181–2; also A. J. Bacevich, *The Pentomic Era: the US Army between Korea and Vietnam* (Washington D.C., 1986), p. 118.
13. See the excellent analysis in Brown, op. cit., p. 83ff.
14. For the readiness problem and its relationship with complexity see F. C. Spinney, *Defense Facts of Life*, (Greenwood Press, 1985), particularly p. 52, table 3.1.
15. Erickson, Hansen & Schneider, op. cit., pp. 197–9.

Chapter 16

1. General J. R. Galvin, 'Getting better: improving capabilities for deterrence and defence', *NATO Review*, April 1989.
2. M. van Creveld, *Fighting Power*, (Greenwood Press, 1982).
3. C. N. Donnelly, 'The Soviet use of military history for operational analysis', *British Army Review*, December 1987.
4. D. M. Abshire, 'A resources strategy for NATO', *NATO's Sixteen Nations*, vol. 30, 1985.
5. Lt Col. M. L. Wildman, 'Sustainability: a shackle on the operational commander', The Collected Papers of the First Higher Command and Staff Course, Staff College, Camberley, 1988.

Index